THE
HEALERS

Your access to perfect health and happiness

KATHLEEN WELCH RAYMOND
WAYNE G. GABARI

The authors are not medical doctors and they do not practice medicine. They do not diagnose, heal, treat disease or prescribe medication. They do not dispense medical advice or prescribe the use of any technique as a form of treatment for physical, emotional, spiritual, or medical problems, either directly or indirectly. Their spiritual energy work is not a substitute for conventional medical diagnosis or treatment for any medical or psychological condition. For such issues, you may want to seek the proper licensed physician or healthcare professional. Their intent is only to offer information of a general nature to help you in your quest for physical, emotional, mental and spiritual well-being. Their work is spiritually based. They believe that when the energy in and around the body is balanced and moving correctly, everyone has an innate ability to self-heal - if they are willing and wanting to. They assist in correcting energetic imbalances in the bio-energetic fields, which in turn, allows the mind and body greater access to its own innate healing ability. In the event you use any of the information in this book for yourself, which is your constitutional right, the authors and the people who shared their stories, assume no responsibility for your actions. They do not make any promises, warranties or guarantees about results of their writings, their work, or of their energy healing sessions, in person or long distance.

ISBN: 1492268798

ISBN 13: 9781492268796

DEDICATION

This book is dedicated to:

All of our loved ones – both family and friends – who
believed in us and our work; to those who gave of their time,
encouragement and guidance to support us throughout this
journey; to the people who participated in the healings and
were courageous enough to share their experiences with the
world; and to the people reading this book who bring the whole
process from a dream to reality.

And to Kathy's sister and Wayne's friend,

~ Lynn Esposito Raymond ~

She began this journey with us from one side of the veil and
finished from the other. You are with us always.

We could not have done it without ALL of you!

We are forever grateful.

ACKNOWLEDGEMENTS

We would like to give special acknowledgment and thanks to:

~ Patricia Gruning Higgins ~

who opened her home to us and relinquished her dining room
table for the creation, editing and re-editing of this book
– which turned into a five year process –
We thank you for your generosity, love, wisdom and
commitment in support of our dream.

~ Eileen Giuliani ~

whose knowledge, objectivity and
courage to 'ask the tough questions',
in conjunction with her professional editing skills,
added tremendously to the final culmination of this book.
We thank you for your generosity, love, and
extensive contribution of time and expertise.

And to the many pioneers and teachers who went before us
on this journey of healing and enlightenment.

We are blessed and we thank you.

TABLE OF CONTENTS

Preface ... ... *ix*

Introduction ... ...*xiii*

CHAPTER 1 : THE HORSE WHISPERER 1

CHAPTER 2 : A MAGNETIC ENERGY HEALING. 9

CHAPTER 3 : THE GIFT OF TUCKER'S LEGACY.. 14

CHAPTER 4 : REBIRTH OF A SHAMAN 25

CHAPTER 5 : GET THE WAGONS ROLLING 34

CHAPTER 6 : MIRACLE ON THE MOUNTAIN. 44

CHAPTER 7 : CHARADES WITH THE ANGELS... 50

CHAPTER 8 : A STAR IS BORN... 58

CHAPTER 9 : TAKE A RIDE ON METRO NORTH 66

CHAPTER 10 : PICKING UP THE LOOSE
CHANGE ON WALL STREET... 77

CHAPTER 11 : GIVE THEM A HAND 89

CHAPTER 12 : BACK TO SCHOOL WITH PATRICIA HIGGINS 96

CHAPTER 13 : IN AN INSTANT 106

CHAPTER 14 : EXTENDED FAMILY. 116

CHAPTER 15 : HEALING OF THE PUTNAM VALLEY MARKET... 123

CHAPTER 16 : FORGIVENESS HEALS A BROKEN HEART... ... ... .150

CHAPTER 17 : TOUCHDOWN MIKE SPINELLI.. 160

CHAPTER 18 : MAMA'S BOY. 169

CHAPTER 19 : EGG SHELLS FROM HEAVEN.. 182

CHAPTER 20 : COURAGE TO CHOOSE... 216

CHAPTER 21 : AN ANCIENT ART 230

CHAPTER 22 : I AM THAT AM 251

CHAPTER 23 : WHAT IS A HEALING.. 255

CHAPTER 24 : HOW CAN I GET THERE FROM HERE. 261

Our Gift to You 271

Resource Guide 273

Notes 280

PREFACE

This is a book of hope and healing.

It is our hope that you will develop a new perspective on healing and that you will open to new possibilities for greater health and well-being. Whether it happens in an instant or over time, there are options available for people who have previously resigned themselves to a life of pain and suffering.

Our natural survival instinct is to move away from pain. We do this by stuffing our emotions, numbing feelings we do not want to feel, diminishing ourselves to make others feel comfortable, or hiding our emotions and pretending that everything is fine. These may be useful survival techniques for the moment, but over time, the accumulation of these behaviors will eventually take their toll on our body, mind and spirit.

Our bodies are our vehicles in life. Pain is our indicator when something is not right. When a warning light appears on a car's dashboard, it's time to take action and address the problem. If we choose to not take action and continue to drive, there is a high probability that our car is going to break down. The same is true of our bodies. The more we disconnect from our bodies, the more we will suffer and the greater the pain will be.

Whether physical, emotional, mental or spiritual, there is some action that needs to be taken when the warning light of pain goes on. If we learn to be still, listen for the message and have the courage to take action - the pain will go away, and we will not suffer. When that tiny course correction in life is made the indicator light goes out.

Unfortunately, most of us are more afraid of change than we are of pain. We'll ignore the situation and avoid making changes until the pain becomes so loud we cannot stand it and outside intervention becomes necessary.

If we do not go inward and deal with these stuffed emotions, or are not true to ourselves and courageous in the face of change making little course corrections as we go along, these accumulated experiences will eventually become our *prescription for illness.*

In our society we can see the results of this. We would be hard pressed to find a family that does not have one or more members dealing with physical, emotional, psychological or spiritual problems. This book contains true stories of people who fall into one or more of these categories. You may see the mirror of their stories in your own life or in the lives of people that you know.

In many cases you will read actual quotes about how their lives and health improved after receiving an energy healing which was experienced either in person, through physical touch – referred to as "the laying on of hands" - or by "long distance".

The ability to heal is not limited by distance. A long distance healing means exactly that - wherever you are, it will reach you. Distance healings differ from hands-on-healings only by the physical touch of the healer. They are just as powerful and life altering as a hands-on session. Many people who have experienced both hands-on and distance healings report that the results and the experience are the same - just the feeling of being physically touched is missing.

As you read through our book, you will learn about healing techniques that have been used for thousands of years. They can be used in conjunction with modern medicine, or they can stand alone. Even though modern medicine is capable of many remarkable recoveries, it is not the end-all solution for every situation. At a time when humanity is suffering from an inordinate number of afflictions, this book offers an alternative to as well as an enhancement of modern medicine for the healing process.

OUR PRESCRIPTION FOR WELLNESS

As healers, it is our intention to reconnect you to your Self, so that you can hear your own internal guidance system, open the connections to Source Energy so your body can heal itself, and awaken you to the knowing that resides in each and every one of us. Be true to your Self!

Through the generations, this knowing has been pushed to the sidelines in favor of something outside of ourselves having the answers. Our desire is to create an awakening of each person's internal guidance system, and foster an awareness of these healing possibilities.

As you read this book and develop an understanding and awareness of the human energy fields, as well as our innate power as human beings, there will be new opportunities for you to use this knowledge to enhance your life. Look for the mirrors that reflect similar experiences in your own life.

By sharing our journal of actual healings as well as the perceptions of both the healers and the recipients of those healings, we intend to enlighten our readers as to what is possible. The effects these healings have had on the people and animals involved will broaden your awareness of spirit and the different modalities available.

Some will be adamant and say, "Show me scientific evidence!"

We say absolute proof is not what an x-ray or microscope indicates but rather that a person who could barely walk now has pain free strides. How about a person suffering from depression who has been to the best psychologists with no improvement? All of a sudden the depression is gone. Life looks good. Pain, suffering and worry disappear. Upset and despair are replaced with smiles and possibilities. Aren't results like these, achieved through non-invasive techniques, the desired outcomes one hopes for?

As you read through our journals, you will be able to enjoy actual uplifting events that have changed peoples' lives.[1]

The possibilities for health and wellness are unlimited.

Remember our prescription for wellness:
Be true to your Self!

When you are true to yourself, well-being becomes a way of life.

The body doesn't need to break down to get your attention.

Life can be "…and they lived happily ever after!"

---

1 In some cases, the names have been changed at the request of the client.

INTRODUCTION

KATHY'S STORY:

We had just dropped my two older sisters off at Grandma's house for an overnight stay. My mother was driving with the three-year-old twins, Richy and Susie, up front with her in old-fashioned car seats, and my other little sister, Patty, was standing between them, hanging on. It was 1962 and there were no seat belts in those days. At seven, I was considered one of the "big" kids, and was responsible for holding Vicki, my seventeen-month-old sister, in the back seat of the car. It must have been a hundred degrees out, and the breeze from the open windows felt great as we headed home.

Suddenly, I was on the pavement!

I don't remember feeling the impact of the car that hit us, nor do I recall being thrown through the air and sliding thirty feet down the road. The only thing I remember is that as one of the big kids, I had to hold onto my baby sister.

As we lay on the pavement, the tire of the car only inches from our heads, someone pried Vicki from my arms. She was screaming at the top of her lungs. I was carried back to the car, and the lady who was a passenger in the car that hit us held Vicki in her lap and me next to her. She had an odd smell about her which years later I realized was the smell of alcohol. I did not feel good about this woman holding my sister and me, as my mother frantically drove to the hospital.

I must have been in shock. I remember thinking what a baby Vicki was for crying over a few scratches. My favorite white eyelet sundress had been ruined, covered with blood, and I would never be able to wear it again, and I wasn't crying!

We were rushed into the emergency room where our cuts and abrasions were cleaned and the pebbles and road rubble removed from my head and skin along the right side of my body. Although that hurt a lot, I still didn't cry. I was promised ice cream after they finished dressing my wounds, and that sounded good to me. A member of the medical team couldn't believe that we only had minor injuries. Someone referred to me as a human sled. "This is a miracle! How could either of these children still be alive?" Somehow Vicki and I had been spared from what appeared to be a sealed fate.

This is where my journey as a healer began.

That summer, my mother took special care of me. Among the many wounds I suffered from was a scab extending from my shoulder to my elbow. Several times a day, Mommy would soak my wounds to keep the scabs soft to avoid scarring. She taught me that the body heals from the inside out. She also knew that salt water promotes healing so we went to the beach a lot. I healed with amazing speed, and as remarkable as it may be, I do not have one scar on my body from that accident.

Later that summer, as I lay on moss-covered ground next to a quiet little stream in the woods, I thought about what happened. It seemed as if someone or something had taken us out of the car, a two-door Hudson, and placed us on the pavement. We were either thrown through the open window or hurled out under the door that flew open during impact.

This was the day I realized I wanted to help people heal naturally, the way my mother had cared for me. I remember hearing a gentle voice in my head, "You're going to be a healer" and I thought back "Like a doctor? Or a nurse?" And the voice said, "No, different". And I thought, "Okay". And off I went to play with my siblings, not giving it another thought until years later…

WAYNE'S STORY:

I spent sixteen years of my life in parochial schools, from grammar school right through college. A facts-and-figures guy, I wanted a solid Wall Street career, and as a senior vice president of an investment banking firm, becoming a healer was the furthest thing from my mind. However, you never know when life is going to throw you a curve.

Working at a desk for over thirty years, in front of a computer and under constant pressure made me the perfect candidate for poor health. It started small with aching joints and loss of flexibility. Then my vision and memory started to deteriorate. Eventually, I underwent surgery for my gallbladder. When my shoulder started hurting, not wanting to have another surgery, I began looking long and hard at different modalities. There had to be something out there that would stop this deterioration. There had to be a natural way to restore myself.

I discovered magnetic products which made a huge difference in my shoulder pain. Next was the addition of nutritional supplements. After discussing the supplements with biologists and doctors, I started to take several. My health took another giant leap forward. I could now throw a baseball without pain and in addition to an incredible increase in energy, my memory greatly improved. This was amazing! I started to read more about natural products. Next on the agenda was a vitamin for the eyes and soon my vision got better. With results like these, an unquenchable thirst to learn more was building within me.

I had a very bad stiff neck and went to a traditional chiropractor religiously. The results were mixed - sometimes better, sometimes worse. My son, Jason, recommended a chiropractor who works with energy instead of manipulation.

So I went.

Amazingly, these gentle treatments resulted in improved flexibility in my neck, and I have not had to take painkillers since. In the chiropractor's office, there were several patients in the same room, on individual tables, simultaneously receiving treatments. During one of these sessions, an event happened that completely changed my perspective on life.

A fellow patient, Susan De Robertis, was also receiving treatment. I had never met her, yet following her treatment, she waited for me and introduced herself.

She said, "This was the second time I was in the room with you during a treatment. The first time I felt this fantastic wave of energy coming toward me. I thought it was from you but was not sure. This time I am sure! The wave of energy coming from you was the most peaceful, powerful and loving, that I have ever felt."

I was floored by the fact that someone could feel my energy and benefit from it. This was the first time that I had an awareness of how my energy could have an impact on another without any physical contact.

The next leg of my journey was with Kathy Raymond who was working in the chiropractor's office. Kathy was always very cheerful, and one evening while I was laying face down on the table, the chiropractor asked her to do some energy work on me. She placed her hands gently on my body, moving them along my neck, shoulders and back. I had no idea what was happening, and could not believe how good my neck and back were feeling. I was intrigued by this newest event.

At my next session, I noticed Kathy was doing the same procedure on other clients. I asked the doctor what she was doing and was told, "She is doing energy healings."

"What is that?"

"It's something that you really have to experience."

The doctor scheduled me for one session with Kathy. During that session, I realized he was right. I had an exhilarating experience which was to alter my life forever. I asked Kathy how she did it and told her she was gifted. She told me, "Anyone can learn to do this."

In that moment I became determined to learn these skills and enrolled in the two-year training program in Torrington, Connecticut, the same program from which Kathy graduated.

During the training, my skills grew with each amazing healing, and I knew that helping people in a positive way was what I wanted to do with my life.

CHAPTER 1

The Horse Whisperer

KATHY

Ever since I was a little girl, I have had a loving attraction to horses and I never missed an opportunity to watch *Fury*, *My Friend Flicka* or *National Velvet* on TV. My greatest pleasure was to watch their majestic beauty. Whether frolicking in a pasture or running as fast as the wind in all their splendor the joy that I felt inside remains with me even to this day. It was this attraction that enticed me to learn to ride at an early age, and I wanted to spend as much time as possible on the back of a horse.

I was eight years old when I took my first solo ride. My older sister, Lynn, boosted me up onto the bare back of our friend's huge horse, Bobbie, and I was beaming! With all of her eleven-year-old wisdom, Lynn told me, "Just get on, and Bobbie will walk around the corral." All was going well, until we reached the end of the corral and turned the corner where Bobbie's natural routine was to start trotting. I was bouncing all over when I heard Lynn yell, "Kick her, and she'll go smoother."

When my tiny bare feet banged against her sides, this gentle, well-trained horse shot into a canter, leaving me sprawled out flat on my back on some very hard ground. As I laid there gasping for air, Lynn ran over and said, "Why didn't you hang on?"

Finally catching my breath, I said, "You didn't tell me to!"

Even though the landing was no fun, this experience did not diminish my love of horses. In fact, it increased my determination to learn to ride, especially because when I fell off, Bobbie stopped, came back and nuzzled me, as if to find out why I left her. She really was a great horse and we became friends. Over the next four years I got much better at riding - and at falling off.

Although I never owned a horse, many of my friends did. I would often accompany Frances when she went to ride, and we would take turns or ride double. Afterward, I would help her do her chores. That's how I met Mr. Rogers, the owner of the barn, where Frances boarded her pony. Being at the barn gave me an opportunity to be around the other horses and get to know Mr. Rogers, who would often come out to say hello when he saw us. Standing about 6'4" and skinny as a rail, he looked a lot like Abraham Lincoln. He was a kindly man who loved his three horses and treated them very well. Although he and his wife were not riding much anymore, they were not planning to give them up any time soon.

One lucky day when Mr. Rogers came out to the barn to see how things were going, I mustered up enough courage to ask if he would let me ride one of his horses in exchange for helping him take care of them. He explained that two of the horses were not suitable for me to ride. Kyron was a massive bay, and Mr. Rogers' personal horse. He thought Kryon would be too strong and aggressive for me. Ivy, a beautiful dapple-gray thoroughbred, was too mean to ride. She had been a race-horse, and Mr. Rogers showed me the numbers that were tattooed on the inside of her upper lip. He went on to explain that she had been injured at a young age and because of this, and her bad disposition, she was not suitable for riding. However, he agreed to let me ride Geordie, his wife's horse. He thought it would be good for Geordie to get some exercise.

I was thrilled! Geordie was my favorite and the one I secretly wanted to ride. A twelve-year-old Standardbred gelding, the same age as me, he was the most elegant looking horse I had ever seen. Standing 17.2 hands, or 5'8" at his withers, it was a stretch for me to reach his back. With his head held high in the air, there was no way I could ever reach his ears. He was huge! His coat was shiny golden brown and glistened in the sunlight. With a reddish-blonde mane and tail, white stripe down his face and four white socks, he was absolutely beautiful. He was a "retired trotter" and when he ran his tail would go up in the air and flow out behind him. Not only was he an impressive sight to behold, he had the friendliest, most gentle disposition, and I got to ride him. What a great deal. I was on cloud nine!

This great deal was also a very challenging endeavor. Each day I would either walk or, when lucky, get a lift to the barn to do my chores and then ride. Kyron and Geordie were easy to handle and a pleasure to care for. I cleaned Ivy's stall but only Mr. Rogers took care of Ivy. However, over time, as he began to feel more comfortable with my skills, and as I got to know the horses better, I took on more responsibility, and that meant Ivy.

Despite her beauty, Ivy was one of the meanest horses I had ever known. In her early years she raced before large crowds. Her career came to a screeching halt when she suffered a badly bowed tendon in her front leg that never seemed to heal. Ivy went from the cheering crowds to a nag no one wanted. She could no longer be ridden and had no value in the racing arena. This was what you might call a painful, early retirement. Many horses suffering similar injuries were done away with. Fortunately for Ivy, Mr. and Mrs. Rogers gave her a home. These kind people knew that this was a major responsibility, saving the life of an unhappy horse that could not be ridden. Ivy must have known this, too, because she was always respectful of Mr. Rogers, and he had no problem handling her. However, she didn't want anyone else near her, or her stall, and she let you know it. For a twelve year old to handle a horse as mean as Ivy, this would be no easy task and was not something I was looking forward to.

When Mr. Rogers' niece, Ellen, came to visit for the summer he gave us the responsibility of caring for Ivy. Ellen was fourteen, an accomplished rider, with horses of her own. Yet it took all three of us to control Ivy during her grooming. The other horses enjoyed being groomed, but not Ivy. It was a production!

She had a halter on, but we couldn't get near her head without the risk of being bitten. We needed a better plan. Food! Sweet feed to be exact. We found a leather feedbag to use as a muzzle which would keep her from biting us, but we still had to get it into place. This was a dangerous endeavor. We agreed that whoever drew the short straw would install the muzzle.

The plan was; with the lead rope already attached to the muzzle, we would fill the bottom with sweet feed in an attempt to entice her nose into it for a tasty nibble. With her mouth in the bottom of the bag, there would be slack in the strap, and we would quickly slide the strap over her head and behind her ears, thus securing the muzzle in place, protecting us from her teeth. To make this happen, the person who drew the short straw would shake the bag in an effort to lure Ivy to stretch her head and neck out of the stall. While holding the feedbag in one hand, at arm's length and ready to jump backwards, Ivy would put her nose to the bottom of the bag and in that instant, you would use your other hand to slide the strap over her head and voila!

We all agreed that it was a good plan. Ellen volunteered to go first. We protested that it had to be fair. Short straw loses. None of us forgot the time Ellen first arrived and unknowingly entered the stall, only to be grabbed by Ivy's teeth and hurled against the wall. She was extremely lucky not to be seriously injured. Although she had been pretty shaken up when that happened, she recovered and was now cautious around Ivy.

However, Ellen was determined to handle this horse and declared she would go first.

More than once, Ivy head butted her way out of the trap. It took several tries, and none of us wanted to get bitten or hit by her flying head. She wasn't just a mean horse; she was a smart, mean horse.

Eventually, it worked!

The next challenge was to lead her out of the stall without anyone being injured. If she pulled back into the stall, no one would go in after her. It was simply too risky.

Once out of her stall, we hooked Ivy to the crossties to hold her head in place. Crossties are two lead ropes, hooked to mounted rings on each side of the center aisle of the barn. Once in place, Ivy's movements were limited. Out of her stall and hooked up like this, Ivy had fairly good manners as long as she could see us. We needed her as still and safe as possible for the grooming.

We developed a series of procedures specifically for Ivy. Nothing was part of the norm when caring for this horse. As part of the grooming, we would brush her and clean out her hooves. The only way to effectively accomplish this without someone getting hurt was to keep Ivy off balance.

The first girl would pick up Ivy's front leg and hold it in the position necessary to clean out her hoof. This would leave her standing on three legs. The second girl would pick up her back leg on the opposite side. Now Ivy was standing on two legs. The legs had to be held close to her body to keep her as still as possible so she was focused on maintaining balance and not on kicking us. Two girls controlling 1,200 pounds of explosive horseflesh! The "leg girls" would clean out the inside of Ivy's hooves, while the third person brushed her down, including her mane, coat and tail. The two girls on the legs had all they could handle and yelled at the brusher to go faster. We then had to switch sides to clean the other hooves and added grain to the muzzle when we switched to keep her occupied. She had to be kept as docile as possible.

It was during one of these grooming ordeals that the healing instincts within me were aroused.

I was a 'leg holder' and as I ran my hand down her leg to lift it, the leg seemed unusually tender and swollen. I thought, "It's no wonder she's always so mean, she must be in awful pain. Maybe she was not as mean as we believed. Maybe she was in constant pain and as a result frustrated and scared."

I asked Mr. Rogers to come to the barn and examine Ivy's leg. He said, "She has a bowed tendon as a result of an injury from long ago. Nothing can be done for it. It's been like this for several years. We've tried all kinds of treatments but nothing has worked. She can never be ridden again. We're just providing a home for her to live out her days." He also hinted that because she was so mean, he was not sure how long that would be. They were considering putting her down.

After hearing the story, I knew they had given up hope of healing the leg.

Immediately, my whole attitude toward Ivy changed. I now had a growing compassion for her. She was only six years old, strong and healthy in every other way. Even though her owner had given up all hope of rehabilitation, I was just getting started. I asked Mr. Rogers if we could try again. It was not right to leave her in such pain. This was a former racehorse that had the finest of medical treatment. They all said nothing more could be done. How was a twelve year old going to make a difference? The odds were stacked against me, but I guess Mr. Rogers could not resist the pleas of a little girl. He agreed to give it one more try, stating "Come spring, we'll make our decision."

Although Ellen went home at the end of the summer, Frances and I continued to care for Ivy. We had a pretty good system in place and Ivy was getting more cooperative.

As the weather turned colder and the snow began to fall, we were not riding as much. I loved being with the horses and still had my chores to do, but now I also had more time to focus on Ivy. Mr. Rogers said he would concoct a mixture for me to put on her leg every day in the hope of reducing the swelling. He was happy to be trying something again, although he did not hold much hope for success. But I was determined.

Winter was the time of "Sunday Evening Mash". Every Sunday, throughout the season, we would gather in Mr. Rogers' kitchen to cook for the horses. We made a huge pot of warm stew with sweet feed, carrots, oats, and bran. It may not seem like much to a human, but boy, did the horses love their mash! This was their Sunday dinner and after the inaugural meal, they expected it every week, snorting and stomping out in the barn in expectation of the feast they knew was coming. They all loved it, even Ivy.

While the mash was cooking, I went out to the barn, pulled up a bale of hay across from Ivy's stall and sat quietly for a long time, trying to figure out how to help her. She was pacing inside her stall and seemed very nervous and agitated. I spoke gently to her and explained what we were going to do, and that we needed her help. I apologized for any pain I caused her during the groomings, and for the added weight on her front leg when we kept her off balance, realizing the entire grooming procedure must have been very painful. Ivy seemed to calm down, and she let out a few snorts. It was as if she understood what I was saying. I felt a greater connection to Ivy, like I understood what she was thinking. A spiritual bond was developing between us. I could actually feel her start to relax and for the first time in a long time, trust a human other than Mr. Rogers.

The next day, I told Frances my plan. She thought I was crazy but agreed to help. We went through the normal routine for getting Ivy out of the stall to the crossties. She still needed to be groomed and have her stall cleaned and we needed the muzzle to protect us from her teeth. There was one big difference - I was now the only leg person.

After attaching her to the crossties, we sat in front of her for a long time so she knew where we were. I was the only one who spoke telling her about our plan for healing and how good she was going to feel. I lovingly explained how we were going to care for her and make her leg feel better. We were both onboard with this, and you could sense the positive energy in the air. It was very different from the past. We were no longer there to defend ourselves from Ivy's wrath. There was now a spiritual connection. We were there to heal this fabulous thoroughbred and instill that feeling in her.

Ivy seemed to understand and started to show signs of relaxing. I kept speaking gently to her and then gradually rose to my feet. She became a little nervous, bouncing her head around on the crossties, but as Frances didn't move, she settled down again. I continued talking to her. Something was happening, she was very different. Ivy was nervous but not mean. I placed my hands on her shoulder and slowly ran them gently down her leg. I continued speaking to her until I reached the injured area in the lower part of the leg. Gently, I held the swollen area between my hands, telling her how much better she was going to feel and that we were all going to take better care of her. Although I did not know what was happening, I felt there was a tender loving energy passing into this area.

What we saw completely amazed us. Her demeanor changed right before our eyes. Ivy's body, usually tense and twitching, started to relax. Her eyes stopped rolling back, her head lowered, and her ears came forward. Her heavy breathing calmed to a steady gentle breath. The years of pent up anger and frustration seemed to dissipate.

After about ten minutes, I told Ivy that Frances was going to groom her. I remained where I was, with my hands on her leg and nodded to Frances, who slowly walked over to Ivy and began to brush her gently. Ivy was slightly startled, but I spoke softly to her and she quickly relaxed. Frances kept silent and we were both cautious to make no sudden movements. We couldn't believe it! Could this really be happening? How did I know what to do? We did not lift her legs to clean her hooves that day, and for the first time, Ivy stood peacefully, without fear or apprehension, as she received a thorough brushing. We sensed she was enjoying our care, even the grooming, and we were both smiling. It seemed like a miracle and we were elated! A trusting bond had been created. She knew we were her friends and there was nothing to fear. We were there to restore her quality of life.

This procedure became our daily routine. Although Ivy still remained agitated when she was in her stall, she was quiet out on the crossties. At these times, I would work on her leg from shoulder to hoof while Frances brushed her. We were absolutely amazed! I continued to work on her leg long after the brushing was completed and was soon able to move my hands all over her body. Ivy seemed to be irritated by the mixture Mr. Rogers had prepared, so I stopped applying it as my touch seemed to be much more effective.

Mr. Rogers was absolutely thrilled with Ivy's improvements. I told him I was not able to use the mixture. "Don't worry. Just keep doing what you're doing because it seems to be working. I've never seen her so calm, she's like a different horse!"

By spring, Ivy had completely transformed. Although she was still frisky in her stall, when she was out, she was pleasant to be around. Her limp was completely gone and she was a much happier animal. Mr. Rogers could not believe the difference and asked the vet to examine her. We were all there, waiting for the verdict.

The vet declared, "The leg seems to be healed. Amazing! Looks like she can be ridden again. Who wants to go first?"

Yes, Ivy could be ridden, and she was a pleasure to ride. In fact, when Ellen returned that summer, she was able to ride her in a horse show. Ivy had been given a new lease on life and a twelve year-old's healing gifts had been awakened.

COMMENTS BY WAYNE: When Robert Redford starred in the hit movie, "The Horse Whisperer," it was the rage of the day. Mr. Redford had a great performance in this movie but not as great as the real life performance of a twelve year old named Kathy Raymond. This story opened up a new awareness in me that animals can benefit from these healings, just as much as humans, if not more, because animals have no pre-conceived judgment.

CHAPTER 2

A Magnetic Energy Healing

WAYNE

When I was a kid, I loved playing with magnets. My favorite ones were made in the shape of horseshoes, painted red with silver ends, and I would use them to pick up all sorts of metal objects. I remember holding one in each hand and when I tried to put them end to end, they would repel each other, which was always fascinating. I also had a game board with a man's face on it. It came with a magic wand which had a magnet on one end. Moving the wand over the tiny metal shavings, which were under the plastic game board cover, the shavings would magnetize to the wand. Then I would drag the shavings over the face to create a beard, hair, moustache, sideburns, and eyebrows. When the shavings were over the right place, I would lift the wand and the shavings would drop from the magnet. I had no idea how this worked, but was intrigued by what I could do with these magnetic toys.

Today I have a whole new perspective of magnets.

I was in my early fifties when I told my mother I was contemplating surgery on my elbow and shoulder. Suffering from old baseball injuries, I was tired of being in constant pain and could barely throw a baseball anymore, something I loved to do. My mother worked at the Westchester Medical Center and suggested I speak with a gentleman at her office who was exhibiting wellness products, before having any surgery.

He spoke to me about magnets and said that they may be able to help. Interested but skeptical, I did some research of my own first.

I discovered that magnetic energy has been a basic life force since the inception of the earth. As the planet is magnetic, every human, animal and plant that exists on this planet needs magnetism to survive. If a person were to be isolated in a room with no magnetic energy, their body would gradually deteriorate. In the early days of space travel, when the Soviets launched cosmonauts for missions that lasted for a prolonged period of time, upon their return to earth, their joints had significant deterioration. The old newsreels show them being carried from the returning spacecraft, as they could not walk on their own. This problem ceased when the spacecrafts were magnetized. During the early days of mankind, peoples' activities were close to the surface of the earth and many actually slept on the ground where the magnetic energy is the strongest. Thus, their bodies received a steady input of this necessary energy. For the most part, those days are gone.

People now work in buildings constructed of steel, our homes are elevated above ground, and we drive in automobiles that thwart magnetism. It's no wonder joint deterioration is so high. Today, more people than ever are having hip and knee replacements, and various other surgical procedures for joint problems.

If you have a joint problem, ailment, or injury and put a refrigerator magnet on that area, you would probably not notice any improvement. These simple magnets lack strength and therefore have little effect on the body. However, Wellness companies have researched and developed high-tech healing magnets which can have a major impact on people's lives.

Healing magnets increase magnetic flow over a larger area in a continuous manner which balances the energy fields throughout the human body, creating ideal conditions for restoring health.

Wanting to avoid surgery, I was willing to give these magnets a try!

I followed the gentleman's recommendations and purchased a magnetic mattress, innersoles, and various other magnets for my shoulder, neck, and elbow. Within a few days the pain was gone and flexibility returned to my joints! By the end of the week I jumped out of bed one morning and proclaimed, "I feel so good I could run a marathon!"

The Nikken[2] distributor my mother had introduced me to was absolutely right. I was hooked! I began attending meetings to learn more about magnets. Nikken produces the best magnetic products that I know of. Although they cannot make medical claims, there are an infinite number of testimonials to back up the success of their products.

The injuries to my shoulder and elbow which I once cursed - became my gifts that opened a new doorway on my path to becoming a healer. I knew these products must be shared with others who were suffering.

Filled with a burning desire to help people, along with this newly discovered knowledge, a monumental healing was about to take place. This was the first healing where I had a major impact on someone's life. Cathy and Paul Nolte were about to receive the full blast of my enthusiasm as I visited them in their home.

When Paul removed his shoes to try a pair of the magnetic innersoles, my exuberant feelings quickly changed. I must have looked like a deer caught in the headlights on a dark night. Paul's legs were ravaged by the terrible side effects of

2   Nikken, Magnetic Energy Therapy and Wellness Products; http://www.nikken.com

diabetes. Lack of circulation to his extremities had caused his toes and lower legs to turn blue. Two toes had already fallen victim to this horrid disease and been amputated. Cathy and Paul were well aware that he would soon be losing more toes and eventually his legs. Despite his best efforts, which included going to a podiatrist and soaking his feet in hot whirlpools, Paul's feet continued to worsen. No matter what the doctor tried, there was no improvement. What a sense of hopelessness and depression. I thought to myself that under these conditions, how could anyone have hope?

As soon as Paul tried the magnetic innersoles, I asked him, "Do you feel anything?" He responded, "I feel tingling in my feet and toes." Paul didn't know what that meant, and even though I was inexperienced, I felt that something good was happening.

After three days of faithfully sleeping on a magnetic sleep system and wearing magnetic innersoles, Paul's natural color returned to his feet and legs. He went to his podiatrist, who couldn't believe what he was seeing, and asked incredulously, "What did you do?"

Paul said it was simple. He slept on a magnetic sleep system and used a comforter made of Far-Infrared material that drove his natural energy back into his body. During the day, he wore magnetic innersoles. Furthermore, the tingling he felt using these products indicated an increase in circulation. After a few days, the natural color returned to his feet.

The doctor lost a great patient/customer. Paul had been visiting him several times a week. I was obviously ecstatic. This was revolutionary, and if these products were capable of restoring the quality of life to one person, they would help others.

Shortly after this I attended a meeting with people who had significant experience with magnetic products. I asked if anyone had seen the effects of these products on people with severe diabetes. A woman came forward and told a story even more striking than Paul's.

She had met a man whose legs had turned black and was scheduled for surgery to amputate them. A week before the operation, she begged him to try the products. He agreed and followed a similar pattern to what I used with Paul. In a few days, the natural color returned to the man's legs. He had come within an inch of the knife, from the jaws of defeat, to a new beginning!

The woman went on to say that the doctor was "shocked" to see the change! When he scheduled the surgery he had assigned certain finality to the outcome that both he and the patient had accepted. "There is no way out of this, the legs are coming off." To his credit, he wanted to know how such a miraculous transition had taken place. He asked to speak with her and a meeting was arranged. She explained what she had done. The surgeon had nothing to say.

After hearing this story, I was excited to know that these magnets would be a miracle to many people suffering from diabetes and overall circulation problems. However, my spirits were quickly dampened when I realized that these two highly educated doctors would do nothing to bring this discovery to the forefront of diabetes research. The wellness company that produced the products was forbidden to make medical claims and the doctors who saw the results were not going to promote what they had seen.

I look forward to the day when the medical community will promote products such as these, that they have seen work, so that people throughout the world no longer unnecessarily suffer loss of limbs.

Several years later, Paul passed on from heart related problems caused by the diabetes, but he never lost his toes or legs and the lack of circulation ceased. He maintained his dignity and quality of life from a simple magnetic energy healing. I recently spoke to his wife, Cathy, who referred to it as a miracle. For me, this instilled a deep-rooted determination to learn more about magnetic energy and natural treatments.

CHAPTER 3

The Gift of Tucker's Legacy

KATHY

I met Tucker when I was twelve years old while out-and-about the neighborhood with a group of friends. His electric smile and infectious laugh were magnetic and we became close friends. This was a friendship which lasted throughout our teen years of parties, bonfires at the beach, and dances.

Tucker, and his best friend Lenny, had a band that played '50s, '60s and the new '70s dance music. Tucker was the lead singer and guitarist, Lenny was the drummer. They built a large fan base that loved the music and went to all their performances. What better way to spend an evening, than at a dance where your friends were in the band and everyone loved their music?

As years went by and I began to date Lenny, the three of us did everything together and what a blast we had. We felt that the bond we had would last forever, but as time passed, it became clear that we each had our own directions in life to pursue. Lenny and I broke up, which left me heartbroken. He was my first love. They said "time heals everything", but I knew "they" never felt like this. Although we still hung out in the same circles, Tucker and Lenny remained best friends and eventually, I lost touch with them. I heard Lenny moved away to follow his entrepreneurial dreams in real estate. Tucker headed for the entertainment world and created his own band. I went to see him perform a few times, and the crowds just loved him. He was a rock star and in his element! I went off to college and moved away, but every now and then I would come back home, and Tucker and I would get together for a short visit and catch up on life.

I was twenty-three when I got the call that Tucker was dead. I was shocked! He was only a year younger than me. He was one of the most alive people I knew. He was headed for fame and fortune...what could have happened? How could that be? His family must be devastated!

They said it was a gunshot wound to the stomach, a self-inflicted accident. There was no one to blame. They said that Tucker's girlfriend had allegedly cheated on him and in his rage he took his father's revolver intending to scare the new boyfriend away.

The son of a police officer, Tucker had been raised to know better than to touch a gun in such an emotionally upset state. They said that when he slid the gun into the waistband of his pants, the trigger caught on something, and the gun went off. Tucker was home alone and by the time help arrived, he was in really bad shape. Every effort was made, but they could not save his life.

It was surreal being at the funeral of a friend. Kneeling at the casket and looking at him was one of the strangest experiences I ever had. The body in the casket didn't look anything like the Tucker I knew.

Closing my eyes, I remembered the last time I saw him. He was a rock star! On stage, singing his heart out and playing the guitar, his long wavy blond hair flying wildly about. He was young, healthy, vibrant and full of life! With a smile that lit up his whole face, and his contagious laugh, you could not help but feel happy just being around him. That was my Tucker.

I opened my eyes and looked again at this young man before me. A motionless body, dressed in a suit, with short hair parted down the middle. Every hair was in place. There was no smile on his face. I wondered if God would recognize him. My Tucker was gone ...

Or so I thought.

A weird feeling suddenly came over me. My attention was drawn to the right corner of the room where the wall met the ceiling. I got an overwhelming sense that Tucker was up in that corner. I didn't see or hear anything, I just had this feeling that he was there, like someone was pulling at me, watching me. Like someone was watching all of us. I looked again at the body, then back at the corner. The corner had all my attention.

A very small part of me wanted to point and yell out, "He's up there!" But after observing the other people in the room, no one else seemed to be drawn to that corner, and the larger part of me thought, "Keep your mouth shut." I never had any kind of supernatural experience before and was afraid to say anything to anyone. There was a history of mental illness in my family, and I didn't want any part of it. I convinced myself I was just upset and tried to shake it off.

Many of Tucker's childhood friends came to the wake, and I knew Lenny would be one of them. Lenny and Tucker were more than best friends...they were like brothers. Although Lenny and I had gone our separate ways, over the years we had run into each other on occasion and it was always uncomfortable for me because I never really got over him. A few years had passed since our last meeting, and I was hoping it would be different. I knew Lenny would be there, I just didn't know when he would arrive.

Lenny did arrive that first evening and like Tucker's family, was devastated and looking for someone to blame for this horrible tragedy. I, on the other hand, was more concerned with shaking off this feeling that Tucker was still with me, only now it felt like he was following me around! Lenny and I tried to console each other over the loss of our friend. It felt good to reminisce about the old days and there was a peaceful feeling between us.

That night, while driving home - alone in my two-seater MGB sports car - the feeling of Tucker was so strong, I pulled over and stopped the car. It felt as if someone was sitting behind me in the compartment area. Apprehensively, I looked in the rear view mirror, praying no one was there. I saw nothing, however, the feeling persisted. Although I was really scared, enough was enough. I spun my head around and shouted at him, "OKAY! What? What do you want? I can't see you but I know you're there, and I don't know what you want from me. You're going to have to find some better way to communicate because all this is doing is scaring me and creeping me out!" This was 1978 and I didn't know anyone who talked to dead people. I especially had no idea who to ask for advice. People would think I was going crazy. Heck, I was beginning to think I was going crazy. Although I didn't get any response from the back seat, thank God, I did feel braver. At least I had faced my fear.

Over the next few days, Tucker's presence remained constant and powerful. Although I didn't understand what he wanted, I was becoming more accepting of feeling his spirit. Soon it became comforting, knowing that he was with me. Lenny and I spent a lot of time together, not just at the wake but between calling hours as well. We were inseparable, even going to the funeral service and cemetery, together. The finality of the burial - it seemed so permanent, so surreal. Tucker's life was over because of some senseless stupid act of machismo. His family was heartbroken.

I wanted to tell them he had not gone anywhere - he was right here with me! I wanted to tell them his life was not over, he was just no longer in his body. That it seems as if death is not such a permanent ending and when life as we know it ends, the spirit continues.

But I didn't. My fear was too great. I was afraid of what people would say. I kept this to myself and didn't even tell Lenny.

The day of the funeral was horribly sad. The guilt and self-punishment on his father's face was unbearable. After all, it was his gun that killed his son. I could not be with his sadness. The same held true with his mom and siblings. Such grief, such a loss, so young, what could be said to comfort them? I wanted to say, "Hey, he's right here and has something to say – maybe one of you can hear him." But I didn't. I knew what happened to people who hear voices – they locked you up or put you on heavy doses of medication to keep you in a numbed state of existence.

Lenny and I had spent a lot of time together over the last few days, being upset and sharing our sorrow. He suggested that it might be a good idea for us to get away from everything and everyone, and I agreed. We booked a weekend get-away to the Bahamas and left two days after the funeral.

We boarded the plane and settled into our seats. As soon as the doors closed, and we were locked in together, I felt a different sense of loss. Tucker's presence was suddenly gone! As strange as it felt when he first came to me, once I got used to his energy it became a comfort. Now that he had so abruptly left, I must have made a sound because Lenny said, "What's wrong?"

"It's Tucker, he's been with me since the first night of the wake, and now he's gone." I couldn't believe I said that out-loud. Lenny stared at me in disbelief.

"He was with you too? He's been with me since the first day of the wake." I was astounded. We had *both* felt Tucker's presence but neither of us said anything. And, how was it possible that he was with *both* of us? How many others had felt Tucker's spirit and not said anything? This became our conversation over the entire trip. We shared our experiences of Tucker's presence as well as our memories of him.

As it turned out, Lenny and I were not meant to be together, but were able to bring a healthy, mutual closure to our relationship and remain close friends. That was Tucker's final gift to us, the completion and closure of our incomplete relationship.

The legacy he left was my awakening to the knowledge that although people die, they are still with us, and I will be forever grateful to him.

It would be more than twenty years before Tucker came to me again.

COMMENTS BY WAYNE: My own experience took place in 1982. My wife's grandfather, Tony Guardino was a family oriented man who loved to laugh and have a good time. He was bigger than life and had a particularly close relationship with my three-year-old son Brett. Brett was a very active little guy, always on the move, and grandpa Guardino adored him. They were emotionally linked.

At the age of 79, Grandpa Guardino passed away.

What does a three-year-old boy know about death? Brett had no knowledge or understanding of what happened. Yet, the next morning, he came scooting out of his room, screaming, "What is grandpa doing sitting on a branch outside of my window?"

We all went to his room but the vision was gone. We never discouraged Brett because he had obviously seen his grandfather. Yes, Grandpa Tony stopped by to say goodbye to his little pal, and I am sure that his energy is around Brett to this day.

I believe that most families have similar experiences but refuse to believe what they see and discourage any conversations about such happenings out of fear. If you, or someone you know has had a spiritual experience, do not doubt yourself. Give credibility to the event and ask that spirit to help you, or see if they need help. By trusting in your intuition and discarding your fears, your life will be greatly enhanced.

THE RE-AWAKENING...

It was twenty-five years after my experience with Tucker before I felt anything like that again. The experience of Tucker was stored away in my memory, and other than Lenny, I never told anyone. I was not interested in having this type of supernatural information held against me by society. I wanted a normal life.

Over the years, I married, had children, got a dog, two cats, a home in the country, and had the normal ups and downs of that lifestyle. But life happens and some things I dealt with and some I didn't. The things I didn't deal with eventually accumulated until I had my own *prescription for illness:*

At 48, I was diagnosed with severe arthritis and told that I would be on painkillers for the rest of my life. Not only would I be on painkillers, I would slowly begin to lose my flexibility and ultimately have to face the reality of being a cripple.

Months before I received this depressing diagnosis, a series of events occurred. It began just before Easter, or so I thought.

Every morning, for years, I would go for my two mile walk and I was in good shape. However, my marriage was starting to disintegrate and in order to give myself quiet time to think, or as a way to vent my upsets, I would go for a walk. It was one of those times when I stormed out of the house to "walk it off".

Imagine my shock when after walking only about 150 feet, I was suddenly paralyzed with excruciating pain. My lower back locked, my legs were in terrible pain, and I was twisted and bent to one side. I could not walk another step, and was all alone. After standing for what felt like an eternity, the pain subsided just enough that I was able to turn my head and see my house. It was a short distance, but this would be one of the longest walks of my life. Very slowly, each step agonizingly painful, I made my way back home, thankful that I could move at all. When I reached the house, my husband was there to help and gave me some over the counter pain relievers.

I had a history of lower back pain and although this was extreme, it was not the first time I experienced my back locking up. Not one to go to doctors, I spent the next few weeks pretending I was feeling better but getting worse. My automatic answer to anyone who asked was "I'm fine," a lie that could not have been further from the truth.

After much suffering and not much improvement, I finally went to a doctor because the pain was so grueling. I remember standing in the kitchen, holding my breath, being afraid to breathe. Terrible pains were shooting down my leg, from lower back to ankle. Tears ran down my cheeks. I wanted to cry out, but it was already so painful, I thought if I made noise it would hurt worse. I did not know what to do. I saw the telephone book on the counter, found a phone number for a pain relief center, and made an emergency appointment.

Upon my arrival, I was examined by a physician and sent for x-rays. I received prescriptions for pain killers and muscle relaxers along with a recommended set of floor exercises, which I could not do because I could not lay down.

Ultimately, I was diagnosed with arthritis of the spine and told I would be on painkillers for the rest of my life. Although I needed medication to stop the pain,

I knew in my gut that this life sentence was not one that I agreed with. I *had* to do something different in my life, something non-medical, or I would be living out my days on painkillers, my body twisted and contorted in odd directions. Not exactly what I had planned for my future. This is what I now refer to as *forced behavior modification.*

I discovered the book *Healing Back Pain – The Mind-Body Connection*[3] by John E. Sarno, M.D., that emphasized listening to our bodies because they speak to us. An odd concept for me at the time, but I tried it with some success. By using medications and exercises in this book, I was able to lie down again, walk more erect, and much of the pain dissipated. However, I was constantly vigilant of how I moved and fearful of the pain returning.

Somewhere, somehow, I knew there was more. The search continued.

I attended an introduction to a therapy called Network Spinal Analysis[4] – also known as NSA and its companion therapy, SRI or Somato-Respiratory Integration[5].

NSA is a gentle yet powerful therapy, designed to release spinal cord tension. The theory is that over time our bodies store all unresolved negative, emotional experiences and traumas as energy, in the spinal cord – or the "back of our mind" so to speak. As life happens and we don't fully process our experience, the remainder of the experience gets pushed to the back of our mind to be dealt with at a later date. Over time and for me that time was about forty-eight years, I had built up quite a stockpile of unfinished experiences that needed processing. These accumulated experiences were reflected in my body as severe arthritis.

I would later come to understand that arthritis is the physical manifestation for criticism, resentment and feeling unloved. The part of the body that it manifests in, for me the lower back, is about fear of money, lack of financial support and feeling safe. That would fit with someone whose marriage was disintegrating. I recommend everyone buy, read, and use - *Heal Your Body*, by Louise Hay[6], who cured herself of cancer – without surgery, chemo or radiation. *Heal Your Body* became my healing roadmap. It remains a cornerstone in my life and without a doubt one of my most valued books.

---

3   John E. Sarno, M.D., *Healing Back Pain – The Mind-Body Connection* (New York: Warner Books, Inc., 1991)

4   Donald M. Epstein, D.C., *Network Spinal Analysis / NSA Chiropractic,* http://wiseworldseminars. com

5   Donald M. Epstein, D.C., *SRI/Somato Respiratory Integration,* http://wiseworldseminars.com

6   Louise L. Hay, *Heal Your Body* (California: Hay House, Inc., 1987)

NSA is an advanced form of chiropractic that requires many years of special-ized education and training. An NSA office is about community entrainments, using one large room containing up to six massage-like tables. Usually soft music is playing, and the environment is warm, safe, and loving. Lying down on a table with your face comfortably supported in a head cradle, the practitioner makes a sequence of contacts at the base of the skull and at the sacrum using as much pres-sure as you would to touch your eyelid. This gentle touch whispers to the brain, "look here." The brain locates the tension, you bring your breath to that area, and on the exhale the tension you were unknowingly storing gets released. As the ten-sion releases, the spinal cord relaxes, and the vertebrae realign. Stress is relieved from the body, and from your life.

As tension released, less energy was being used to maintain my body in a defensive position, or the fight/flight/freeze syndrome. I was amazed. I hadn't realized how tense I was, until I wasn't. The extreme amount of tension I stored just became "the norm."

It was during one of these NSA sessions that the spirit of the mother of some-one I knew came to me with a very distinct message. Here I was, lying on the table, totally relaxed, enjoying the feeling of peace that permeated my entire being. Suddenly, these thoughts pop into my head: "Tell my son not to get mar-ried! You must stop the wedding!"

I thought to myself "Where did that come from? My sons are teenagers, they're not getting married!" I realized those first two thoughts were not mine. I knew I was Empathic (someone who feels other people's feelings), but until that moment, I had never heard messages like this. At least not since I was seven years-old laying by the little brook. I believe the level of relaxation and lack of resistance of my physical body, along with the extreme peace I was feeling, re-opened a channel from long, long ago. "Tell him not to get married." There it was again. Suddenly, the memory of Tucker, long since forgotten, rushed back into the forefront of my consciousness. Although the voice I heard in my head was my own voice, the thoughts were not mine. I must be making this up. I wasn't telling anyone anything! Over the next few months, during my NSA entrainments, the thoughts continued and I resisted. It got to the point where I was actually having arguments with this voice in my head. I now knew who it was and also that it was a woman who I had never actually met while she was alive. However, her message was never ending. "Tell my son not to get married, you must stop this wedding!"

At the time, I was not willing to share this experience with anyone. My old belief system was still running the show – *you don't tell people that you hear voices!*

However, she was not going away, and I was not comfortable delivering the message. This was a real dilemma.

How different would life have been for Tucker's family had I said something at the time of his funeral? This was a second chance and I realized this gift might alter someone's life, and should be delivered.

Finally, I figured out what to do.

During my next NSA entrainment, she was back. My "thought" to her was, "I will tell your son that I have a message from the other side and if he wants to know, I'll tell him. If he refuses, I'm relieved of my responsibility to deliver the message, and you'll stop the incessant badgering." She agreed. I fulfilled my agreement, and her son declined. The voice never returned.

I felt a sense of relief, but I also felt a sense of regret. My lack of courage amazed me. I was only the messenger. Very clearly I thought to myself, "Yes, and they shoot the messenger." Now there's a thought. Embedded in my belief system, this rang loud and clear. The next thought was whose belief system?

Here I was, almost a half a century old, and still afraid of what other people would think of me. Still avoiding my gifts, living my life through other people's "shoulds" and "what would the neighbors think?" Where was my wisdom, my courage?

What would my life have been like had I learned to embrace my gifts instead of avoiding them? How many people might I have helped over the years? I remembered my experience with Tucker. How might his family's lives been different if I had let them know what I was experiencing at the time of his death? Some may have been able to find peace as opposed to loss and grief. I myself had an amazing sense of peace because of my experience. I knew that death was not so much an end as it was another doorway that we all eventually go through.

From that point forward, I was committed to being courageous, open to new experiences and exploring the possibility of living a life exposed.

It was not long before Tucker returned. Again it was during an NSA entrainment, in a totally relaxed state, that I heard his message, "Please tell my dad." This time I was not afraid! Immediately, I got off the table, left the office, got in my car, and headed for the house Tucker had lived in over twenty years ago. An hour later, I knocked on the door, but Tucker's family had moved. The people who resided there did not know where they went. As hard as I tried, I could not locate any family member. Eventually I heard Tucker say, "It's okay, let it go." My thought was that while I was searching, Tucker's dad may have passed away. A beautiful feeling of peace came over me.

I have not heard from Tucker since, however, there have been many new messages from others, including one from the brother of a chief of police. This occurred during the time when I was a real estate agent. My sister, Lynn, and I were on the office computer trying to get tickets to see John Edwards, the famous psychic who had his own TV show. Phyllis, another realtor, asked what we were doing. She said, "You don't have to go there. I do what he does. I can tell you whatever you want to know." We said, "No way!" We had known Phyllis for years and never knew she was a psychic. I said, "Okay, tell me if there is anyone around me."

"Yes, Archangel David is with you all the time. I also see a young man who died of a gunshot wound. I think his name is Tommy. He has very short brown hair like in the military. Does this sound like someone you know?"

"It could be my friend Tucker. He died of a gunshot wound, and his name was Tommy but no one ever called him that. The hair's not right but it could be him." She said, "I'm getting J.C. Does that mean anything?" "No, but I'll think on it." The phone rang and I had to get back to work.

After work, Lynn and I went to her house. We were to meet up with our friend Jack and go to dinner. Excited about having Phyllis as our own psychic, we discussed what she had said. Somehow "Tommy" didn't feel like Tucker. Suddenly, I felt an incredible rush of breath come into my chest and I blurted out, "I think 'Tommy' is Jack's brother. He wants Jimmy to know. Tell JC. We have to tell Jack!" "Tell him what?" Lynn asked. "I'm not sure. I just know it's about Jack and Jimmy. Tell JC it's okay to heal."

I knew Jack's brother, Tommy, had died but had no idea how. I thought it was during his tour of duty. Jack also had another brother, Jimmy, who was still living, but had been badly injured years ago in Vietnam.

This wasn't just a voice or thought in my head, it was a whole new feeling, like an invisible pushing energy. I knew I had to tell Jack about Phyllis and what I had felt. Even though Jack and I were close, he was a Police Chief, and I was certainly not looking forward to telling a chief of police that I had a message for his living brother, Jimmy, from his dead brother, Tommy, on the other side. Oh boy! This was going to take some courage.

When Jack arrived, I relayed what had happened. I told him that he had to tell Jimmy what Tommy said. "Tell JC it's okay to heal. He has 'survival guilt' and cannot heal. Tommy says it's okay to heal." Jack was surprised, but open to what I said. He agreed to tell Jimmy.

During dinner, I again felt pressured to remind Jack to tell Jimmy. Jack then confirmed the message, "Tommy always called Jimmy, JC. No one really knew that. Tommy did die from a gunshot wound. He was in a bar and went to the aid of a woman who was accosted by an unstable man. The man became enraged, pulled a gun and shot him. Tommy died instantly." Jack also told us, "Jimmy had been in Vietnam and stepped on poisonous bamboo shoots which went completely through his feet. In all these years, Jimmy's feet have never healed. The skin is always falling off and they are continuously infected." All of this validated what Phyllis had said. Jack promised to relay the message.

During our ride home, the relentless need to implore Jack to pass on the message continued. I wanted to say over and over "you must tell him tonight, you must tell him tonight." By the time we got to the house, and before I could get out of the car, I had to say it! "You must promise Jack. You must tell him tonight! Tommy's real pushy and won't leave me alone unless you promise. Tonight!"

When Jack assured me he would tell Jimmy that night, Tommy stopped pushing.

Self-punishment and guilt is the worst kind of prison. The only way out is through forgiveness, of self or another. After decades of suffering, just a few words from the other side, delivered to someone who needed to hear them, made all the difference to this man. Jimmy is free and his feet have started to heal. Tommy has not visited me again.

The healing power of spirit is amazing. Although they are in another dimension, they will find a way to reach us if we are open to their way of communication. Often, during a healing session, spirits of loved ones are present and I welcome them with open arms, for there is only love once they are on the other side. Sometimes they communicate directly with the person and sometimes through me, which I willingly deliver. If you have the ability to communicate with the other side, embrace your gifts!

You are a Lightworker!

If you are the parent, sibling, spouse, friend, or know one of these people, encourage them to share their gifts and allow yourself to be open to yours. We are all connected, and are here for a larger purpose. We all have gifts to bring to the planet. Be adventurous and explore the possibilities!

Thank you, Tucker, for the wonderful legacy you have given me. I am forever grateful.

CHAPTER 4

Rebirth of a Shaman

WAYNE

What could a person with a background such as mine, know about Shamanism? The answer is: almost nothing. As I related in the Introduction, my Roman Catholic upbringing and attending of parochial schools, followed by a long career working in the financial markets of Wall Street, did little to make me aware of Shamanism.

I remember the old western movies where the soldiers chased the Indians and the medicine man, who wore some kind of animal skin on his head, was always the bad guy. He was usually shaking a rattle around a roaring fire and stirring up the tribe to battle the cavalry. What could I possibly have in common with this life style? My belief system was primed for a rude awakening.

Soon after I started going to Kathy for energy healings, amazing things began to happen during the sessions; things that were inexplicable by the standards of this modern day businessman.

During one healing, I had my first out of body experience. One minute I was lying on my back enjoying the peace and relaxation of the healing, and the next, it felt as if my chest concaved to the back wall of my spine and became about an inch thick - like it just collapsed! The rest of my body stayed normal. Suddenly, I, or more accurately my spirit, was above my body looking down at myself on the healing table. How could this be? This was no dream; the clarity was remarkable. I was viewing my physical body from several feet above! Although it seemed as if it lasted a long time, the whole experience was probably just a few seconds. Then I was back in my body, which returned to normal size. I became acutely aware of my physical body which was now *alive* with energy, the likes of which I have never experienced and for which I had no rational explanation. If I were asked to swear under oath how many hands I felt on my body, I would have said eight. Yet, I knew that Kathy was the only other person in the room. It was only by sneaking a peek that I verified there were only her two hands actually touching me. What was going on here? Closing my eyes again, I began to see an array of beautiful colors. They held indescribable beauty displayed in varied shades of reds, greens, blues, oranges, and yellows. My eyes, although closed, burned to see more. This was the most beautiful thing I had ever seen. It was a show that I never wanted to end.

There were also times when my body went through a period of what I call "ultimate euphoria", when every cell in my body was tingling with love and joy beyond expectation. This was a level of elation I never knew existed. If this is what we can expect in heaven, then we all have it made.

These healings were, up until now, imbued with joy. It was not in my realm of consideration that I could possibly have a healing with any sadness. What I did not realize is that as I received each healing, a clearing was taking place not only in my body but also in my thoughts. Daily worries just disappeared and I now was able to laugh at the idea of even having them. Fears that I lived with every day, including the fear of dying, were now gone.

At one of these early sessions, Kathy made a statement that I could not understand. "At some time, in a past life, you were a powerful Indian Shaman. I saw you as a leader among your tribe in a full headdress. You had long dark hair, and were wearing some sort of ornamental breastplate. You had a place of honor and people came to you for your wisdom and medicine."

Up until this moment, the healings had been all about the feel good experience and the colors. I couldn't get my mind around a past life, never mind being a Shaman. I could not fathom what this meant. However, my thought process was beginning to change. Never had I dreamt that a person could funnel energy through another person's body or that the effects could be so altering. Kathy clearly saw me as a Native American Shaman. In the past, I would have immediately dismissed this as nonsense, but now I did not rule out the possibility.

It was around this same time I commented to Kathy that she had a spectacular gift which enabled her to channel energy into someone's body. Her response was, "Anybody can do it."

How? How can anyone create such uplifting energy in another's body? I had my doubts but my imagination had been tweaked. If I could learn this skill, think of the family, friends and other people I could help. I asked her how?

Kathy told me that she and her sister, Lynn, had been healers for years and had gone to the Transformational Energy Healing Program in Torrington, Connecticut to enhance their knowledge. She suggested I attend an introduction to the program.

At the introduction Maureen Goodhouse, who developed and ran the program, explained the two-year curriculum. I enrolled, and during the first semester my Native American Shamanic background started to become apparent on a regular basis. Many energy healers, both first and third year students, and a psychic, observed the very same trait within me. Initially, I paid little attention to these assertions, but as they kept coming, my interest grew, as did my knowledge. There was no collusion going on here. These people had never discussed this. What was happening? Where was it coming from? My inquisitiveness was growing and I wanted to know more.

Patricia Higgins, a fellow student, worked for the Rockefeller Family for many years managing major special events for such luminaries as Nobel Peace Prize winner Desmond Tutu, President Clinton, the Council on Foreign Relations, the Museum of Modern Art, and the Nature Conservancy.

Patricia, who had just performed a newly learned healing technique on me said, "I saw you as a young Indian and then as an adult Indian paddling a canoe across a lake." She saw it very clearly but had no concept of what it meant. We became great friends and Patricia has since given me a framed picture of an Indian, books about Indians, and a book about Shamanism, by Tom Cowan, entitled *Shamanism, As a Spiritual Practice for Daily Life*[7]. This book illuminated an unexpected path for me on this journey.

---

7   Tom Cowan, Shamanism, As a Spiritual Practice for Daily Life (California: The Crossing Press, 1996)

My next encounter with a Shamanic link came in consecutive healings performed on me by Kathy and her sister Lynn. Not every healing creates tremendous elation and monumental shifts of energy. No one can predict what will happen. Sometimes there is sadness or depressed feelings. Usually when these arise, they are cleared, and they never bother the person again. I was expecting a healing filled with elation, but somehow I ended up in another dimension.

Shortly after Kathy began the healing, I saw myself in a teepee with a large fire in the middle. The heat from the fire was warming to my body, as several great chiefs entered. There was an Indian name mentioned that I cannot fully pronounce, "Milachichonk", or something sounding like that with guttural tongue clicking sounds accompanying it. The chiefs were happily greeted, and the atmosphere was filled with camaraderie that could only be shared by warriors whose lives and adventures were intertwined. Everyone was happy, and there were thrilling stories shared about successful buffalo and other hunts. It was a time of comfort, and we all felt a high level of bravado. My senses were heightened. I reveled in the sweet smell of mother earth, and the sound of the melodious trickle of a brook, just outside the teepee. Things felt good!

Just as quickly the mood changed and things felt very bad. I have no specific recollection of what went wrong, but whatever happened, it was not good for the tribe. It felt as if our way of life had disappeared, and only hardship and decline lay ahead. These feelings were so powerful that tears streamed down my cheeks. This continued throughout the remainder of the healing, and for a significant period of time thereafter.

Following the healing, I felt nauseous and upset. It took me quite a while to get myself together. Kathy shared her experience with me. "I saw you inside a teepee. There were many men, elders, gathered around a fire, and I could feel the heat. I was surprised to be in the teepee because I was a woman. I quietly moved among the gathering, bringing food and drink. There was arguing among the chiefs. I heard an Indian name that I can't fully pronounce. Something like "Milachichonk", pronounced with a guttural clicking of the tongue. It was your name. You were a powerful tribal Shaman. Across the fire from you was a very confrontational man, an adversary. He is your brother, in this lifetime. You did not see eye to eye. He wanted to go to war. You did not. He thought you were weak."

I don't know how she had heard the same name that I did, but she had. Although this healing was traumatic for me, it was another link to my Indian background.

The next day was my healing with Lynn. She was going to do an Astral healing, which allows your spirit to travel through time and space, wherever it chooses, while remaining tethered to your body.

It started slowly, but I soon began to feel energy shooting through my body. The buildup was so strong that it felt as if energetic jolts were coming from everywhere, and the overflow was released through my mouth by making sounds. I felt as if I was shaking, which was caused by the space between the cells of my body vibrating at an extremely high level.

A high vibration level in the body creates an atmosphere where disease cannot exist. In the 1920's and 1930's, a brilliant man, Royal R. Rife[8], invented a frequency machine that was designed to cure cancer by increasing the vibration level in the body and thus making it impossible for cancer to survive. He discovered "that all life forms vibrate at different frequencies. For example, the viral form of Herpes vibrates at a different frequency than Malaria. These frequencies are measurable, and can be programmed into software in the form of binary numbers. The same way sound waves can break windows, can be used to explode or implode different cells."

It is interesting to surf the Internet to see the diversity of frequency machines that are available and being marketed today. The energy healings that we perform raise the vibration level both in the healer, and the person receiving the healing, to a level that creates maximum health in both bodies. This is the situation Lynn created that day.

As the session continued I began to see a magnificent spectrum of colors. While I often see colors, I rarely see the color pink, and yet my entire view was filled with a solid pink. From the upper right hand corner of my vision I saw something white flying down across the center of my view. At first, I thought it was a spacecraft, but as it came closer, I quickly realized it was a magnificent white eagle. He had a huge wingspan and I was in awe of the gracefulness of his flight. As soon as he reached the mid-point of the pink, he flew directly into the center and disappeared. Shortly thereafter, the pink color also disappeared.

At this point, I was vibrating at such a high level, it felt as if every inch of me was shaking, as if I were outdoors on a cold winter's night wearing only a bathing suit.

The healing took a long time to wind down. When I felt ready, I sat up and found Kathy in the room with me. She said, "Lynn went to take a shower and asked me to keep an eye on you. How are you feeling?"

---

8   Royal R. Rife, *The Website of Royal Rife*, 1888-1971, http://www.rife.org/

> *COMMENTS BY KATHY: When I arrived at Lynn's house, she met me at the door and said, "Wayne's off flying on the back of an eagle. Keep an eye on him while I take a shower." I went into the healing room to find Wayne lying on the table. His body was twitching and shaking. As I had seen this many times before with different people, I was not concerned. I knew this was the body releasing stored energy that was not needed. I call it an energetic clearing, a healthy process.*

I was drained and the high vibration level left me partially dehydrated. I drank a large quantity of water then and over the next few days. It seemed as if I could not consume enough water to quench my thirst.

When Lynn returned to the room, she said, "Did you see all that pink?"

I was flabbergasted! "Yes, but how did you see the pink that I saw?"

She responded, "That pink was your father. He was here and wanted you to know that he is very proud of you."

I had never spoken to Lynn about my father and she could not have known that he had passed away several years before. This obviously blew me away. She then commented, "Did you see that eagle?"

This blew me away. "I saw it, but how did you?"

Lynn added, "I saw the eagle and you were riding on its back."

This whole experience almost seemed like a cartoon. Could this be real? Here I was, relatively new to this whole realm of healing, never experiencing anything like this before, having visions of eagles. Even stranger than that, someone else saw what was going on in my mind. Yet, I knew what I had seen, and without any prompting from me, Lynn shared what she had observed and provided confirmation. However, despite the strangeness of all this, I felt very comforted that my father was there and proud of me.

It was almost a year later when I realized what all this meant to my Shamanic background. Patricia Higgins was reading the Cowan book on Shamanism when she felt an overwhelming urge to stop reading, and get the book to me as soon as possible.

According to Cowan, each Shaman has a power animal that he uses for its power and as a guide. As I read through the book, I thought that my power animal was a mountain lion, but as soon as I followed a simple ritual outlined in the book, it became evident that it was an eagle. A few days later, I remembered the eagle in Lynn's healing. I wondered if the eagle in that healing had some link to this being my power animal. As I read on, Mr. Cowan stated that a power animal helps the Shaman fly by carrying him on his back to a place where the Shaman asked to go. Could it be that a year earlier I had requested the eagle take me to my father? How could this be a coincidence? I have no doubt that my latent knowledge of Shamanism led me to my dad.

Kathy and Lynn introduced me to the book *Medicine Cards*9, which provided an in depth description of our power animals. For me, the Eagle represented power and the ability to stay connected to spirit and the divine, while remaining grounded to the earth. In addition, the Eagle is about owning one's personal power and overcoming fears.

It was after reading Tom Cowan's book that I understood another shamanic experience that happened, while vacationing with my son Brett, my brother Bruce, my nephew Little Brucie, and his six-year-old son, Aidan. We were in one of the largest wilderness areas in the mountains of Idaho.

It was a beautiful June day as we left our base camp and headed deeper into the Selway Wilderness Area of the Rocky Mountains. Brett and Brucie headed off together on an ATV, and later separated further down the trail. Aidan, Bruce, and I, traveled in a different direction on another ATV. Aidan was my partner for the day, and Bruce dropped us off several miles down the trail, and was scheduled to pick us up later that afternoon.

It was fun for me to see the world through a child's eyes as he explored the various insects, birds, plants, animals, and their tracks, along the trail. Shortly after enjoying our picnic lunch, the wind started to pick up and it began to rain. As I turned to look in the direction of the oncoming storm, I knew this was going to be bad. Weather can be unforgiving at any time of the year in this country, and today was no exception.

A ferocious storm was rolling in. The wind was howling, trees were bending over, and the skies were turning black. Bolts of lightning were getting closer as were the thunderous booms that accompanied them.

Aidan was beginning to get scared. I was concerned about our safety, as well as the safety of our entire party. We were spread out, several miles apart, with no way to contact each other and in for an ominous storm.

My newly awakened intuitiveness guided me to send what I now call a "peace and serenity healing" to the sky. I had never done anything like this before, and have no idea why I did, yet it felt totally natural. I stood facing the storm, eyes to

---

9 Jamie Sams & David Carson, and illustrated by Angela Werneke, *Medicine Cards,* (New York: St. Martin's Press, 1988)

the heavens, arms outstretched. It was as if I was part of the sky, and just as when I perform a healing on individuals, I sent my guides to see if they could calm the angry forces of nature. In very short order, the wind died down, the lightning and thunder ceased, and the rain eased to a drizzle before stopping. I thanked my guides, and those from the skies, for honoring my request. This is the closest I have ever felt to the elements of nature. I was stunned and absolutely amazed by what had taken place.

Later that evening, I told the group what I had done, running the risk of being ostracized as a lunatic. I have no way of knowing what they actually believed but they all knew the storm that was riding our backs and covering the entire horizon had completely and inexplicably stopped. No one said a derogatory word because they know I'm a healer, and they knew something beyond the norm had happened.

It was months later, while reading the book, that I received insight to this event. Tom Cowan's comments, on how the shaman can sometimes influence the weather, gave validation to my experience.

Several weeks after this I met psychic, Dennis Levesque. I have never been one to pay any attention to psychics or even believe in them. However, since Dennis worked at The Holistic Center of Healing Arts & Personal Growth that Kathy and Lynn co-owned, he came highly recommended. Dennis shook my hand and looked into my eyes with a gentle but piercing stare. He said, "You were a great Indian shaman in a former existence." He perceived buffalo and saw turquoise, which is often used in Indian jewelry and ornaments. Although he did not know which tribe, he thought it was of the Great Plains.

At another healing with Kathy, in my mind's eye, I saw two portraits of the same magnificent Indian. One portrait was with a beautifully adorned headdress while the other was without the headdress and bare-chested. Each portrait was from the waist up. Although the vision did not last long, I felt that these portraits were definitely of me.

During the last weekend class of my first year the program gave each of the student healers a special gift. The third year students read the inner cores of each individual in my class. As they viewed student after student, I had a strong premonition that something to do with Indians was going to be revealed when my core was viewed. Sure enough, I was observed as being a wise old sage, an Indian shaman, and turquoise was seen. After the readings were done, I asked if any of them knew which tribe and one woman said she felt I was a Chippewa, but I am still not sure. However, I know that this background makes me a better healer and

I will continue to recall my Shamanic abilities and utilize them in conjunction with my energy healing skills to maximize what I can do for humanity. I view these instances as a rebirth of Shamanic knowledge that has been dormant in me for many years.

COMMENTS BY KATHY: I have actually shared some of the same visions that Wayne has experienced during his healings. I have seen many of his past lives and on multiple occasions, I have seen him as an Indian shaman and leader. At each of his healing sessions, he is in such a place of surrender, having no agenda of his own, and allows himself to experience the ultimate benefits of these healings whether it be physical, emotional, mental, or spiritual. Wayne is a "yes to life"! I can only imagine what lies ahead now that he has remembered his Shamanic abilities.

CHAPTER 5

Get the Wagons Rolling

KATHY

In August of 2004, Danielle called to schedule a healing. For months, she had been suffering with extensive pain and pressure in her abdomen which prompted her to go for medical tests. She had just left her doctor's office with distressing news and was extremely concerned about the medical diagnosis. Danielle had several large fibroid tumors attached to her uterus. After reviewing the test results, her doctor immediately scheduled an appointment for the next day with a surgeon, to discuss having a partial hysterectomy.

Danielle was distraught. This was her worst nightmare!

A warm, loving person, Danielle yearned to have children, but at the age of thirty-two, her plans hit a brick wall. She was crushed, but not ready to give up hope. She knew the power of the healings and wanted to try to shrink the fibroids and avoid surgery that might make conception impossible.

As a healer, I believed Danielle's fibroids were created from an emotional hurt to her feminine ego which manifested in her physical body. My intent was to have

Danielle understand the root of her problem, release the pattern that created it, and create a life of perfect health and joy.

As soon as I placed my hands on her abdomen, the area of creativity, I experienced feelings of overwhelming sadness and confusion which persisted throughout much of the healing. The image in my mind was a mass of vines and branches intertwined, entangled and congested. These were all wrapped around the largest fibroid, choking off her center of creation. I cleared out the area, and filled it with glowing green energy leaving the entire abdomen rejuvenated, refreshed and healthy. At that time, the fibroids were not willing to dissolve, but they were willing to diminish in size. Danielle needed to take actions in her life, some small and some large, and the fibroids were to stay as a reminder, a motivator. This was the message I received from her body. I proceeded with the healing, re-charged and balanced her chakras[10], re-energized her fields, closed the healing and gave thanks.

Afterwards, Danielle felt much better and I shared my insights. We spoke about her dreams that had been stowed away on the back burner until someday, one day, somehow, down the road, maybe they would come to fruition. My explanation that the fibroids were willing to reduce, but not willing to go away, was somewhat consoling. However, although she understood the concept that the fibroids would remain as a reminder for her to pursue her dreams, she was not totally thrilled. She wanted them gone!

As a highly creative person, she was not expressing her creative gifts or realizing her dreams. In fact she had been selling herself out. She realized the profession she was in, although it provided her with financial security, was not aligned with her spirit. There was *no* outlet for her creative side. Her spirit was suffocating. Knowing her fibroids were not something to be afraid of but were actually giving her powerful guidance for her life, she agreed to take action toward finding an outlet for her creativity. When she left my office that evening, she was grounded, empowered, and confident.

Danielle decided to keep her appointment with the surgeon. She wanted to see if the tests showed any change in her condition.

The following afternoon she called. Frightened by what the surgeon told her, Danielle was electing to have the surgery. This was her final decision. She accepted the surgery as the best solution to eliminate the pain and pressure from the fibroids. She was to have a partial hysterectomy.

While recuperating from what ended up being a full hysterectomy, she came to terms with not being able to birth any children. Accepting this outcome, she

---

10 Chakra - See Resource Guide

began to explore her creative possibilities and looked forward to her new future. Danielle had an incredible eye for color and design. She started her own interior decorating business.

The following February, Danielle came for another healing session. The operation had been successful and her uterus removed, however, the pain returned.

She asked, "How could this be? How can I have such pain when the cause of the pain had been surgically removed over five months ago? I thought I was done with this."

I recommended a past life[11] healing suggesting it might reveal the cause and provide guidance for healing this phantom pain. Past life healings can clear patterns of behaviors, memories, or fears that originated in a past lifetime but are manifesting in the current one.

Danielle was intrigued and wanted to know more.

Have you ever met someone, looked into their eyes, and had the unmistakable feeling you knew them? Yet, at the same time, you know you have never met them before ... in this lifetime.

Life is a series of experiences that develop us into the people we become. As we go through life we all have loving and joyful, as well as hateful and traumatic experiences. Like individual snapshots, these are embedded in our cellular memories and stored in our minds, for all time. Some we can easily remember, while others we cannot or do not want to recall, but they abide within us just the same.

When people have mental or physical breakdowns, they usually go to the medical community for help, including specialists skilled in handling specific ailments or parts of the body. Each patient is required to fill out a form regarding medical history for themselves and their immediate family. I have never heard of a doctor asking about a person's past life history, and yet something in a former life may be causing the current ailment.

What about the person that the medical community cannot help?

We've all heard of people who exhibit phobias of things, or situations, linked to spiders, heights, water, elevators, bridges, or even a specific building, and so on. Often there is no logical reason for the phobia as the person has not experienced anything in this lifetime that would perpetuate such a fear. This condition is very often the result of some traumatic experience that happened in a past life and has carried into the person's current existence.

---

11   Brian L. Weiss, M.D., *Many Lives, Many Masters,* (New York: A Fireside Book, Simon & Schuster, 1988)

These traumatic experiences may also cause physical problems.

A past life healing can reveal problems from the past that are affecting the current, and thus provide a path to resolution in this lifetime. For instance, people who starved to death in a past life may over-eat because they always feel hungry. People may get sick every year at a certain time because they got sick and died at that time of year in another lifetime. A person who made a poor traveling choice in another lifetime and ended up dying in the mountains may now continue to punish himself by making poor choices in this lifetime. People who are afraid to take on a leadership role may have made decisions in a past life that resulted in people being killed. These scenarios are endless but events that happened in times long, long ago have a profound effect on our current lives.

Past lives are not something to be frightened of but are a record of our historical past as eternal beings. We may change the vehicle we travel in but we keep on going. There is an incredible sense of freedom and peace that comes with the recognition that death is not the end. It is merely part of the process and the energy that is us, goes on forever.

Danielle said, "Let's do it!"

A past life healing is performed in a different energetic field. Grounding myself, inviting our angelic teams for support, I raised my vibration level and began at Danielle's feet. Moving up to her left hip, I detected an arrow imbedded between her hipbone and abdomen. I thought, "Okay, this is what is causing the pain. The arrow needs to be removed." I asked Danielle's spirit for permission to remove it, which is not always granted. Permission was given. The arrow which felt very long and hot in my hand, released easily. "Now I can seal up the hip area and fill it with healing light and maybe this was the cause of the phantom pain she was having in her abdomen." As I cleansed the wounded area, a scenario about a spinning wagon wheel and Indians came into my head. There was no noise but, a progression of snapshots through time, played out. Moving to her head, there was a scalping, which was disgusting and seemed uncomfortable for both Danielle and me. I felt nauseous and opened my eyes to observe Danielle. Her face was contorted so I quickly healed that area and moved on. The healing of her scalp brought peace to the area and to her face. So I thought, "Great, past life done."

I continued with the healing moving to her right side and leg. Aha…another past life. Her leg was very cold from the knee to the ankle. It seemed Danielle had been a fur trapper who'd been caught in a trap for a very long time, got frostbite and ended up having the leg amputated above the knee. My hand was directly on the area funneling energy into it. I cauterized the wound and sent warm, loving energy down her leg and into her foot, reconnecting all disconnected parts, cells and consciousness.

When I got to her abdomen, the wagon wheel was back again, and it seemed that Danielle may have lost a baby because of the arrow. Between the arrow, the scalping and the baby, this was a very traumatic death. Feeling some anxiety coming from Danielle, I knew that the past life portion of the healing was complete and our angelic teams confirmed this to be true. I sent love, light, and compassion to all areas affected and finished with a gentle balancing of her chakras, connecting each to the next and creating an open flow of energy.

I asked Danielle to turn over and performed a spinal cleansing to support her immune system. When the healing was complete, I allowed her time to process the experience.

When Danielle was ready, she sat up and said, "Wow! That was wild!"

She had received her own past life information when my hand was touching the back of her neck. "I was a witch and was persecuted and then killed for speaking my truth." She saw how that affects her life now and her ability to speak out. She continued, "There were, and still are, many Ancient Ones in the room with us, and I felt very safe. I can still feel their presence."

I told her what I had seen. She listened, laughed at the strangeness of it all, and accepted the information. She said that at one point during the session she started to get anxious. I told her I perceived her anxiousness as an indication the healing was complete and our angelic guides confirmed she was finished.

We laughed, thanked each other and our fabulous team of guides, angels, and others. It was an extraordinary healing for both of us, safe, incredible. Wow!

A few days later, Danielle brought me the hand-written pages she wrote of the past life that came to her after our session.

August 26, 1874

The day is our best yet this summer in what is now known as 'modern day Montana.' I step out onto our porch and breathe in the fresh air as I admire the beauty of the rolling hills. The bustle around me quickly brings me back to earth as I realize it is getting late and there is much still to be done.

The workers are loading our coach with all our belongings and Emma Sue – my lady in waiting – packed us a full lunch for our long journey.

Today is moving day!

As I tidy up and pack the final piece of clothing in my luggage, I hear his voice out by the barn, the voice which soothes my soul and warms my heart, for four years and going strong. My husband, Anthony, is leaving last minute instructions to his brothers as they will be taking over in his absence. My husband is a prominent business man in our community: he owns our county's largest mill. Not only do I love him, the whole county has a high level of respect for him and loyal trust in his abilities. So much so, they have voted unanimously that he head further west to become the mayor of a small village recently settled. I am so proud of my love; he has done a fine job in this community.

"Ready Sweetheart? We have a long journey ahead of us and in your condition I don't want to put in any more than eight hours a day."

I am expecting our first child – a son! We have already named him – Sydney – after Anthony's great, great, grandfather.

"Yes, my love. All packed and ready for our new start!"

He drew me in close, held me tight, and said "All of this is not possible without you."

I feel a wave of warmth wash over me, and I feel like I did the very first time I saw him when he entered the room and my heart jumped into my throat. The minute our eyes connected, I felt our souls combine as one, and I immediately knew he was the man I was going to marry. We were put on this earth to find one another.

A few clouds begin to roll in. Emma Sue gives me a hug goodbye and helps me into the coach. Anthony comes down the porch steps, pausing briefly, fixing his watch in the pocket of his freshly pressed navy blue suit. I smile, so proud, knowing he's all mine, forever.

"Ready to begin our new life in the western territory, wife?"

"Absolutely!" I say, grinning ear to ear.

He smiles sweetly, tucking a loose strand of blonde hair behind my ear, giving me a wink. And with that, our driver calls out to the horses and we were off on this bright and sunny August day.

THE HEALERS

Several days have passed and so far, for the most part, the weather has held up nicely. Today is no different with a clear, blue, sunny sky and a few white puffy clouds. I glance over at Anthony, sitting across from me in the coach, as we slowly make our way across the prairie. He grins widely while gently rubbing my belly. At eight and a half months, he knows it won't be long before our Sydney makes his grand appearance.

Suddenly, our coach takes a jolt. The horses begin whinnying, and there is some screeching. Anthony opens the door of the coach and is immediately struck in the heart with an arrow. He falls to the ground, lifeless. He does not move. I scream in disbelief, my love is dead. In horror, I see through the window our driver and most of our horses are dead, all by arrows.

Tears well in my eyes, as I can't believe what is happening. My soul mate, the man with whom I share my innermost secrets and thoughts, the man I love with every ounce within me – will never take another breath. I will never again see his deep brown eyes look into mine and travel deep into my heart. I will never hear his laugh again or feel his touch.

I am frozen. I want to jump out of the coach, run to him and hold him one last time. Before I move, I see them. Their faces painted red with white and black. Their manes of black hair, some shaved on the sides, some braided. They head straight for me.

I scream and hold my belly. What is going to happen to me and Sydney?

They reach in and yank me from the coach. "My baby! Please don't hurt my baby!" I scream and plead. I securely fasten both hands to my belly. Another man pushes me to the ground, and they all begin kicking me in my head, hips, and stomach. "Oh, Sydney!!!" My eyes are puffing and swelling by the minute. It is no longer clear what is happening. My pain is severe. I feel an arrow puncture my thigh.

Oh no, Sydney! No please no! I am your mother and I have to raise you and give you a happy life.

Another arrow punctures my stomach – Sydney – No! – Sydney!!! "My baby boy! No, please, no!!" I scream out at them.

I feel a knife puncture my stomach and my skin ripping open. The pain is unbearable. What are they doing to my baby?

Out of my swollen eyes, I can barely see my baby's back hunched over, facing away from me. I feel warm blood flowing out and all around me. I immediately feel cold. I am losing consciousness. I don't hear Sydney crying. I see nothing other than his back – my beautiful Sydney – being taken away by a man with many feathers.

I feel a fistful of my hair being pulled, lifting my head from the ground. A jagged knife rips down my scalp and blood falls over my face and down the back of my neck as I am scalped.

Where is my baby – where is Sydney? Is he alive? I hadn't heard him cry. Was he alive? Where were they taking him? If he was alive, would he be hurt by the Indians? Will he ever know he had a mother and father who loved him more than life itself? Will he grow up hating the woman who brought him into this world because he looks different than everyone else? Or is he dead? Is my beautiful boy who was created out of the most pure form of love not even going to breathe a single breath or be given a chance in life?

The cold washing over my body increases by the moment. I know it won't be much longer. My weeping gets softer. I use whatever strength I have in me to turn over to see my love for the last time. My eyes rolled closed – forever.

Danielle also wrote to her son – Sydney:

To my Sydney –

My beautiful boy: Not knowing if you lived or died has been following me for several lifetimes. The guilt I feel over not protecting you with all of my ability has haunted me – no matter what lifetime I am presently in. I have not forgotten you. Not in this life or the next as you live in my soul. I want you to know about your father. I have found him again – in this life, and he is a large part of my life. I fell in love with him the moment I saw him and the last few years he and I have connected on a soulful level. He does not know about our history together as he is caught up in his present day pain and has shut down.

But let me tell you this, Sydney. I know deep in his heart, in an area he is not capable of reaching yet, lives an incredible amount of love for you. He was so excited for your arrival and he was the proudest father-to-be. I wonder if you would have had his brown eyes or my green eyes.

I hope your soul knows that wherever you are Sydney – in whatever lifetime you are in – that I will always love you. I hope you can connect with your heart and find the love I have for you.

I am sorry you were abandoned. I am sorry I never got a chance to hold you and nurture you.

I love you Sydney, now and always.

Love,
Mom

After reading this, Danielle and I sat and talked. I shared with her my intuition that although this may sound strange – I believe Sydney is actually her father in this lifetime! She looked shocked! She said her father, who she feels she raised in this lifetime, has moved to New Mexico and is living on an Indian Reservation – the right hand man to the chief of the tribe. Now it was my turn to appear shocked!

After this, Danielle had an incredible sense of peace come over her. She is no longer in any physical or emotional pain. This healing permeated her life and it was not too long after, that she chose to leave her marriage and job to pursue a more desired lifestyle and career.

By addressing the reoccurring pain from a past life perspective, Danielle was able to uncover the core cause of her medical problems, created over several previous lifetimes. Healing this traumatic memory in this lifetime means it is complete and will not carry forward into lifetimes to come. She has accepted the fact that she will not bear children in this lifetime but intuitively knows she will have children in her life, through a future marriage.

Danielle recently wrote me, "…I am living in upstate New York, happily married and step-mom to three great kids. I'm enjoying my life and living it to the fullest!"

COMMENTS BY WAYNE: After Danielle had the operation and the pain returned, she was at a crossroads. She could have returned to the medical model and I have to wonder, what new diagnosis or treatment awaited her?

Every experience in this life and our past lives is maintained like a series of videos in our spiritual being. Danielle's feminine ego received a severe blow when her family was violently killed and she was helpless to stop it. As she lay dying a traumatic death, unsure if her son lived or died, Danielle was consumed with guilt that her son might hate her because she would not be there for him.

Danielle also saw the hurts she was stowing from her current relationship. The heavy burden that Danielle was bearing created the perfect environment for her fibroids.

Danielle wanted to be healed and her intuition guided her down the path to Kathy. The power of this healing goes far beyond any words that describe it. How could both Kathy and Danielle have the same vision of an incident that happened in 1874? How could Danielle remember every intricate detail of that fateful day and document it the way she did? I wonder what would have happened had Danielle had this past life healing before the hysterectomy. If this had been cleared she may very well have been able to have children.

The end result of this fabulous healing was that Danielle achieved a new level of comfort and peace from a past life event and moved happily on with her current life.

CHAPTER 6

Miracle on the Mountain

WAYNE

I believe most people would describe a miracle as an event leading to a result that goes far beyond anything viewed as possible within their belief system. Yet, there are those who live in a world surrounded by miracles. For these people, miracles have become the norm. As my experiences in healing have grown, I expect miracles, and although they do not happen all the time, I see them more and more.

A classic example might be a young woman crossing the street when a tragedy occurs. She witnesses a multi-car accident, and one vehicle lands on top of a small child. There is no time to think. The young woman races to the auto and effortlessly lifts it off the child. We have all heard stories similar to this. How could anyone lift several thousand pounds? Was this a miracle? The most common explanation given is that the woman was empowered by an adrenalin rush. Yet common sense will tell you, adrenalin or not, anyone lifting that amount of weight would have ligaments torn, joints ripped out of their sockets, and bones snapped. So how did she do it?

A few years ago, on a frosty November morning, I had my own experience. I was riding my all-terrain-vehicle (ATV) along a mountain ridge. I turned off the main trail and began winding down an extremely steep mountainside moving gingerly between closely cropped oak and ash trees. About half way down I arrived at my destination. To avoid flipping over backwards on the return trip, I loaded 150-pounds of cargo on the front of my machine and started back up the mountain.

Although it was a treacherous, straight up climb, I had little trouble and was relieved when I could see the crest of the ridge where I knew it would level off. About fifteen yards from the top, my front tires caught in the intersection of two trails and the weight on the front shifted and flipped the ATV. Time seemed to slow down yet there was nothing I could do. In what felt like extreme slow motion, I was thrown off the machine and it followed me through the air. I landed flat on my back, my shoulder up against a stump and a large rock on the downhill side, with over 800-pounds of upside down vehicle resting squarely on my chest.

Time returned to normal.

It was difficult to breathe and I realized if the machine tilted even a little, it would crush my lungs. I assessed my condition and even though I couldn't move, nothing seemed broken. Screaming for help would be useless as I was deep in the woods and no one would hear.

What should I do? What could I do? My arms were pinned along with the rest of my body, and all I could manage was modest squirming. Amazingly, I never panicked.

I had no idea how much time passed, but all of a sudden, the stump and rock gave way and rolled down the hill. Squirreling myself out from under the load, I stood up facing downhill and breathed a huge sigh of relief. I was euphoric, thankful to be out of that trap!

As I brushed myself off I realized my knife, which was kept in a sheath, had dislodged and disappeared into the leaves on the side of the mountain. Expecting it would be like looking for a needle in a haystack I surprisingly found it in short order. Turning around to face the machine, I was astonished to see that the ATV was no longer upside down, but was on its side!

A series of thoughts and questions rushed through my mind. "I don't remember lifting the machine." "I must have done it and not realized it." "How could

I lift so much weight from the downhill side of a sixty degree angle when I can't even budge this machine on flat ground?" "How?" I could not figure out exactly what had transpired, and could not dwell on it while I still had the ATV on its side on such a steep grade.

I knew if I could somehow turn the machine so both the front and back tires were facing up the hill, I might be able to put enough of my weight on the side to turn it upright and keep it from catapulting over me and down the mountain. I tugged as hard as I could to move the back tires. They grudgingly shifted a little, and when I thought I could flip it, I gave it a whirl. It almost started to tumble, but I was able to stabilize it by using the weight of my body.

I turned the key and it started immediately. After a quick scan, I realized that nothing was broken. The handlebars were fine and other parts that were breakable did not have a mark on them.

I checked again and there did not appear to be anything wrong with me. I looked at the stump and the rock that had rolled down the hill and couldn't believe I dislodged such solid weighty objects.

As I drove away from the scene, I couldn't believe my luck. Or was it luck? My mind played the scenario over and over again. The best I could come up with was that I must have lifted the ATV, but how?

When I got to flat ground I tried to lift one side, but couldn't budge it!

The next morning there was not so much as a black and blue mark on my body, but I was achy and called Kathy. After telling the story to her and Lynn, I asked them to send me an energy healing for my pains. Before long they called me back and had part of the answer to this puzzle. They said, "You didn't lift the machine off of yourself, a spirit named Uncle Charlie did. Your father was in the background." Lynn thought that Uncle Charlie was the spirit of some distant family member.

My mind began to race. I knew I couldn't have lifted that machine, and their explanation made more sense to me than my lifting such a massive weight.

But who was Uncle Charlie? I never remembered hearing anyone in my family mention that name. The healing Kathy and Lynn sent took away my aches and pains, but I craved to know about Uncle Charlie.

Later that day, Kathy and Lynn were visiting Kathy Pepe, a psychic. They told her about the ATV rolling over on me, the healing and Lynn's perception of the event.

Kathy Pepe immediately knew what had happened:

While Wayne was on the ground, his father protected him so that he would not be injured. Uncle Charlie is not a family spirit. He is a huge guardian angel with an enormous wing-span. As he hovered over Wayne, he gave the appearance of a ski jumper suspended in mid-air, fully extended over the scene. As Wayne lay on the ground, Uncle Charlie touched him on the forehead so he would not panic, and then lifted the machine off of him with one swoop. Wayne's father was off in the distance, leaning against a tree and smiling because he knew that his son was protected and safe.

I had never met Kathy Pepe, but after hearing her explanation, I was in awe of her. How could she see what happened to me on the side of that mountain? From my healings I knew I had three guardian angels – Simon, Cary and Joseph – but never knew about the angel Uncle Charlie. I now invite all four of my angels, along with my guides, to assist when I do healings.

Months later, I had the opportunity to meet Kathy Pepe. I was leaving Kathy Raymond's home and getting in my car, when Kathy Pepe saw me through her window and came outside to introduce herself. She said, "You're the man I saw on the side of the mountain with the huge angel hovering above you! You must be Wayne!" She reiterated how clear the vision was. It was so clear she was even able to recognize me despite never having met me before.

Kathy Pepe still receives visions of me, and each time, it's the same. She describes a specific place in the wilderness with trees off in the distance, a meadow, and two babbling brooks coming together creating a river. The land between the two brooks is covered with rocks. On the other side of the river there is green land and some sort of fence. Kathy's observation is so vivid that she has drawn a sketch of the setting. Although I have neither an association with the images nor understanding of what they mean, I'm sure that at some time in the future, I will.

After going through my own experience, I now believe adrenalin isn't the only thing involved, if at all, with a person lifting massive amounts of weight to save themselves or others. In such situations, there are times when one's guardian angels step forward to save the day. I believe that because I constantly request my guardian angels to assist me in healing others, and in my everyday personal life, that Uncle Charlie got the message and came to my rescue.

From the human viewpoint, this was a miracle. It was a disaster in the making that resulted in a non-disastrous outcome. I now see miracles both big and small on a regular basis, and with the team I have working with me, there will be many more in the future. As for Uncle Charlie and my dad, this is what they do, business as usual.

COMMENTS BY KATHY: Wayne's abilities and skills to connect with, ask for, and accept help and guidance from his spirit guides, guardian angels, Source, and loved ones that have crossed over inspires me!

Many people don't believe they have this kind of supportive team, but we all do. And we also have something called "free will". This means that unless we request or want their help, our team cannot assist us. They cannot intervene without permission. Just say, or think, "Please always help me."

If you would like to discover the name of your angel, follow these steps:

1. *Close your eyes*

2. *Take three gentle breaths*

3. *Think this thought ... "Dear Angel(s), please tell me your name(s).*

4. *For some, the answer will come right away. For others, especially if you're new to this or use to doing things on your own, it may take a few times.*

5. *Give thanks.*

6. *Ask for their help. Start to play with them. The more you ask the more familiar it will feel. Eventually, it will become the norm.*

7. *Watch for miracles!*

There is a great book called The Parables of Kryon[12], *and in this book is the story of "Wo." Kryon tells us that there are angels with us from the time of our birth. At the end of the story, Kryon wants to know, "Have you hugged your angels today?"*

Well have you?

12   Lee Carroll, *The Parables of Kryon,* (California: Hay House, Inc., 1996)

CHAPTER 7

Charades with the Angels

KATHY

The coffee was already brewing when I heard the doorbell. Always punctual, my sister, Lynn, arrived precisely at 7AM. We had set aside this entire Sunday to work on our plans for the Grand Opening of our new venture and dream – *The Holistic Center of Healing Arts & Personal Growth!*

As I opened the door and bid her "good morning" she announced, "Pack your bags and order some airline tickets. We're going to Florida!" Pausing just long enough to pour herself a cup of coffee she added, "Oh yea, we'll need a rental truck and car carrier."

I stared at her as if she had two heads, "Today? You're kidding, right? It must be a hundred degrees down there!"

"Yes. Today! I've had enough! I have to go down there now. Will you come?"

"We're supposed to have the grand opening next week and there's still a lot to do. Why are we going now?"

"I'm tired of my 'loved ones' taking advantage of me and disrespecting my home and possessions. I've repeatedly asked them to stop using my car, my bed, and my home without permission and to stop stealing my stuff. They don't seem to hear me. Rather than calling the police, I've decided to remove my belongings."

"Do you realize this is the 4th of July weekend? Are you sure this can't wait?"

"Absolutely not! *Your* mother *("my mother?")* called just now to ask why *my* car was making such a horrible noise when she backed it out of *my* garage. When I asked her why she was stealing my car again, she laughed and said, "I'm not...I'm borrowing it." I said, "Didn't we just have this conversation about the difference between borrowing and stealing when you stole my car last week and called to ask why the convertible top would not go up? Didn't we discuss then that borrowing is with permission, stealing is without permission? Not only did you *not* ask for permission, you think this a joke. You're stealing my car! Why don't you use your own car? To which she replied... "I look better in your shiny convertible than I do in my car." (*Our* mother is 83 years young!)

For Lynn this was the final straw, but it was far from the only incident.

"Other family members have repeatedly taken advantage of my generosity and in my absence, abused, used, and ruined many of my belongings and physically violated my personal space. This home that we (my sister and her children) shared was an in-law setup where my living area was separate from the rest of the house. This was supposed to be my vacation home and I trusted my family members to respect the boundaries. Unfortunately, the boundaries were continuously violated. Each time I went to enjoy my home I was always upset by the lack of respect for my space. The agreements that were made at the time we purchased the property were never honored. I've had enough!"

Since we had our Holistic Center to open, and deadlines to meet, we needed to be back by Friday morning.

Thus began, what was to be, an amazing journey!

From the moment I made the first call, this trip was serendipitous. Airline tickets, rental truck, and the special car carrier were easily secured on the Internet at close to normal or even discounted prices.

Four hours later, we were on a flight headed to Orlando. Our mom and eldest sister, Cricket, agreed to pick us up when we arrived that afternoon – yes, in Lynn's convertible...with permission.

Monday morning, we picked up the truck, and headed for the house. We only had until five that evening to pack all Lynn's belongings, load the truck, clean the house and get back to the rental facility before they closed for the 4th of July.

They could not attach the car carrier until the truck was completely loaded. If we missed the deadline, we would have to wait until Wednesday and lose a travel day. Needless to say, we were on a tight schedule.

Because of the holiday weekend, there was no one available to help load the truck. Even Cricket, usually very helpful and strong, hurt her back and was unable to lift anything.

So, there we were, two women, each barely five feet tall, with no help to move what can only be described as "castle-size furniture". The bed alone was enough to make us shudder – a massive, four pillar king size bed with mahogany and leather head and foot boards. And, there was more - the huge sectional sofa with queen sleeper, a dining room table with a thick, round glass top, heavy chairs, giant mirrors, pre-plasma TV's, rugs – plus all the items that needed to be boxed.

As if the furniture wasn't enough of a challenge, we also had to deal with broken air conditioning and no running water on a day that was already eighty degrees at eight-thirty in the morning. We had not yet begun and were already sweating. This was a $300,000 home, nothing was working, and we had to start packing.

Lynn sat down to cry, and I said, "Look at the bright side – there's a pool full of water we can use to flush the toilets. It's a good day!" We both started to laugh. "There must be some reason for this. Thank God for our senses of humor and our Angels. Oh yeah! We forgot. Let's ask them for help!"

Our Angels, those magnificent entities we strongly believe in, did not disappoint us.

Each time we had to lift something, we asked the assistance of our "Moving Angels". We were able to move everything into the truck without difficulty or damage. We had been particularly anxious about moving the glass tabletop as it was very heavy and our hands were slippery with sweat. The floors were tiled so dropping it would be disastrous. Thanks to our Angels, we managed to roll it out to the truck without incident.

Time was running out. It was already four o'clock and there was still more to load. We called the rental shop to tell them we wouldn't be able to make it there by five. They told us, "Don't worry, we're running behind with paperwork, we can wait."

Packing finished at 4:45, and we headed to the rental facility just twenty minutes away. Upon our arrival, the manager hooked up the special car carrier. Unfortunately, the car didn't fit. The front end bottomed out and it could not be loaded. After checking his company's inventory, he said there was not a carrier on the east coast that would fit our model. He suggested we drive north and check with different rental facilities on Wednesday, when they re-opened.

We thought, "Okay, there must be a reason. Perhaps as we drive up the coast, we will find a dealer open after the holiday that has one."

We went to our mom's to spend the night and called friends in Hilton Head, South Carolina telling them we were heading north the next day. Aileen had been our teacher throughout the three-year Energy Healing Program we graduated from. She and her husband, Gil, invited us to celebrate the 4th and stay overnight. In that moment we realized had the car carrier been attached we would not have stopped to visit anyone. The overall length of the truck and carrier would have put us at 45 feet, too long to maneuver around a coastal community.

Next morning, bright and early, we said our goodbyes. I climbed into the truck, Lynn slid into her convertible, and we headed north. Today was the 4th of July and for Lynn... *Independence Day!*

Six hours later we arrived just in time for lunch. Afterwards, we took a scenic bike ride around the island. Lynn and I were amazed that we could ride eight miles on a bike, and still had so much energy after all we had done. Thank you, Angels!

That night, the four of us went to dinner then back to their house where we talked non-stop for hours. The conversations were fast and furious. These were not the normal everyday conversations of life. As the four of us were Healers, these were "channeled" conversations about Universal downloads, geometrical languages, spiritual guidance and insights. Some conversations included the four of us, some were paired off, and the pairs kept changing. Abruptly, all conversations stopped. It was time to sleep.

The next morning, the conversations resumed at high speed. The information was being channeled by each of us, for each of us. Suddenly, abruptly, the conversations ended again. We all knew we were done. Each of us had received knowledge and wisdom that would benefit us as healers and individuals.

We called the closest rental facility, which was only three miles away. As miracles would have it, they had the special car carrier we needed!

"This is incredible!" the manager told us. "A man from Texas who reserved it just called and cancelled. There's not another one on the east coast that will fit your car. This is amazing!" She was shocked, but we had these Angels ...

The rental facility was on the same road we were taking toward the highway. Had we kept driving north yesterday, there would not have been a car carrier available all the way home! Once again, "Thank you, Angels!"

The installer hooked the carrier to the truck, but something seemed wrong. Lynn and I had experience with campers and trailers, and knew this wasn't secured properly. We expressed our concern, but he assured us it was fine.

Just then, he went off to answer a phone which gave us the opportunity to inspect the hitch for ourselves. The hookup was incorrect. We reset the connection properly and secured the cross chains, before the installer returned. Had he not gone back into the building, the car carrier could have disconnected from the truck while we were driving. "Thank you, Angels!"

It was very clear – we were receiving messages to pay attention and trust *our* own intuition.

We were finally on our way and together, it was much more fun than traveling in separate vehicles. The plan was, I'd drive and Lynn would read to me. Didn't happen!

Each time Lynn tried to read or turned on the radio, the chain attaching the carrier to the truck, on the passenger side, disconnected. In fact, when either one of us was not present or in the moment, the chain disengaged.

It was Lynn who saw a pattern. The chain would fall off, Lynn would get out to reconnect it, and we would notice the time and road sign directly in front of us. The sign would have a number on it, such as Route 101 – and that would indicate the next time the chain would fall off – 1:01PM. There would be no apparent reason for the chain to disconnect. Bumpy roads, potholes, craters – the chain would stay on. Then, a patch of smooth asphalt, Lynn opened a book or turned on the radio and wham! The chain fell off. We tried hooking the chains this way and that. It made no difference.

One time when the chain fell off right after being reconnected, we realized that for whatever reason, "our Angels" were slowing us down. Another time, Lynn was talking about selling her belongings, buying a camper, and going on a grand adventure to explore the world. I thought, "Okay, I can open the Center by myself."

The chain fell off.

There was no room to pull over so we took the first exit ramp. Right there, at the end of the ramp was a sign – "DO NOT LEAVE HOME." Okay, no mistaking that one. I looked at Lynn and said, "Perhaps that's not a good idea after all." We both laughed. This was a game and we were getting the hang of it.

We decided to test the chain action. It was now 15 minutes away from the next indicated number. We parked, waited, and thought nothing would happen if we weren't moving. Maybe we were making it up after all.

We watched the clock. Right on time, the phone rang!

We jumped, screamed and laughed! We were expecting the chain. Apprehensively I answered the phone. "Hello, Kathy speaking."

"Hello, this is Patrick."

"Patrick who?"

"I'd like to make an appointment for an energy healing session." He was calling from a New York number so I suggested we meet at my Katonah office.

"No. I understand you have a location in Connecticut. I'll be returning from Rhode Island Monday morning, and would like to come for a session on my way through. Ten would be perfect."

I hung up and stared at Lynn. "Well…we have our first client! We're opening the Center on Monday morning!" We both laughed. Now we knew what the chain was all about.

The rest of the ride that day was uneventful until we started talking about stopping for the evening, having dinner, and calling it a day. Yup, you guessed it, the chain fell off. Again, there was no place to pull over so we took the first exit. Right in front of us was a motel with a parking lot big enough to accommodate our rig with ease. Perfect. Game on!

Lynn fixed the chain and tried to open the back of the truck to get a book for our ride home. The padlock was jammed. Okay, we're still not supposed to be reading. Clearly, we were to be in the "now"[13] and stay completely aware.

We registered and walked across the street for dinner. As soon as we returned to our room, the phone rang.

"This is Marilyn at the front desk. I have a horrible headache. Do you have any aspirin?" Ordinarily, this would seem weird – a desk clerk calling guests for medication – but on this trip, everything was weird.

Lynn and I just looked at each other and laughingly responded, "Wrong number! We don't have any aspirin, but we can help you get rid of your headache. We'll be right there."

Marilyn was in severe pain. She was feeling pressured in life. Working too many double shifts, her boss ignored her request for fewer hours, and to make matters worse, this was not her ideal job. In addition, her home life was stressed as her husband paid no attention to her concerns.

She made a commitment to stick up for herself at work, even if she got fired. At home, she was going to be heard, even if her family was not happy about it. Her headache immediately disappeared. She felt refreshed and empowered. To her surprise, she was pain free, aspirin free, and feeling happy and hopeful about her future.

---

13   Eckhart Tolle, *The Power of Now – A Guide To Spiritual Enlightenment,* (California: New World Library, 1999)

She exclaimed how lucky she was that we had chosen her motel. We replied, "Luck had nothing to do with it. You see, we have these Angels…" and proceeded to tell her the story. Lynn ended with, "You have your own Angels working on your behalf. Just talk to them."

The next day we played the time/chain/message game all the way home.

Still wondering who we were playing with, the answer appeared loud and clear, right in front of us. As the next designated time approached, we were nearing an old bridge underpass. At the exact time, we looked up and there it was!

Written on the nameplate of the bridge … RAPHAEL!

Archangel Raphael was playing charades with us! We were elated, joyful, laughing! It felt as if he was riding in the cab with us, right between the seats. There was an almost audible sigh that Lynn and I both heard and felt. Finally – we got it – Raphael!

The rest of the ride home was amazing now that we knew who was playing with us. We would go over roads with potholes big enough to disconnect the trailer, never mind the chain, and it would stay connected. It only came off when it was time for the next message. Sometimes, it seemed stopping to fix the chain served the purpose of slowing us down. A few times, we would find that just up ahead there was an accident. Perhaps if we had not stopped to fix the chain, we would have been in it. We'll never know for sure. What we did know was that we were protected all the way home!

The next number received was 11:11. We thought for sure that would be the time we arrived at our final destination. WRONG!

At 11 PM we were still an hour away from home and exhausted. As the time neared, we saw signs for a rest area and realized we needed to get a few hours of sleep. At 11:11, we pulled into the rest area and slept for a couple of hours. We both awoke at the same time, completely refreshed!

There was one more number that Lynn noticed – 222 – and we thought this was to be the time of our arrival. The plan was to park the rig in front of Lynn's son's house and get help unloading in the morning. As the time approached, we were still traveling on dark, country roads. Knowing that something was about to happen, we became very present, slowed down to a crawl, and at 2:22 AM, out jumped a deer – right in front of the truck! We missed it!

"Thank you, Raphael!" With the help of our Angels, we arrived safe and sound. What a great trip. What an experience.

Later that morning, after unloading the car, Lynn's son, Jesse, commented on how weird it was that one chain was so extraordinarily shiny, looking brand new, while the other was dark and rusted. "Have we got a story to tell you," we said laughing!

When we returned the car carrier to the rental company, the man that disconnected it asked, "How did this one chain get so shiny and new while the other stayed so dirty and rusted? It's like a brand new chain!"

"You wouldn't believe us if we told you." And so we did...

We went to Lynn's house to unload the furniture and our sons were there to help. The padlock was no longer jammed. As they started to unload, they were shocked at the weight of the furniture. "How did you two ever lift this on your own?"

"We weren't exactly alone..."

Two years after this trip, Doreen Virtue published her new book, Angel Numbers 101.[14] This book assigns angelic guidance to each number from 0 to 999. It was exciting and validating for us to realize that we had experienced this connection long before this book was written. It broadened our connection and understanding of what they want us to know.

COMMENTS BY WAYNE: Obviously, Archangels have a sense of humor. From the beginning, this was an improbable journey interspersed with obstacles, roadblocks, play and games. Our Angels are not only at our beck and call for the healing of serious ailments but in this story proved that they love to help and play. Kathy and Lynn were able to understand the game and became willing participants. Their "Moving Angels" helped them load the truck while Archangel Raphael both guided and protected them on this long journey, making it a fun trip.

There is a powerful lesson to be learned. Often, we get stuck in habitual patterns that diminish our lives. Lynn was stuck in a pattern where she allowed people to overstep her boundaries. As a result, she was losing her luster, becoming angry, and starting to look and feel like that rusty old chain. By taking an action step, she broke a pattern and altered her life.

Which life do you want to live? One that's stuck, dull, rusty, but safe – or one that's got a few bumps in the road, filled with new adventures, and is alive and vibrant?

---

14   Doreen Virtue, *Angel Numbers 101*, (New York: Hay House, Inc., 2008)

CHAPTER 8

A Star is Born

WAYNE

I overheard several ladies at work saying that Maria DiLorenzo, our receptionist, was having physical problems.

I knew that Maria had been in a funk regarding her musical career and
lifelong dream to be a singer/songwriter. For the past several months, she
had been unable to sing or write any songs that were worthwhile. She was so
blocked that she was modestly depressed and thinking of giving up on her
ambitions. I had no doubt that this frustration contributed to her ailments
and suggested to Maria that she visit Kathy for a healing. I explained the benefits of a healing and how the energy channels in a person's body can open up,
thus creating positive changes in many areas of their life. Maria immediately
scheduled a session.

On the day of her appointment, Maria took the one-hour train ride from Grand Central Station to Katonah, NY. As I was scheduled for the next session, I was waiting outside the room while her healing was taking place. As soon as the session ended, Kathy opened the door, and they invited me in. Maria's first comment to me was, "You never told me it was this good!" At that point, I immediately knew that something terrific had happened. I fully expected that Kathy's healing of Maria would be a life-altering experience.

KATHY

At our first session, I instinctively knew that Maria's physical ailments were the result of creative blockages manifesting in her second chakra (lower stomach area). Placing my hands on her feet, I sent a flow of energy up through her body. It was evident that she was energetically depleted, for much like a dehydrated person stranded in a desert for a prolonged period of time craves water, Maria soaked up the energy like a sponge. I was amazed at how much energy she was pulling through and able to absorb. I had never experienced that magnitude of energetic need or receiving before.

Once she felt fully saturated I began working up her body and perceived blockages clearing out rapidly and being replaced by a glowing euphoria of body and spirit. I had no doubt that change was taking place. Maria's initial lackluster aura was now gleaming and radiant. My observations indicated that this healing was exactly what Maria needed, but I was reluctant to make any conclusions until she finished processing.

Maria felt better than she had in a long time. She was bubbling! When Wayne entered the room there was no holding her back as she raved about her experience and how good she felt. That day Maria's star began to once again shine and her creative juices started to flow. Her self confidence was restored, and she knew she was capable of overcoming any obstacle tossed in her path.

Maria later told me that on her return trip, she wrote three of the best songs she had ever written, amazingly accomplishing this during the one-hour train ride home. Both Maria's husband, Danny, and her producer, were in disbelief.

Maria's career was rejuvenated. She was singing with a new focus and passion that had long been lacking and began to land small jobs both singing and composing. Her lifelong desire was coming to fruition.

COMMENTS BY WAYNE: How incredible is it that a talented performer such as Maria can be so blocked that she was on the verge of giving up her lifelong dream? Just one session with Kathy opened up new possibilities and hope. I have no idea how a person can write three of the best songs that they had ever put on paper in an hour, but somehow, Maria was so inspired, that the words just flowed. I believe the songs were composed during the healing and when the blockages were cleared, it was only a matter of putting the words on paper. Creativity, inspiration and passion were there all along; they had just become pinched off and inaccessible. Maria realized that when the energy of the body and spirit are maximized and balanced to perfection the results are limitless.

What happened to Maria can be compared to a stream that has been dammed up for a long period of time. Depending on how long the flow has been blocked, determines how the land above, and below, is impacted. The land above is flooded, drowning and suffocating growth. The lower part becomes dried out and dies off. Once the dam/blockage is removed, and the water flows smoothly, the eco balance is restored. Plant life above and below, begin to rejuvenate, grow and blossom.

The same was true with Maria. When the flow of energy was restored, her creativity, inspiration, and joyful passion were ablaze. Her internal orchestra began to play, creating harmony for Maria's body and spirit that enabled her to fulfill her dreams.

Maria made the trip to Katonah several times and, as one healing grows upon the other, she continued to progress. Although each healing fulfills a different need, the unification that was taking place within Maria became evident to everyone around her. Her enthusiasm overflowed into the workplace as well as her personal life. Many people in the office started to seek out Wayne for his healing skills.

Shortly after Maria started to come to me for healing sessions, she encouraged her sister, Chrissy, also a singer, to come for a healing. From the beginning, Chrissy had experiences that began to change her life for the better:

When I first went to see Kathy, I had a lot of emotional pain. Depressed feelings, nervous energy, and anger that I had held onto from years ago had left me unhappy in my career, relationship and current living situation. Basically, my life was not working.

The healings really helped me let go of any negative feelings. I now experience much more laughter and joy. I feel way more easy-going. I don't really stress over anything anymore because I have found myself.

Every time was different for me. On more than one occasion I felt as if there were warm hands on my feet and chest area near my heart, at the same time. I always saw vibrant colors of reds, blues, and greens. I felt pure happiness like I wanted to laugh so loud! That feeling would last me for hours. When I would meditate I could totally go back to that feeling.

Immediately after I began going for healings, I started to attract more positive energy. These healings actually helped me make better choices, more positive decisions, and helped me get rid of fear.

I was able to change a large part of my life. I moved to Nashville (which is so amazing) and made great friends – friends I feel that I've known all along. My singing and acting career has been way more productive than ever before. I finally feel like I am where I belong.

Each healing was individually amazing and exponentially advancing. Ultimately, I believe they definitely brought me closer to finding the peace that I now have!

Chrissy's ability to recognize the impact that these healings had in her life was absolutely brilliant. Some people want their pain to go away immediately, which is one possible outcome. However, the deeper value of a healing is recognizing where your life is misaligned with who you really are. Chrissy found herself, and once she was connected, she took the action steps in her life to reach for her dreams and move forward. What could be more freeing than to release negative thoughts, worries, stress and fear?

Chrissy began to feel joy, happiness, and empowered to make positive changes in her life. She attracted more positive energy, and made better choices and decisions for herself. She was now free to create the future of her dreams and live into it.

Maria's husband, Danny, also a musician, decided to come for a session after observing the dramatic changes in his wife. After witnessing the rebirth of her creativity around her music, he wanted to access this for himself. He also saw her new levels of joy and playfulness. Each time she returned from a healing, Danny would notice another positive change in Maria. When he observed the same things happening to

Chrissy, he made an appointment. Although he was skeptical that a healing could make a difference for him, he did not want this opportunity to pass him by.

When I first met Danny, he was discouraged and disappointed by his lack of success in the music industry. Music was his passion and he and Maria had worked very hard to achieve their dreams, but the effort had left him physically, emotionally and spiritually exhausted.

When our energy flow becomes restricted because our energy centers are depleted or shut down, just getting up in the morning can become a struggle allowing little, if any energy, for joyful creation.

This was how I perceived Danny's energy. As we began the session, Danny seemed quite tense, which is not uncommon for a first session. I asked him to lay face down on the table and began by placing my hands on his back. His tension and apprehension quickly dissipated. Danny became open and available which allowed the replenishing of his energy. When I felt this was complete, I asked Danny to turn over onto his back and moved to his feet, placing my hands gently upon his ankles. Danny quickly returned to a state of relaxation, and we began the second part of the hands-on healing. As Danny absorbed more and more energy, his consciousness moved from a place of 'fight-or-flight' into a place of gratitude and joy, our true state of being. By the end of the session, Danny had tears of gratitude from the connection he felt to Source.

For many of us, the problems of life come at us fast and furious, and a life of defending becomes a life of existing. When you are constantly up against it, facing these problems head-on becomes exhausting. Life wears you down, becomes a struggle, and uses up your life force energy.

This is not how it is supposed to be. When our energy is aligned with Source and restored, the problems of life will still come at us, but we then have the ability to step aside and let them go by. This is called the practice of pivoting.

Pivoting is similar to the art of Kung Fu. When you feel that you are being attacked, instead of defending yourself by fighting back, you actually lean out of the way (or pivot your body) and then use the oncoming force to propel the attacker past you; thus, you neither resist, nor receive, the impact.

What you resist persists. Step back and look at your upsets from a different perspective. Look from a bigger picture point of view.

Practice the behavior of stepping out of the way for a while. Learn new ways of being, and eventually, the attacks will stop. You will begin to create life from a place of non-resistance. Joy will become the norm. You will become a magnet for all good things and draw the best of life to you. You will be the creator of your own life.

On this evening, Danny began the pivoting process. He left the office rejuvenated with his energy back in alignment.

WAYNE

It was several months after her initial healings with Kathy, while I was attending the healing program, when Maria asked me to perform a healing on her. It proved to be one of the most incredible healings that I ever performed. At the time, I was a virtual rookie, and I could not believe what I was seeing and feeling throughout this experience.

As soon as my hands touched Maria, things began to unfold. My hands were vibrating so rapidly that I constantly looked at them and wondered what was happening. I later realized that Maria was pulling so much energy through my body, that it was causing my hands to vibrate in a rapid, noticeable manner. I saw an incredible spectrum of color, and felt as if Maria's need for energy was endless. As soon as the healing ended, she excitedly shared her visions:

I saw a knight, holding a gold-handled sword laden with rubies. His name was William and he was of royal lineage. Both of his hands were on the sword and he was forging it in a fire. There was a sequence of letters that I observed – G-O-U-A-I-X. I had no idea what the letters meant.

Then, I saw my soul expand around the earth and flip over backwards. I viewed myself laughing hysterically and jumping from rooftop to rooftop around the world. During my travels, I saw a Sphinx and the pyramids of ancient Egypt.

There was an array of beautiful colors that consisted of exquisite blues and oranges.

I saw a golden angel with a large book tucked under his arm. He turned around, smiled at me and nodded. I recognized his face immediately; it was YOU. I will never forget that face; it was yours, Wayne!

Lastly, I saw myself in an ice cave. There was a crystal opening at the mouth of the cave and a glowing golden yellow light from the outside that reflected beautiful prisms of blue and white through the ice.

COMMENTS BY KATHY & WAYNE: This was an amazing healing for Maria that led to an astral travel experience and a past life remembrance.

The letters that Maria saw and the story of the man in armor, who Maria referred to as a knight, perplexed us all.

At first, we thought the letters were some kind of Roman numerals, but that made no sense. After going on the internet, we discovered that GOUAIX is a small town in France, southeast of Paris. We could not believe that these letters actually represented a tangible place.

We then discovered that a famous warrior named William the Conqueror was born in Normandy (France) in the year 1028. He was an illegitimate child. William was the Duke of Normandy and became the King of England in 1066 when he led a Norman army to victory over Anglo-Saxon forces in the historical Battle of Hastings.

Throughout his life William was constantly battling in England and Normandy against those who were eager to seize power from him. He died in 1087 after burning the town of Mantes, which is west of Paris. He fell off his horse and suffered fatal abdominal injuries. He bequeathed England and his sword to his second living son. The sword is nowhere to be found.

The town of Gouaix is approximately 100 miles from Mantes and much closer to Paris. Somehow, Maria had a vision of something that happened at a time when a man of royalty named William, clad in armor, was forging a ruby-laden, gold-handled sword in a fire in or around the town of Gouaix, France. Maria may never figure out what role she played in this vision, but she certainly had a vivid recollection of these occurrences.

The combination of the healing and these visions gave Maria the courage to uproot her life and pursue her dreams. This is why we encourage multiple healing sessions. As one healing grows upon the other and each one offers something new, this last healing with Wayne empowered Maria to conquer her fears and expand her connection to the world.

The fears which once dominated her were replaced with the joy and laughter of jumping from rooftop to rooftop around the world. She also discovered a newfound wisdom when the angel smiled and nodded at her with the book of knowledge tucked under his arm. We believe that the ice cave she was in was the Cave of Creation, where she was surrounded by ultimate peace and joy.

Maria and Danny signed a contract with a recording studio and moved to Nashville, Tennessee where they are excelling in the field that they love. Maria appeared in a short film and went to California to audition for a role in a major motion picture production. They have since had a baby and are enjoying their lives at a level previously not open to them.

Chrissy, following her passion, has joined them in Tennessee and is thriving in the community that immediately felt like home to her.

Chrissy Porcelli and Maria DiLorenzo

CHAPTER 9

Take a Ride on Metro North

WAYNE

I have been commuting on Metro North railroad for many years. Each day, I travel from Peekskill, New York to Grand Central Terminal in New York City then take the thirty minute subway ride downtown to the financial district. Although my daily roundtrip commute is approximately four hours, my ride on Metro North is about one hour each way.

Over the years I have experienced almost every type of calamity that a commuter could imagine. When Conrail managed the system, there was often no heat in the winter and no air conditioning in the summer. I remember boarding a train in Peekskill with the temperature below zero. The car I entered was freezing and there were no other commuters so I began to walk through the cars in my quest for heat. Everyone was walking through the train until we approached a car that was filled with people. My first thought was that this car must have heat but upon entering, I quickly realized the only heat in there was body heat.

There were times when it took five hours to travel one way. Fires and mudslides, suicides and burning engines have all added to my commuting perils.

One day, after arriving at work, a massive snowstorm hit New York City and closed train service out of Grand Central. It was announced that the only trains leaving for upstate were starting at a small station in the Bronx called Marble Hill. I told a fellow worker that our only hope of getting home was to make it to that station and if we left now, it would take us an hour to get to there by subway.

When we arrived, a police officer said that there had been no train activity at that station whatsoever. We were disappointed and disillusioned, but with no other options, we waited on the platform, exposed to the elements, for over an hour in blizzard-like conditions, hoping the media had been right. By the time a train finally approached, the platform was jammed with commuters. The train was twice the normal length, and to make matters worse, the doors were frozen shut. The conductor had to individually open each door with a key. People were so desperate they were jumping through the conductor's window to board the train which was so full that every seat was taken and people were standing with no room to move. As the train crawled to the north, we stopped at each station. The conductor had to manually open each door and wait for the people to shift their bodies around so that the people trying to exit could get off. Then he had to manually close each door. Because of the length of the train, it had to stop twice at each station in order for people to exit onto the platform. So the manual opening and closing of the doors also happened twice at each station. This trip was a five-hour undertaking.

On several occasions, the train engines caught fire. One time, I remember deboarding the train and sitting on the bank along the tracks with several hundred other commuters, watching the engine fully engulfed in flames.

Another time we were in the tunnel approaching Grand Central, when the train broke down. After a long wait with only emergency lighting, a railroad crew arrived to lead us through the train, out into the tunnels, through the underground passages where we emerged through one of the grates of the sidewalk in mid-town Manhattan. Walking through those passages reminded me of a scene from a well-staged horror film. They were dimly lit, damp, musty smelling and there was always the concern of rats who live in the endless caverns that make up the underground system.

Probably the most excruciating commute I have ever experienced was on September 11, 2001. With the World Trade Center being attacked by terrorists, I stood on the street outside of my office building and saw pieces of two planes protruding from each of the Twin Towers. It was unreal. It looked like a Bruce Willis movie.

We were mandated to leave the area as New York City, the gateway of the world, started to shut down. I began a surreal walk from lower Manhattan to Grand Central Terminal. Along the way, I met several new friends. One woman in particular revealed a hideous narration of how she witnessed people holding hands and jumping from the Twin Towers.

Arriving at Grand Central on 42nd Street, no one was permitted entrance, so I proceeded to walk all the way to the 125th Street Station. Throughout this 10-mile trek, I had the impression that a colony of ants were on a march and that no stop-light or stop sign could hinder their path. We were just a mass moving forward. All traffic was grid locked.

After arriving at 125th Street, there was a several-hour wait and much confusion before the next train arrived at which time we were able to board and head north along the Hudson River. This was a full day commute, one-way.

This day forever altered my commute on Metro North. People that I saw every day, just taking for granted that they were there, never returned again. There were stories about some that had died, some that retired, and some that I will never know. Daily card games that were played both to and from NY abruptly came to an end. People started to stay more to themselves, isolated with their own thoughts. It was during this time that I was probably the most depressed I have ever been in my life. I felt completely violated, like the world was out of control, and I was totally helpless.

COMMENTS BY KATHY: As a healer and SRI facilitator, I have seen the horrific impact of 9/11 on the bodies, minds, and spirits of hundreds of people. The events of that day were so traumatic and life altering, that many people are still physically stuck in a defense pattern, going through their lives, day in and day out, ready to fight or take flight in any given moment.

Unaware that they are stuck, the tension stored in their cellular memory has become the feeling of normal. When you add the stresses of everyday life, for many, it becomes over-whelming. In fact, many people are so overloaded that the tiniest thing becomes an irritant. For some, if another human being even breathes loudly, they become irritated (this can even include our loved ones). Others are walking around holding their breath, afraid if they feel what is actually emotionally locked away inside them they will implode or explode from the intensity of it. Sorrow, anger, frustration, and fear are stored in our cellular memory, even if we have blocked them from our day-to-day thoughts. Emotions are energy in motion. When we are unwilling, or unable, to connect with the emotion, we create a perpetual resistance, or block, to the flow of energy. The result is we feel numb inside. Life loses its spark. Passion fades away. We live life resigned and cynical. Connection and community disappear. Abundance is replaced with scarcity. The world becomes a pie; we have to get our piece before it's all gone. Protect what we have. Don't let people too close, they'll take advantage or just leave eventually anyway. Fearful of being alone, we push people away, trying to avoid the feeling altogether. Our thoughts become a self-fulfilling prophecy.

When we are locked into a defense pattern, we cannot create a new thought. Our body has to use so much of its energy, just trying to get through the day, that there is nothing even available to self heal an injury, illness, or dis-ease. Sleep patterns get interrupted. Thoughts race around in our minds like a hamster on a wheel; negative thoughts and worry, not positive thoughts. There is no peace. There is only exhaustion. Our bodies start to break down.

I have seen many women (and men) who endured much sorrow, grief and suffering because they were unable to conceive or carry their unborn child to full term, when after receiving care, deliver healthy, happy babies. I saw a man who was losing the use of his legs arrive with his cane, and after treatment actually walk out without the cane because he forgot he even had one.

Unfortunately, I have seen many people who were having tremendous results leave care because of the fear of having to face making a change in their lives. The fear of change was greater than the fear of not walking again. Perhaps the fear of returning to a job, or the energy of New York City, was just too overwhelming. Perhaps it was easier to be with the illness and the attention that it brings, (negative attention is still better than no attention) than to be with the unknown that change brings.

None of this is on a conscious level, and this is not only about 9/11. This is the result of layer upon layer of stress and trauma (physical, chemical, emotional, and spiritual) that gets stored in our cellular memory over our lifetime, as well as our past lifetimes.

For Wayne, what was once a community of people who knew each other by sight if not by name, traveling back and forth to their daily jobs became a group of traumatized commuters. Where they use to laugh, play games, and talk amongst themselves during their commute, they were now alone in their own thoughts, wondering and worrying about the unknown and what might await them as they headed toward New York City.

Wayne was one of the lucky ones. He was on a healer's journey. As a person who prefers natural ways of keeping himself healthy, he had been receiving different types of healing modalities (i.e. massage, vitamin supplements and magnetic therapy). Eventually, he found his way to NSA, SRI, and the Transformational Energy Healings (TEH). Using these additional healing modalities, he has been able to release much of the cellular traumas, which he experienced from 9/11 and the days, months, and years of traveling back and forth to the Ground Zero area, since that horrific day. He was able to break his defense pattern and become open to new possibilities.

One of those new possibilities was discovering Transformational Energy Healing work, and he enrolled in the two-year program. From the very beginning, and throughout his years of study, his commitment to bringing his healing skills to everyone he can get his hands on has never wavered. For me, Wayne embodies the meaning of healer, giving endlessly of his time and Self. His love of humanity is limitless and his intention is always the same… to be the vessel of which pure energetic love flows to fill every cell within the body to allow the person a complete, back to brand new, recovery.

Travelers on the Metro North Railroad have no idea how extraordinarily lucky they are to have this particular healer riding their train.

Through the earlier years, I spent my commuting time speaking to friends, playing cards, reading or napping. After 9/11, I stayed more to myself and napped or read. But as I began my life as a healer, this started to change. Once I learned how to perform distance healings from Kathy and Lynn, I discovered that this peaceful travel time could be used to help others and the first person was Flo Rich.

Flo manages the His & Hers Dry Cleaning and Laundromat Service at the Peekskill train station as well as the lot where I park my car. I told her I was studying to be a healer and shared many of my success stories. Flo suffered with left knee pain for five years and although she had been to doctors and received cortisone shots, still walked with a limp and endured severe pain that was always with her.

One morning I offered to send her healings from the train on the commute to Grand Central and on the return trip that evening. The next morning Flo excitedly told me that both the pain and limp were gone! She was amazed that at the times I was sending healing energy, she actually felt extensive heat going into her knee. The groundwork had been established for an apprehensive Flo to become a believer in the power of energy healing.

A few weeks later, Flo awoke with a terrible headache that wouldn't go away so I offered to do a healing. When I placed my hands on her head, she said, "I feel my heart beat rising, and the headache is completely gone." Literally, in seconds, the pain went away.

Months later, I entered the store to find Flo hobbling around in excruciating pain. She was walking with a limp and said her Achilles tendon was killing her. I did a hands-on healing and followed up with distance healings from the train that morning and evening. The next day when I saw Flo, the limp and pain were gone. She said that at the time when I was on the train, she felt a warm sensation come over her and the pain went away. It has never returned.

Another morning when I entered the store, Flo was speaking to Mrs. Mooney who had painful bursitis in her arm. Flo immediately began to tell her about the healings I had done and the great results she had received. Before long, my hands were on the back of Mrs. Mooney's neck and arm. I ran channels of energy from her shoulder to her fingers and literally felt the pain releasing through her fingertips. As I left the store to catch my train, Flo had an all-knowing smile on her face as Mrs. Mooney raved about her new pain-free arm.

One evening, Flo intercepted me before I could reach my car and drive off and asked, "Do you have a minute?"

"Certainly I do."

Flo told me about her close relative who was suffering with major back problems. He had been going to a chiropractor several times a week with minimal results. She asked if I would come to her house and do a healing on him. I agreed, she immediately closed her store, and I followed her home. That night no one would get their clothes from His & Hers Dry Cleaners as there was more important business to be done.

He was waiting for us when we arrived and I was amazed to see how big he was, like a linebacker on a football team. He could barely walk, had a terrible limp and a look of pain covered his face. He explained his physical problems and although he could hardly move without pain, managed to travel at a snail's pace down the hall and get himself facedown onto a bed.

From the instant I touched his spine I could feel energy shooting through his body, opening the blocked energy channels within him. Moving my hands up and down his whole spine several times, I filled it with all the energy colors. He then turned onto his back. Beginning at his feet, I ran channels of energy up his legs and throughout his body, filling every cell with the magnificent glowing, golden light of healing energy. At the same time, I was receiving numerous healing colors and envisioned beautiful spectrums of blue, red, and green.

The healing lasted for over an hour. When I finished, he immediately said, "I felt tingling in different parts of my body. I also felt energy moving throughout my entire body."

After allowing time for his body to process this new balancing of energy that took place within him, I helped him to his feet, and he was like a new man. Much of the pain was gone. He took a few steps and noticed the limp was greatly reduced. He was amazed how such a simple light touch could have such an effect on him. He walked down the hall to the family room to show everyone how much better he was and by the time he arrived, the limp was completely gone.

As we talked, Flo's little grandson entered the room. He had been suffering from a head cold and fever. I asked them if they would permit me to do a healing on him explaining that it might help. They agreed, and I put my hands on his head, back, and neck for a short period of time.

The next morning when I saw Flo at the train station, she was elated. Not only was her relative feeling so much better, she also told me that as soon as I left, the fever in her grandson disappeared.

It was not long after receiving the healing that her relative stopped visiting the chiropractor because his back was so much better.

COMMENTS BY KATHY: It's amazing how quickly a body can heal, young or old, when its "life force/energy" is freed up and back on line. In a matter of minutes, a person's focus can turn from illness and pain to wellness and joy.

A strange thing happened one morning when I walked into His and Hers Dry Cleaners. Flo met me with her usual warm greeting to which I responded, "Good Morning!" That day was a little different as there was a man I had never seen before sitting and chatting with her. In what was a matter of a few seconds the man greeted me and said, "You are something holistic!"

I was shocked! Immediately, I knew he was an intuitive. "What makes you say that?"

"I can tell from looking at you. You fill the room and have a wealth of knowledge about healing."

I was amazed and told him that I was a Certified Holistic Health Practitioner and was involved in healing people. He said that people often focus on the negative and if they do not see any results after a few healings, they immediately claim that holistic healing is all garbage. How right this man was. His ability to recognize me as a healer and state the common thought about healing was a gift for me, and I will never forget his words.

After I left, Flo asked him how he knew who I was just by my saying "Good morning." He told her that he saw an aura around me and everything he said just came to him. She still cannot believe that he intuitively knew this about me.

The realization that there are people who are able to read my aura, which reflects my inner core essence of a healer, left me in awe. Despite the fact that I have worked in the financial industry for these many decades, he saw none of that, and only viewed me as the healer that I am.

COMMENT BY KATHY: I think it is wonderful that this man had the courage to speak out to Wayne, a man he had never seen before, and shared the words he received from his guidance. How often have you received guidance to say something wonderful to someone but held your tongue for fear of looking weird or being laughed at. Perhaps next time, when you get the urge to say something to someone, you will speak the words, even if they do not make sense to you, and you will absolutely make their day.

Riding the train daily, you get to know the regular commuters. A young woman named Mia, whom I saw almost every morning, came limping onto the platform at the Peekskill station.

I asked, "What happened to you?"

"My left knee has been bad for 15 years, and last night I was dancing at a concert and completely aggravated my chronic condition."

I told her I was studying to be a healer and would like to do a distance energy healing on her knee once we boarded the train.

At the same time, another everyday commuter, Jimmy Agosta, overheard our conversation and said that he also had a painful left knee.

Now I was really excited. This was an opportunity for me to test distance healings on two people simultaneously. I was thrilled and could not wait to see what impact it would have on each of them.

We all sat in the same car. Jimmy was across the aisle from me and Mia was going to sit next to us, but I told her to follow her normal routine and sit with her friends at the other end of the car. During the train ride, as I sat in my seat, I closed my eyes and performed the healing. I focused on the left knees of both Mia and Jimmy and felt I had great connection with both of them. A tremendous serenity came over me as I envisioned perfect knees for both. I felt as if every fiber in my mind, body and spirit was a part of their knees. I saw a rainbow of colors and felt a gentle, loving, vibration in both their knees. I requested that my guides, and their guides, give them perfect knees. My intuition told me that it was a good healing and I expected perfect results.

As we arrived at Grand Central, I could not wait to see the outcome. Before Jimmy could get out of his seat, I asked how he felt. He replied, "Let me get up and see how it feels."

We walked onto the platform where he exclaimed, "I feel so good I could run down this platform!"

I was ecstatic with Jimmy's results but would have to wait until tomorrow morning to find out how Mia's knee had benefited from the healing. That evening on the commute home, one of Mia's friends approached me, "I think you got it!"

I responded, "What do you mean, you think I got it?"

"When Mia left the train this morning, we were all waiting to see what happened, and she said that she was pain free!"

The next morning, Mia approached the platform with no limp and immediately announced she was pain free. As the train was pulling into the station, and blew its whistle, she and Jimmy celebrated by doing a little dance on the platform.

Jimmy's healing lasted several days before some pain returned to his knee. Mia related the following story of her experience:

Shortly after I sat down on the train, I felt this insane sensation come into my left knee. At the same time, there was a tremendous amount of heat that engulfed the entire area. I felt a hand digging into the muscle that was hurting. I felt it, but I knew it wasn't there. I continued to look at the knee expecting to see the hand that I felt. There was a thumb digging in and under my patella (knee cap), and it was accompanied by incredible heat. I could not believe what was happening. The sensation that I felt during this healing was unbelievable and indescribable. Without the use of X-rays, how did Wayne know exactly where my problem was? When we arrived at Grand Central, I stood up, began walking, and there was no pain whatsoever. I was shocked, but knew that the true test would be when I had to walk up and down stairs. The pain was always the worst at these times. As I walked up the first flight of stairs, there was absolutely no pain. I was in disbelief.

This healing lasted for six months, and Mia's pain only returned after an intensive workout. When I heard of this setback, I told her I would send another distance healing later that evening. When she awoke the next morning, the pain was gone. Mia had been asleep and did not feel anything, yet when she awoke, she was pain free:

Initially, I was willing to give this a try but really didn't think it was real or even possible. Now, I am an amazing believer even though I cannot understand how this incredible healing can take place without surgically going inside my knee, or even touching it. Not only am I pain free, but the other positive aspect of this experience is that I am no longer plagued with the constant worry about my knee collapsing.

In addition to being elated for them, I also received validation of my ability to perform distance healings simultaneously. I now perform many healings while riding the train and consider this my second office. Anyone who asks me for a healing will often receive them during my commute times.

If the current health resources that are available aren't working so well for you, or someone you know, and you're not quite ready to make an appointment for a distance or hands-on healing, then who knows, you might just want to take a ride on Metro North!

CHAPTER 10

Picking Up the Loose Change
on Wall Street

WAYNE

As I began to learn the techniques of an energy healer, I found myself constantly talking about these skills to my colleagues on Wall Street. Little did I know that people were actually hearing what I had to say and before long my co-workers began to approach me regarding ailments that were affecting their lives. It was almost like picking up loose change off the street. Everywhere I went there was another one.

Rita Critelli was the first person to approach me. She appeared at my desk saying, "I heard you're doing something with healings, and I want you to try it on me. I've had a terrible stiff neck for the past two days."

I told her I really couldn't do much here in the office on the Fixed Income trading floor. "What would these traders think if I started to grab you by the neck?" Rita persisted, and chaperoned by another woman, we went into a conference room. She sat in a chair, and I told her to relax.

As with every healing, I focused on raising my own vibration to a level that would provide the greatest healing for this person and requested that my guides and inner core heal Rita's neck and restore flexibility. I placed my hands on the back of her neck, and felt a channel of energy flowing into the area. About ten minutes later, I felt a distinct relaxing of her neck muscles. Removing my hands, I asked how she felt. Rita began to rotate her neck in a circular motion and exclaimed, "It's gone! It's completely gone!" She stood up, left the conference room, and as she walked across the trading floor, declared her astonishing announcement for all to hear.

The next morning, I followed up with Rita. She awakened with slight stiffness in her neck which immediately dissipated. The pain never returned, and Rita is now a big believer in the efficacy of this healing modality.

Ed Gaffney was walking down a flight of subway steps when simultaneously, the quadriceps tendons, in both legs, tore away from his kneecaps. He collapsed, fell to the bottom of the stairs and could not get up. An ambulance rushed him to the hospital where he underwent a delicate operation to reattach the tendons.

After hearing about Ed's injuries, I visited him in the hospital. Both legs were in casts from his feet to his thighs, and he was very uncomfortable. At the time, I didn't know how to do distance healings and asked if he would accept my gift and receive one from Kathy. After giving him a general explanation of what it entailed, he accepted, even though he did not fully comprehend. I completely understood his skepticism because, until most people experience a healing themselves, it seems unbelievable. Kathy sent the healing that evening.

The next morning I spoke to Ed who described what he felt. "My room was very cold and yet I felt tremendous heat throughout both legs at the time of the healing." He knew that something happened. From Kathy's perspective, she felt that Ed was receptive and yet skeptical. She sent as much energy for healing as he would accept. Although we don't know the impact of this one energy healing, Ed has since fully recovered the use of his legs.

Months later, after returning to work, Ed came to me with pain and stiffness in his shoulder and neck which limited his range of motion. I placed my hands on these areas. Ed immediately commented that the heat being generated from my hands was similar to what he felt during the distance healing when he was in the hospital. Within five minutes, the pain and stiffness were gone.

Noreen Brody, our receptionist, was suffering from tension and stress and asked me to perform a healing on her. I never actually touched her, but established a set time to send her a distance healing. Here's what Noreen had to say:

I tend to be overwhelmed with the little stuff in life. I now see that these things are not important when you look at the big picture. Wayne Gabari is a gift from God, and he is truly a blessing that should be shared with others. I cannot thank him enough for the overwhelming sense of peace that I feel when he bestows a healing on me. I am truly grateful to have the healing touch of Wayne. It has changed my life! I am more energetic, more focused, and I cherish each day.

As a healer, I am absolutely elated that I had such a life altering effect on Noreen.

She is a deeply religious person and believed that my gifts were truly from the Divine. For a time, she received distance healings almost daily, and it became obvious that the energy healings were improving the quality of her life. She was no longer worried about little things going wrong and was actually enjoying herself. To support Noreen on a continual basis, I created a cloud of energy above her head that she could draw from at will. She loves having this energy available and uses it as needed.

Marie O'Neill, an administrative assistant, was suffering from severe pain in her left wrist and thumb which had been diagnosed as arthritis. Although she persevered, it was affecting her ability to perform her job. At Marie's request, I went to her desk to do a healing. Placing one hand on her shoulder and the other on her wrist, I proceeded to focus a channel of energy from her shoulder to her wrist and out through her fingertips. She immediately experienced a slight improvement and commented on the "tremendous heat being generated by your hands." She said it felt like hot towels were being placed on these areas. After several of the hands-on sessions, I sent a series of distance healings.

There were people on the trading floor who were amused and skeptical as they witnessed these daily events. I wonder what they really thought when Marie began sharing how her wrist was improving and ultimately healed.

Marie's husband, Ed, knew the suffering his wife had experienced and was in disbelief about the complete healing of her wrist. He was skeptical that a simple gentle touch could eliminate such debilitating pain, but he wanted to try it. For several years, Ed had been suffering with excruciating pain in his right shoulder which was radiating into his neck. At Ed's request, Marie asked me to perform a healing.

We established a time for an evening distance healing. Ed fell asleep and when he awoke the next morning, the pain in his shoulder and stiffness in his neck were almost gone. I sent a follow-up healing which removed all the pain and stiffness. Ed was excited. He told Marie that he wanted to meet and touch me.

At the time of Marie's original healing, she was greatly concerned and worried about the well-being of her children. A loving mother, she was upset about the trials they were going through in their lives. Worry brings pain and it manifested in her wrist and thumb. Even though a person can be completely better, if the worry energy accumulates to maximum levels, the pain and situation can return.

About six months after Marie's pain had ceased, it re-appeared with a vengeance.

Monday morning, I performed a hands-on healing in the same manner as before, and the excruciating pain was reduced to a minimal discomfort.

As a continuing support during these trying times, Marie enrolled herself, and her family, in our group program of *Sunday Night Distance Healings*[15], and everyone benefitted. As the energy of each person elevated, they thought better thoughts, made better choices, the worrying subsided, and their situations improved. Since then, Marie has been telling everyone about her multiple experiences, and elation at their success.

Some time later, Marie came to me, suffering from pain running up and down her entire left leg. She had been struggling with this for five days with no relief. She believed in the power of the healings and felt confident I would be able to help her. After receiving two distance healings she was pain free.

A few years later, at a wedding reception, Marie's husband, Ed, got his wish. Meeting me for the first time, he shook my hand, thanked me profusely and said, "I have not had any pain in my shoulder since you sent the healing. My shoulder was so bad, and so painful, all the time. I had torn ligaments and muscles and it's amazing how all that pain just disappeared!"

---

15 Sunday Night Group Distance Healing – a service available to individuals, families and pets.

Reggie Funderburk had Achilles tendon surgery, however, it was actually his knee that was hurting and he requested a healing. As I placed my hands on the thick cast that was encasing his leg, he immediately exclaimed, "I can feel a tremendous heat through the cast and a tingling sensation throughout my entire knee and down my leg!" I sent Reggie several distance healings over the next few days and he has fully recovered.

John and Jeanette Lucciola are caring people and every year invite fellow employees to their home for a cookout. They create a warm environment and treat everyone as if they are members of their family. Jeanette was experiencing great pain in her knee so I spoke to Kathy about us sending her a distance healing. Kathy was in Connecticut, I was in New York, and Jeanette was in New Jersey. This was to be a tri-state healing!

When I arrived at work the next morning, I called John to find out the results.

"Forget about the knee", he exclaimed, "Jeannette slept soundly through the entire night!" Despite not knowing that Jeannette had a sleep disorder, it was remedied by this healing. John was elated that for the first time in a long time, Jeanette had a good, restful night's sleep. Jeanette reported:

I was unable to sleep through the night for well over a year. I could fall asleep but would wake up within two hours and then again every couple of hours. Since I really wasn't able to fall into a deep sleep, I found myself tired during the day and unable to stay focused on important details. I was unwilling to try medication to resolve this issue.

I received a long distance healing from Kathy and Wayne and was amazed with the results. I not only slept through the night, I woke up in the morning well rested, refreshed and had a terrific day. I would recommend this natural option to anyone suffering from this condition.

Even though we had no idea of Jeanette's sleep disorder, our guides knew what Jeanette needed and gave it to her. You really have to love this work.

———

Cynthia Vuong is a vice president in the financial division, one of the best accountants that you could find anywhere, and her dedication cannot be matched. We worked together for many years and became good friends.

One day, while outside of our office building, I noticed Cynthia and senior vice president Liz Clancy in conversation, and decided to join them. Cynthia said she was suffering from terrible wrist and joint pain in her right arm. It was constantly throbbing and bothered her when using the computer, and whenever she tried to lift anything or do any type of work. She had been wearing a brace for almost a year and her wrist was deteriorating to the point where she was planning to see a doctor. I told her I was a healer and would like to help. Because Cynthia was pressed for time, I was only able to touch her wrist for less than a minute, but promised to send her a follow up distance healing, which I did.

It didn't take long to create a stir in the office. I heard through the grapevine that Liz was calling people to say that Cynthia's wrist was not hurting anymore. A little while later, Cynthia called me and exclaimed in awe, "It's really not hurting anymore!"

"That's what I expected," I replied. "I set my intent and my guides took care of the rest."

Several days later Cynthia called to say:

It's a miracle! I did not believe, but now I do. The pain is almost completely gone, and I can now use my right hand and do things that I could not do for a very long time. Thank you!

Christine Esposito who works in the Fixed Income Capital Markets division broke her left wrist and, as a result, numbness was radiating through her fingertips. The initial X-ray showed the bone mending together perfectly, but the next one revealed that the bone was separating at the point of the break. The doctor was hopeful that the bone would eventually come together but knew that it would be a long process, if and when it ever meshed.

Christine was skeptical of the healings but requested I work on her wrist. I performed healings for several days, sometimes twice a day, running a channel of energy from her shoulder out through her fingertips. Usually, when I touched her wrist, there would be a steady pulsating that diminished as the healing continued. Although the numbness would lessen, most of the time it was present at some level.

During one of these sessions, I felt movement as if the bone had come together, and told this to Christine. The doctor, who was monitoring the progress of her wrist, took another X-ray and was astounded to see how quickly the bone had mended. In fact, it was perfect. Christine knew why and told her doctor she had a healer work on her wrist.

Jo-Ann Ciavolella is an executive administrative assistant.

I started to have sharp, prickly pains at the base of my left thumb. At first, I didn't think anything of it and thought that it might have been sprained, however, the pain persisted. I knew that Wayne was a healer and asked him if he could help.

I started Jo-Ann's healing and felt a steady pulsation in the thumb area. I ran a channel of energy from her shoulder down her arm and out through her fingers. As I radiated energy into the thumb area, the pulsation gradually subsided, and when I finished, the pain was gone. Jo-Ann commented:

The area around the thumb started to feel very warm. When Wayne stopped meditating the prickly pain had completely disappeared, and I have been pain free since the healing over five months ago.

Louise Wilkins had been my co-worker for many years, but this was the first time she told me about her chronic bad knee. With one hand on her ankle and the other on her knee, I ran a channel of energy between the two points and felt an extensive pulsating in the knee area. After a few minutes, the pulsation stopped and my intuition told me her knee was better. The following is Louise's account:

I suffered with a very painful right knee for ten years. I have seen various medical doctors with no results. In the summer of 2008, I was having lunch in a park next to my office building, complaining to a friend about my knee problem, when Wayne, a co-worker, explained that he was a healer and might be able to help me. I had my doubts, but allowed him to perform a healing on the injured knee, right there in the park in downtown Manhattan. The results were excellent and my knee has been good for five months. When asked about my problem knee I tell everyone how amazing the experience was and that Wayne has healed it.

Sarah Dioguardi's story is one of the most amazing. A highly respected professional, she works in our legal department and I've known her for over thirty years. While out on the street, I noticed her walking with a terrible limp and asked what happened.

"Last year I fell, and ever since then I have had excruciating pain in my hip that shoots down to my knee. I am unable to stand or walk for more than a few minutes without agony."

Sarah went to orthopedic specialists, therapy and took various medications, without success. Ice and heat treatments were also ineffective. I shared with Sarah that I was a healer and could possibly help. As I could not perform a healing on the sidewalk in downtown Manhattan, and she was located in a different building, I told her I would send a distance healing when I returned to my office. Once back at my desk, I raised my vibration level, focused, and sent the healing to Sarah. I had a good connection to her and felt a healing green energy going into her hip.

On Monday, Sarah related the following:

I quite forgot about the healing. The next day, I went shopping with my sister. Suddenly, we looked at each other in astonishment. Both of us realized that I did not have to stop and rest my leg and I had no limp! With the exception of an occasional minor pain in my hip, the excruciating pain was gone! Wayne sent me another distance healing, and I haven't had even a small ache since then.

For Sarah, these healings were miraculous! She had tried many conventional methods and nothing had worked to alleviate her pain. Needless to say, Sarah is now an ardent believer in energy healings.

Since I first started to share about my abilities as a healer, there has been a parade of people requesting my assistance. I have treated knees, ankles, legs, shoulders, and a host of other ailments. It is very gratifying to help so many people return to health and well-being.

COMMENTS BY KATHY: Wayne's success as a healer comes from his courage and commitment to humanity. Regardless of where he is, who may be watching or judging, his focus remains on assisting his fellow human beings and helping them in any way he can. His intention is always to completely heal the person he is working on and he sets his focus for the ultimate, no holds barred, healing.

CHAPTER 11

Give Them a Hand

KATHY

Lynn and I were cruising down the highway in her convertible. It was a beautiful June day, and we were headed to one of our favorite restaurants, looking forward to a leisurely lunch. Abruptly, our plans changed. Lynn's cell phone rang and the news was not good.

"What? What? I can't hear you!" Lynn could barely understand the person on the other end. "Okay, I'm on my way! We should be there in about five minutes."

Seeing the contortion of her face, I knew this was not a pleasure call and questioned, "Who was it? Where are we going?"

"We're going to the hospital. I'm not sure who it was but he's still breathing. All I could hear was ... 'Mom, I cut? or blew? off my fingers! Meet me at the hospital.' It was hard to hear with all the static, but it was one of my sons."

The number on the phone was not one we recognized. Two of her sons are police officers and the third is a landscaper, both jobs are dangerous.

We arrived at the hospital, and realized it was Lynn's youngest son, Jason, the landscaper. He was breathing, no longer bleeding and all of his fingers were with him and still somewhat attached. These were good signs.

Although he was extremely pale, Jason was in good spirits and talkative. He told us that he was trimming hedges. The weight of the gas-powered machine was borne by his left hand, while his right hand guided the trimmer where it needed to go. Despite working outside among nature's creatures, on this particular day he was startled when an irate yellow jacket flew out of the bushes and landed on his left arm. His immediate reaction was to swish it away with his right hand before he got stung. Unfortunately, the trimmer blades were still running on high speed. Jason recollected:

It happened so fast that it didn't seem real. I will never forget that piercing clatter. It sounded as if the hedge cutter was hitting a metal fence. Click! Click! Clang! Just that fast it was over and I was looking at the fingers on my right hand dangling in a hideous manner. It looked like a Halloween hand.

My first reaction was to pull off my shirt and wrap my hand to stop the bleeding. Thank God my cousin, Jake, and my friend, Joe, were with me. I yelled for help, Joe came running, and wrapped my hand as best he could. When Jake arrived and saw the extent of my injury, I think that he started to go into shock, but regained his composure as they helped me to the car.

The hospital was only about twenty minutes away, but it seemed like an eternity before we pulled up in front of the emergency room. By then, a massive amount of blood had run down my chest, down my leg and into my boot. My sock was soaked with blood. The pain was excruciating, and my fingers felt as if they were on fire - as if they had been blown off!

Lynn and I arrived a few minutes after Jason. Having been emergency medical technicians (EMTs) for almost 15 years, we were accustomed to gruesome sights, but when it's "one of your own," it's not easy to restrain your emotions. Lynn thought Jason's fingers looked like hot dogs on the grill. To me, they looked like uncooked sausages, gray, swollen, lifeless pieces of meat that someone had sort of aligned in place, as his hand lay atop of his belly. They did not look like fingers.

Clearly, this young man needed surgery and a miracle.

As EMTs, we knew that after 45 minutes without blood, the limbs start to die and the chance for full recovery is not as good. However, as healers, we were not discouraged and knew that Jason could fully recover the use of his fingers. Thus, we were already setting our intention for a full recovery!

The emergency room doctor said, "Jason needs a specialist. Is there a surgeon you would like us to call?"

Since there are no coincidences, we knew *exactly* who we wanted.

About a month before Jason's injury, a man we knew had a horrible accident. Buddy was feeding metal sheets into a machine press that flattens metal and curls it around a big drum. While setting the metal in place, his knee accidentally hit the start bar and his hand was pulled into and under the roller, flattening his fingers and squishing his hand. It was literally flattened out like a pancake.

Buddy required major reconstructive surgery and was operated on by this amazing surgeon, Dr. Stanley. During his recovery, and although he was unaware, Lynn and I sent many distance healings to his hand which, we believe, worked in conjunction with the excellent surgical restoration Dr. Stanley performed.

Buddy fully recovered and has complete use of his hand, including every finger.

As I said, there are no coincidences. We knew exactly who we wanted and asked the hospital to call Dr. Stanley. They told us he would be hard to get, but it turned out that although he had another surgery scheduled, he promised to see Jason as soon as possible.

We were willing to wait! By this time, a lot of Jason's family and friends had arrived at the hospital and were allowed to visit him. This was very important in keeping Jason's spirits high because of the length of time we were waiting.

I sat in the emergency room for several hours soaking my hand in some kind of cleaning solution. It was several more hours before the surgeon arrived. There was no way to create a rosy image of my hand and the doctor called it like he saw it.

By the time Dr. Stanley arrived, Jason's severed fingers had been eight hours without blood. I was concerned that the bleeding stopped. It was as if the body just disconnected from these fingers. Even Dr. Stanley, who deals with this sort of thing every day, had a somewhat hopeless look on his face when he saw what there was to work with.

My pinky was cut off almost to the knuckle. The bone on my ring finger was sliced through in two different spots and was terribly mangled. My middle and pointer fingers got off easy. They were only cut to the bone and all of the tendons were torn. This was some mess, and I had no medical insurance.

THE HEALERS

Dr. Stanley came to my rescue. A top surgeon, he took my case knowing I had no medical insurance. After examining my fingers he cautioned I may lose one or two fingertips and that recovering full movement of my fingers was highly questionable.

That evening, Dr. Stanley temporarily stitched Jason's fingers back together so they wouldn't fall apart, then splinted and wrapped his entire hand for protection. He explained that the real surgery would be scheduled for a day or two later when he would make specific incisions opening each finger lengthwise to re-attach the severed ligaments, tendons, and repair the broken bones using wires and pins. He was concerned that, even with the surgery, because of the extensive damage, Jason might lose a few of his fingertips and have limited use of his hand.

After Dr. Stanley completed this initial reattachment, Lynn and I began our energetic healing and repairing of Jason's hand and fingers. Just as Dr. Stanley had his plan for the physical reconnection, Lynn and I had our own plan. Jason's fingers had been without blood for eight hours. Through our intent and in our mind's eye, we visualized placing leeches into the tip of each of Jason's fingers, pulling the blood flow to the very tip so that each finger would receive nourishment and oxygen for complete healing. Once blood flow was restored, these leeches were to dissolve and disappear. It was our intention that each and every cell be revitalized and restored to optimal condition.

During the extensive surgery, Dr. Stanley had to re-cut my fingers and then re-attached them. The surgery lasted eight hours, involved four pins, and about 1,500 stitches. I had no money for the rehab the doctor said that I needed. He thought that it would take at least three months of work before we would know the extent to which I would be able to use my fingers. Knowing that I could not pay for therapy, Dr. Stanley had me go to his office for the sessions that I needed. What a great person!

During the days that followed, Lynn and I did healings on Jason's fingers, imagining a complete restoration of every muscle, tendon and ligament; each and every bone growing back stronger than before; the skin surrounding each finger, completely repairing itself smooth and new; complete restoration of Jason's fingers and hand, fully functioning, strong and healthy.

From the beginning my mother and Aunt Kathy began performing healings on my fingers. They were constantly doing hands-on and distance healings to create healing and blood flow throughout the injured area. My fingers that were numb and swollen early on began to heal rapidly. I would feel tingling and within a month after the surgery, I noticed how much better I was. In fact, I was healing so fast that the pins, *which were scheduled for removal after six weeks, were actually taken out after only four! Dr. Stanley could not believe how fast I was responding and how well I was healing.*

I now have full use of all my fingers and you would never know that I had gone through such an ordeal to keep the use of my right hand. Dr. Stanley did a fantastic job and is an amazingly generous man. I know the healings my mom and Aunt Kathy gave me made all the difference in the world when it came to the full use of my fingers returning.

I recommend that anyone suffering from an ailment or recovering from surgery should try energy healings. I know they helped me.

COMMENTS BY WAYNE: The healing of Jason's fingers is the perfect example of how the medical model and the energy healings can complement each other to create the best outcome for an injured person.

Dr. Stanley, with all his skills, knew that he could reattach Jason's fingers, but still felt that due to the extensive damage and length of time before reattachment, a complete recovery was unlikely.

The healing skills of Kathy and Lynn are just as great as those of this fine surgeon. When Dr. Stanley completed his segment of the process, Kathy and Lynn took over and created a healing environment in Jason's hand and fingers that could not fail. Jason knew exactly what was happening and he set his intent, along with his mother and aunt, to help expedite the healing process.

I recently met Jason and saw his hand up close for the first time. You would never know that he ever had extensive surgery or any kind of surgery at all. His hand looked absolutely perfect.

WAYNE

Mary Gruning, or the "Duchess" as she is lovingly referred to, is a dynamic, energetically charged woman with a great love of life as well as a terrific philosophy which is reflected in her many sayings - "Why look in the rear view mirror? What's the sense of complaining about the past? Let's move on!"

Those three statements tell you a lot about this lady. By the way, Mary is 97 years young. Spirit is everything, and she has it! She lives her life exactly how she speaks and what a role model for us all to follow. She doesn't worry about the past; she is too busy living in the present. She doesn't complain about anything negative that has happened to her, she is too busy enjoying the now. The Duchess does not let herself get bogged down by the weight of past negativity but instead creates a vibrant positive energy in the moment. If she is in a hurry don't get in her way, she has things to do.

One evening while Kathy and I were visiting with Mary and her daughter, Patricia Higgins, Mary told us she had a cyst on the inside of her right hand and was scheduled to have surgery in a few days. Patricia explained that about a month ago, Mary had seen her doctor, and he was monitoring the cyst very carefully. Several weeks after the initial examination, he decided it should be removed and scheduled surgery for the upcoming Monday morning.

Patricia asked Kathy and me to do a healing on Mary's hand. Kathy and Patricia sent distance healings while I held Mary's hand between my hands. It felt as if the cyst went all the way through from the front to the back of her hand. It was bizarre. At first, I felt the cyst disintegrating and then I envisioned it elevating above Mary's hand and being swept away. The space was replaced with perfectly healthy tissue. I saw colors and filled the area with a beautiful healing green, confident that a positive outcome was at hand.

First thing Monday morning, we received a call from a very excited and elated Patricia. She was calling from the hospital.

"We arrived at the hospital expecting to be prepped for surgery and when the doctor examined my mother's hand the cyst was gone! The surgery has been cancelled. Thank you so much."

Patricia and Mary both knew that the complete disappearance of this lump, which had been visible to the eye and perceptible to the touch, was the direct result of our combined healing efforts.

COMMENTS BY KATHY: *While we were all together that evening, Patricia and I sat on the sofa across from Mary while Wayne did the hands-on portion of the healing. Patricia and I sent distance healings to Mary's hand. Our intention was that the cyst would dissolve and surgery would be unnecessary.*

It was also my intention/prayer that whoever came in contact with Mary would be filled with love and would provide the best available care.

Our intentions were honored and all prayers were answered.

Imagine what could be possible if more people gathered together and joined their prayers and intentions with their focus on positive outcomes? Perhaps YOU are the one that will alter the healing world of your friends and families and change the focus from illness, to wellness and complete recovery without surgery.

CHAPTER 12

Back to School with Patricia Higgins

WAYNE

The solo healing was a course requirement and major event leading up to graduation from the Transformational Energy Healing program. After two years of hard work learning the skills of a healer, each student had the opportunity to select a partner and perform the healing of their choice on that person. Through the years we had practiced on each other many times, but this was different. We would now be viewed and critiqued by our teachers and peers. The general feeling of apprehension among the group was similar to that of a cast on the opening night of a play. I knew no one was eager to go first, except two, and as soon as the teachers asked for volunteers both Patricia Higgins and I stepped into the arena. We agreed I would perform the first healing on her while the class silently observed. Each student and teacher had an index card to make notations of their observations.

<u>Wayne's perspective of the healing on Patricia:</u>

I felt a high level of energy and vibration flowing through Patricia's body as soon as I touched her feet. Moving my hands to her ankles, I was aware of a rapid pulsation being generated from deep within her core and could feel it building to an uncontainable level. I could palpably feel the vibrations coursing through her body and knew immediately that this was not going to be a typical healing.

The high level of vibration created a release of stored energy which caused Patricia's upper body to go into violent spasms. Her torso was bouncing up and down so quickly I could hardly believe my eyes. It did not look real. In fact, if you tried to move that fast on purpose, you couldn't. She was not in any physical pain, but was releasing an endless stream of excess energy and habitual emotional patterns from her cells.

We all store these old patterns within our bodies. They block our internal flow of energy, and keep us fearful of making changes. These old patterns thrive on *fear,* also referred to as false evidence appearing real. Everything comes to a standstill with fear. However, once the fear is released and replaced with positive action steps, such as speaking up for yourself, taking a stand on your beliefs, being true to yourself, or being courageous in pursuing your dreams, the old patterns cannot survive and doors open to new possibilities and growth.

As fast as she was releasing old energy, I was filling every cell in her body with beautiful glowing white light. The thoracic spasms continued as I proceeded up her legs to her abdomen. To see anyone's body, at any age, moving that fast and for so long, was beyond my realm of possibility. Patricia was in her late sixties.

My guides were balancing Patricia's energy throughout, and I could feel her chakras spinning in a rapid clockwise manner. My instincts had developed as a healer, and in conjunction with the spiritual connection to Patricia, I knew what was happening and what I had to do.

I was drawn to her heart chakra. It was here that my higher Self felt the pain and anguish Patricia was suffering. It seemed to me she felt unloved and yet, at the same time, was resisting love. Her feeling of unworthiness was paramount at the very core of her being. My higher Self filled her with love, and I can still hear the message over and over again. "Patricia, you are loved: understand that you are loved and are worthy of being loved." Patricia's heart opened and her body and spirit received the message on a very deep cellular level. It seemed as though this was the first time she was truly able to feel and accept this message.

Immediately, the violent spasms stopped, her entire body relaxed and her breathing slowed. The pain that had been firmly entrenched in Patricia was lifted, replaced with the calmness and serenity she craved. As the volcanic, spasmodic energy that made her torso shake and convulse ceased, I felt a great sense of relief from the observing students and teachers.

When I sense an area has pain or is not healthy, I channel energy into that area and start seeing colors. Pain and healing energy/colors cannot occupy the same space therefore, if a person is willing to release the pain, the energy of color pushes the pain out and creates a healing environment. The higher the levels of energy, the more vividly pronounced the colors.

During the healing, I visualized many beautiful spectrums of color. Spirals of blues, reds, greens and oranges spinning across my range of vision created amazing panoplies of colors. These were literally the most magnificent I had ever seen. As one color spun into oblivion, another immediately took its place.

As the healing continued, I moved to Patricia's head, cradled it in the palms of my hands, and performed a healing technique called "brain balancing". The energy in her brain was balanced and enhanced to meet her needs while instilling in her the manifesto of love and its acceptance.

I sprinkled flakes of healing energy from her head to her toes filling any spots that may have been missed and then completed the final balancing of her energy fields. Confident that all of Patricia's needs had been met, standing at her feet and imbuing her body with a calm grounding, I brought the healing to conclusion.

Patricia's experience:

This healing was indeed a milestone. Wayne's intuitive comments about my feeling undeserving of love at a deep core level truly resonated. The issue of being unlovable seems fraught with the most basic of all clichés. While in my day-to-day life I experience myself as being someone eminently lovable and deserving, when it comes to a mutually loving partnership with a man, I had lived with myriad feelings of unworthiness, low self-esteem and a keen sense that at my core, I was truly undeserving and unlovable.

Oftentimes, what might seem to be trite, in fact, possesses a legitimate emotional currency. As someone who has experienced a plethora of healing and therapeutic modalities over the years, I am in a position to discern a given healer's efficacy. Wayne's healing was brilliant! His level of intuition, breadth of focus and healing energy allowed my body to be healed on a deeply cellular level. While my adult mind, intellect, and ego all know that I am worthy of being loved and cherished, the unrealistic systemic belief of being unlovable stems from my childhood and continues to surface. Even as I write this my mind wants to say: STOP...enough of this childish self-indulgence and complaining.

However, what is miraculous about transformational energy work is that despite the noisy and invalidating conversations ricocheting across my synapses telling me to "just get over it", I believe this issue of being unlovable has been transformed and healed on a cellular and energetic level.

Wayne's observations of the healing were incredibly perceptive. On many levels, I was able to release old negative thought patterns of unworthiness which prevented me from receiving love. Many of these crippling old fears and thought patterns have now been miraculously released, leaving me with a blessed sense of peacefulness and a powerful renewal of my life's purpose.

As a result of Wayne's healing, I am now present, in my body and mind, to a new sense of integrated peacefulness and courage vis-à-vis the ability and power to create a loving, joyous and enduring partnership with a great man, one who has the capacity to mirror the abundant love, energy, compassion and playfulness that is at my core being.

COMMENTS BY KATHY: Wayne was completely attentive to Patricia, and what she needed, to be free from the ingrained and false belief that she was unlovable. I believe the intensity of this healing for Patricia could only have occurred by the coming together of these two powerful healers.

The willingness of Wayne, with his strong yet gentle male energy, to create and hold a sacred healing space allowed Patricia to experience the full depth of this transformation. Wayne was the only man in a class with fourteen women so it's quite a sacred space he held. His skills and his commitment to his classmate were courageous, necessary, and for Wayne, very natural.

It took great courage for Patricia to allow her body to release the old habitual patterns of energy, in such uninhibited ways, while being observed by her classmates and teachers. Giving herself permission to be vulnerable, created extraordinary results.

This was a cellular healing, and for Patricia - life altering! As she stated, her belief, or energetic pattern was so deep that she had no awareness on a conscious day-to-day level, it was preventing her from ever having a wonderful partnership with a man.

In fact, a belief like that, at a core level, would actually draw to her men that would prove untrustworthy and not loving, which would ultimately prove her right ... I'm unlovable.

But no more! As she so beautifully expressed, Patricia is now free to..."create a loving, joyous and enduring partnership with a great man, one who has the capacity to mirror the abundant love, energy, compassion, and playfulness that is at my core being."

The following are exact comments by students who silently observed the healing:

- A rainbow of energy around Patricia. She's feeling warm energy. I'm feeling nauseous. A release is happening. Patricia is heavy in her chest, and there are Angels over her. Sparkles of light! There's a pulling from her stomach.

- There is a gentle kindness. Wayne is helping Patricia through labor pains to remove stuck energy. There is a safe strength and calmness. Peaceful grounding at the end.

- Strong energy connecting to Patricia. Feeling a pull in the right neck and shoulder. After, there is a balance between the right and left shoulders. There is a great release and calmness when Wayne is at her feet. I feel a strengthening of the inner core. Patricia is now participating in the healing – there is a sweeping, almost brushing of her energy fields.

- Tranquility; focus; total submersion; Patricia releasing; comforting; reassurance for child/Patricia; total calmness; grief followed an anger release through energy waves; Wayne created a safe environment for whatever Patricia needed; peaceful grounding.

- Tears being held back; small child – abandonment – release; nausea bubbling up; orange; tightness in throat – fear to release – tightening; release; guardian around her heart; no holding back of tears; lightening of energy; thank you Wayne.

- 2-3 minutes for grounding – bent into it – concentrated experience; healer's response to crying – cradled her ears (head) in hands; healer swaying a little with Patricia's head in his hands; one hand on her abdomen and one hand at her knees – great!; Patricia – exhaled an audible release; physical releases – flinching, kicking, 5 minutes crying as Wayne worked up right side massaging temples – clearing/waving of hands; immense clearing; Why stop/fix the emotion? One hand on her abdomen and one hand on her solar plexus; rubbing of belly, placed entire forearm up torso; panting as in childbirth, scream; release of fear/sadness; focus on right side of Patricia; fearless → fearful; hands in open clench. End: consoling at her knees / reconnected at feet; Patricia relaxed, placed right hand on her heart, Wayne put his head on her knees and hands to Patricia's feet for several minutes – nice! Rose colored light, sweeping, sprinkling of silver.

- Warm glowing light at ankles and legs; warm amber color – true intention is seen. I could feel the intense sadness escaping as the energy was being grounded. While working on the crown of her head and her forehead, the anger began to escape from her. Nice job working with this energy – at her abdomen, I could sense something very ugly happened either in this lifetime or a past one. It seems like that is what was bubbling to the surface in the beginning of the healing. Grounding at the end seemed to smooth over all intense releases from her during the healing. She seems more at rest, at peace. Warm glowing amber color all around her at the grounding phase.

- Strong, sudden headache, panic in my chest; Wayne's male energy guide/angel to his right – orange flashes from right leg. Rising up and out – panic in chest intensified, something pulling under Patricia's chest from under table, like a rock on a rope, to hold the pain from release. Pain is Patricia talking to the pain held in Wayne's neck – both held tightly in. "What would I do/be without my pain?" Snakes in the belly; Patricia crying in Wayne's stead; his hand on her belly – sound like water drainage out the feet; large rock anchoring, pain still there – not ready to release. His head to her legs – very lovely. Talking to her about the rope. Rope starts to unravel. Patricia put her hands to her back and sighed. Rope is loosened, frayed, process begins. Molecular movement within the rock, its energy is shifting, losing mass. He moved the particles that were released down and out her feet. It's a big decision for Patricia to let go. Rock is like pumice now, rope is fraying. Wayne very careful to bring back to peaceful place.

After the solo healing, one of the instructors commented, "Wayne has been doing this for years and years." I believe that she was referring to me being a healer not only in this lifetime, but also in past lives, notably when I was a shaman.

COMMENTS BY KATHY: Considering there was no communication or collaboration regarding their observations, notice that many students observed or felt: great release, nausea, orange/amber color, sprinkling of colors, Angels, peaceful grounding.

SWITCHING PLACES:

It was Patricia's turn to perform a solo healing on me. The same students and teachers watched silently, and wrote their observations on new index cards.

Patricia's reflections of the healing on Wayne:

For the solo presentation I selected Native American music to reflect Wayne's connection, and for my healing of choice followed my intuitive guidance.

I had a strong sense of merging with Wayne's core as I positioned myself at his feet. The musical accompaniment was a conduit for me to connect with the depths of my Shamanic core and I was immediately guided to perform a Shamanic healing which was atypical for our program curriculum.

I began moving my hands in the air in a supplicating circular motion calling in Wayne's Indian spirit guides and my own Shamanic guides. Holding Wayne's ankles, I placed my head upon his feet, securing our sacred connection. Elevating his ankles above the table, I began rapidly moving them left to right. Lifting his legs higher with his knees bent, I rotated them in a clockwise then counter-clockwise motion, simultaneously moving my body in a similar fashion. After lowering his legs to the table, I placed my hands on his knees and rocked them side-to-side while rocking my torso over them.

I was next drawn to Wayne's abdomen, his power center, where I had the vision of a tubular, hollow pipe, extending from his inner core to the earth's roots. Stacking one hand over the other, I created a hollow tube and blew air into that area to purge internal toxins and bring in a clear channel of radiant sacred energy.

Moving to Wayne's shoulder blades, I supported and lifted them gently off the table sending him purifying energy. It was there that I saw the vision of an eagle in the area of his chest. Gently moving my hands upward, I cradled Wayne's head in my hands and rocked it side to side with the deliberate intention of releasing old negative thought patterns.

From the moment it started and throughout the entire healing, I felt I was in an energetic trance, knowing that the healing was being channeled.

<u>Wayne's experience:</u>

The moment Patricia touched me I knew she was being guided to perform a healing we were never taught. I felt a wave of energy spread from my feet through my body and to my head. She wrapped her arms around both my legs and swung them rapidly in a circle. This was not the gentle touch that is used in Transformational Energy Healings. I knew this was a Shamanic healing! It felt so good, very familiar, and a sacred partnership was created between Patricia and me.

My norm is visualizing the chakra colors. It's very rare for me to see images and I was astonished by the vibrancy of what I saw when Patricia began to swing my knees. The images were as real and clear as if I were watching a high-definition TV.

The first image was a beautiful slab of ancient green jade, in a geometrical design atop a gold pedestal. It was several inches thick and flat on both sides. My interpretation was that this represented a tremendous sacred healing taking place within me. Green is the powerful healing color of the heart chakra, and jade is revered in many ancient cultures for its unique strength and healing properties. The gold pedestal represented a place of honor.

As the image dissipated, I saw a man dressed in biblical robes holding a shepherd's staff in his left hand. Although it lasted only seconds, I felt a sense of reverence and awareness of this representation of strength and wisdom.

I then saw a tall, sleek, African shaman, dancing above and around my body. Streams of white ornaments cascaded from his hair and white tribal lines were painted on the surface of his body. He was magnificent!

Although each vision was unique, for me they represented a connection in healing strength and kinship between these two very different healers and myself. It was a gift emphasizing that all healers are linked no matter their origin, appearance, dress, or techniques. No dimension of time or space separates the spiritual bond between us.

As Patricia worked on my upper torso and blew into my abdomen, it seemed as if many of the inhibitions holding me back were whisked away. I felt as if I were floating, clearly lighter with much of my baggage gone. The negativity released was replaced by a soothing, peaceful energy.

When Patricia put her hands under my shoulders and down my back, I could feel the energy from her hands rising up through my body. This prompted another great release, and there was a sense of many voids being filled.

When my head was cradled in her hands, a new awareness and clarity emerged. I strongly felt the link to my former existence as a Native American Indian medicine man.

This healing provided growth that will last me a lifetime! The visions rekindled my memories of healing powers, sense of belonging and finding my place in the world, as if I had come home to do what I was always meant to do. The warm feeling that opened my heart and enveloped my whole being is one I will never forget.

Comments from the observing students:

- Medicine man – big Indian headdress on – a very sacred healing.

- High priestess is the word I am getting for Patricia and Indian shaman for Wayne. Very secure in all motions. Trusting in the Divine. Very mysterious yet loving. Patricia was very graceful in her movements. It seems like she followed what Wayne's guides were telling her, and she understood what he needed.

- Strong and confident healer with Divine guidance. Dramatic.

- I saw a lot of orange colors. Patricia was a priestess. This was a sacred ritual. I saw Mesopotamia. In the end, there was a fabulous green clearing.

- Wayne was running off into the woods. Patricia showed much care with his legs – stop running? Compass for the lost. Both Patricia and Wayne kept shifting in time, from girl/boy to grownups as the healing progressed. A pine tree grew out of Wayne's belly. Heart-light. There was a sword to cut through the bonds at Wayne's neck. There was a great yearning and commitment to healing. There was an Angel's hand on the small of Patricia's back for support.

- Reverent but commanding. Not afraid to follow her own intuition. Physical but gentle and guided. Creative – open to all types of healing. Fluid and royal – medicine woman.

- Immediately brought Wayne to his core. No nonsense. Leading the way. All encompassing. Gave her all to Wayne. Uses every emotion within the healing. True surrender – safely brings Wayne to surrender.

COMMENTS BY KATHY: It's interesting that Patricia saw Wayne's power animal, the Eagle, in his chest area having no previous knowledge that this actually was his power animal. Also, when she blew into his abdominal area, she was in such a trance state that she knew she was actually clearing Wayne's power center as she stated. This was evidenced when one of the students observed "a pine tree grew out of Wayne's belly", which reinforces Patricia's vision of the roots to the earth image.

Having done a multitude of healings on Patricia and Wayne over the years, I have seen many of their past lives in which they were shaman/priestess/healers.

I was not surprised that these two amazing healers connected for their solo healings. They allowed their intuitive healing natures to take over and perform the healings without judgments, fears, or staying within the parameters of the program teachings. Patricia and Wayne were completely at ease, felt safe, and welcomed the exchange at the deepest level. These healings were life-altering. However, had they been stopped by "what it should look like" they would have dishonored themselves and each other.

I believe these extraordinary healings were actually mirror healings for Patricia and Wayne. Both released baggage from their pasts and came home to their own power. For each it was an awakening and being true to the Self.

CHAPTER 13

In an Instant

We perform healings on people for many reasons. There are those suffering from all kinds of ailments, others who are "fine" and just want a tune-up, and those who want to expand their consciousness and have new experiences. For some, one healing builds upon another and the person gradually notices changes and improvements in their health and well-being. But there are many times when people are immediately impacted and in an instant their lives are altered forever.

KATHY

I met Gina and Stan Serafin while working at the NSA/Chiropractic office. They are a wonderful couple, and I immediately took a liking to them. As music teachers, professional musicians and entertainers their commitment to each other, their work and the children they teach was consistently evident. They are always searching for ways to improve their own quality of life as well as the quality of life of all those around them.

As our friendship grew over the years, I shared many of my experiences regarding the energy healing training program, but never had the opportunity to do any healings on them. However, as the SRI facilitator and wellness educator in the office, they would have regular appointments with me to improve their breathing and inner connection. I would also participate, with the chiropractor, in the patient re-evaluation visits. It was during one of these visits that I did my first healing on Stan.

He was experiencing excruciating back pain and I asked Stan if I could place my hand on the area. When I did, we both felt a tremendous amount of heat. I held my hand on his back while he and the doctor continued their conversation. After a few minutes, I removed my hand and the pain was gone. Remarkably, in an instant, it had just gone away and never returned.

Many months later, Stan arrived at the office as soon as it opened. His shoulder had been hurting all weekend, and he was looking for pain relief. He remembered how quickly his previous pain disappeared and thought about calling, but not wanting to bother me over the weekend, decided to wait until Monday morning.

We had a "wellness conversation healing" where I teach people how to listen to their body's guidance and heal themselves, ultimately empowering them in their lives. When we learn how to connect with our body's guidance, healing can occur in an instant. I cannot stress how important it is to *breathe!*

RULE #1: BREATHE

When in pain we have a tendency to hold our breath and thus perpetuate the pain. Holding our breath disconnects us from, and shuts off oxygen to, areas in the body we are trying *not* to feel. To promote deep healing it is vital to bring breath and oxygen to the specific area in pain.

RULE #2: CONNECT TO YOUR BODY'S GUIDANCE

It is the only body you are going to get, and you cannot play on planet Earth without it.

Stan was willing to expand his personal awareness and self-healing skills. I instructed him: "Close your eyes. Put your hand on the area in pain and focus all your attention there. Find exactly where the pain is located. Is it in the muscle, the bone, the tissue, or in your energy fields outside your body? Listen for your body's guidance. You will hear it as a thought or see it as a picture in your mind."

There was no answer forthcoming so I had him try a different approach.

"What color is the pain? How big is it?" Although Stan knew his shoulder was in great pain, he could not find the source.

Stan was familiar with the energy fields that surround his body. With his eyes still closed, I had him move his hand off his shoulder and out into these fields, searching for the source. He found it! The pain was about five inches off his body, in his emotional field. He was amazed. Once he found the location, he was able to connect with it. He could see its shape and color. He was able to ask the question, "What do you want me to know?" He heard the message loud and clear: "Stop beating yourself up. You did the best you could, and there was nothing else you could have done. This is not your burden to shoulder."

Stan understood. He agreed to release his guilt (the action step). The pain went away immediately. "I wish I had called you when it first started. I wouldn't have suffered all weekend."

Instead of disconnecting in order to avoid the pain, Stan followed my instructions, was able to connect with the pain and received his own body's guidance. He heard the message, took action, and the pain disappeared.

Gentle, drug free, permanent pain relief!

Gina had her own experience when she won our monthly raffle for a free energy healing session. She loved the healing and afterwards, disclosed a medical recommendation she was not comfortable with and was having a difficult time making a decision about. At her annual checkup, because of the fibrous density of her breasts, her doctor scheduled both a mammogram and an ultra sound. Since neither test was conclusive, it was suggested she have two biopsies. Gina felt the biopsies would be highly invasive and were not something she wanted, yet with all the concern about cancer, she was somewhat scared not to have them.

I suggested she quiet all of the outside influences and check in with herself. Gina had seen this work with Stan, and was in total agreement. Having just had an energy healing, she was very connected to her own internal guidance.

I asked Gina to put her hands on the part of her body that we were speaking about and we had a wellness conversation. She was very clear what her body wanted and needed. She agreed to honor herself and her choice, and left feeling peaceful and confident with her decision.

Eventually, I left the NSA office to open my own practice. In the process, I lost contact with Gina and Stan, but met them again at a Landmark[16] seminar.

16 Landmark Worldwide: Innovative programs for living an extraordinary life, http://landmarkworldwide.com

A few days later, we had lunch and Stan told me about his scheduled surgery. He had a herniated belly button (Umbilicus hernia[17] - that's when your belly button bulges out and according to medical science cannot be healed without surgery). We spoke of the other times we had worked together and he asked, "Do you think it would work for something like this?"

"Yes, why don't we have a wellness conversation?" Having had previous success with this, he was a big believer. I asked him to put both hands over his belly button, close his eyes and listen to his body. He quieted his mind as best he could in a restaurant setting and focused on the injured area. "What does your body want you to know?" I asked.

"To stop working out so hard and to cut back on the amount of weights."

Stan was committed to losing weight and both toning and strengthening his body. He had been going to the gym two times a day, seven days a week and, as a result, his overzealous commitment to health was actually injuring him. He had been abusing himself.

I asked if he was willing to do what his body requested and he said he would. Because his body believed him, the pain immediately went away. He honored his word and reduced the amount of weights as well as the number of times per day and per week he was working out.

Once Stan found a healthier balance, he was able to receive the benefit of the workouts without the injuries. Within a few days, his belly button returned to normal. Just one little course correction and his body healed itself. He no longer needed the surgery.

Our bodies are trying to *communicate* with us and healing happens when we pay attention. In Louise Hay's book, *Heal Your Body*, "hernia" is defined as: "Ruptured relationships. Strain, burdens, incorrect creative expression."

Jane, suffering with stomach and digestion problems so severe she was forced to drop out of an Ivy League university, was referred to me by her doctor. After months of conventional treatments with little success, her doctor was baffled and frustrated. Because so many medical tests and procedures failed to provide any relief, and previously referred patients had benefited greatly from my energy healings, Jane scheduled a session.

---

17 http://hernia.tripod.com/umbilical.html

THE HEALERS

For six months, I suffered from digestive issues, chronic pain, and fatigue. Each day felt harder to get through than the last. Conventional medicine helped, but my doctor recommended I also see Kathy.

I could only imagine how bad this disorder had become to force this young woman to leave school and relinquish her lifelong career dreams. Every time she tried to eat, her inability to digest the food caused her agonizing pain. "It felt as if there were a sharp blade being twisted in my stomach." Jane basically stopped eating, thus suffered from excessive weight loss and malnutrition. She was exhausted. Her ability to focus was totally diminished. She was also losing hope of ever being well again.

She shared her experience of the medical testing she went through, feeling like a pin cushion, and how tired she was of being poked and prodded. I explained to Jane that a healing is very gentle, non-invasive, and sometimes referred to as the *laying on of hands*. I further explained that if she was too sensitive or traumatized to be touched, I did not need to place my hands on her body. She could sit, stand or lie down, whichever was most comfortable for her. Jane chose to lie comfortably on my massage table and listen to the soft music playing in the background. I also let her know that if, at any time, she felt uncomfortable, she could say "stop" and I would.

Throughout the energy healing, Jane's ability to relax expanded. Her tension and guardedness continued to release, allowing her to receive an ever-increasing energetic flow. Her body muscles relaxed which was evident by the angle of her feet, hands and fingers. When we began, her hands were held in lightly clenched fists, but as we progressed they opened and had little twitches in them indicating a state of relaxation and energy fluxing through her. Her facial muscles softened, and her breathing altered to what I call "puff" breathing. This type of breathing is an indication that the body is in an altered and relaxed state where spontaneous healing can take place. All these indicators informed me her body was receiving the benefits and in the process of self-healing.

When the session ended, Jane shared that the constant pain had lessened greatly; she felt much lighter and for the first time in a long time, was hopeful.

I had a sense there was a buried secret that was preventing Jane from nourishing herself. Something she could not digest. I asked her to contact me with any questions or concerns that might surface, explaining the nature of this work is that it continues to process after the session and as one goes about life. She left the office feeling revitalized. The possibility of healing completely and resuming a normal life was restored.

Later that day, Jane called with this exciting news: "When I left your office, I was really hungry. I went to a Mexican restaurant for dinner and ate my whole meal!"

She not only enjoyed the food, she was able to digest it without any pain or problem. Jane was very excited and elated about this immediate result.

A few days later Jane called to discuss something that had been bothering her since the day after the healing. She remembered an incident with her mother at the beginning of this illness which she had blocked out completely, but resurfaced after the healing.

The incident occurred during her first visit to the doctor when Jane's deeply concerned mother asked, "Did you do or take anything that might cause this problem?"

In fear of what her mother would think, Jane replied, "No." But Jane had, in fact, tried something that was considered the norm by her peers. She tried to lose weight by vomiting after eating. This behavior set up a pattern in her body that eventually caused Jane to be unable to eat.

By not telling the truth to her mom, who she loved very much, the foundation had been laid for a festering inside her that grew worse each day.

I suggested she forgive herself and tell her mom the truth. Jane had long ago stopped the unhealthy behavior, and now that the physical pattern was reset by the healing, it would be best to clear up the guilt she had been carrying.

Jane restored her health, her relationship with her mother and herself, and returned to college at the beginning of the next semester. She sent the following testimonial:

I felt a difference after the very first session. I felt completely relaxed, which was something I had not experienced the whole time I was sick. My pain lessened and my digestive situation improved drastically. In addition to helping me feel better physically, Kathy helped me feel better emotionally. She listened to me and showed genuine concern for my health and well-being.

COMMENTS BY WAYNE: *Mostly, if you follow YOUR guidance, and do the right thing for YOU, you will avoid illnesses. We are all born with an internal guidance system that is given to us for protection. It is also referred to as instinct. When a person utilizes their instinct they go within to find the cause and can often root out the problem by themselves. However, in a world that trains us to look outside of ourselves for answers, and treats the symptoms, following YOUR guidance is the opposite of that training.*

As tensions in life have a tendency to mount and get stored within, many people face these problems by cutting their breath short. They have no idea that they are suppressing the oxygen needed to create energy for every fiber of their body. By maximizing our breath to oxygenate not only the area of stored tension that is reflected in pain but also to every area of the body, a tremendous energy is generated to each cell within us.

It is amazing how simple yet powerful these two rules can be when utilized. These practices show you how to identify the CAUSE of the problem and then go inside to cure yourself. When a person is able to follow these two rules, and bring their body in sync with their spirit, by relying on their instinct, there is no ailment that cannot be completely healed.

Stan went within, relied on his internal guidance system which identified the cause, pointed him in the direction of the action steps that had to be taken and avoided surgery.

WAYNE

My family and I were off to Florida to attend the wedding of my nephew. We were all looking forward to the gala event and to start things off I made arrangements to visit my retired secretary, Roz Gold and her husband, Gil. Throughout my business years, Roz and I were the best of friends. She is a beautiful person, always willing to help anyone, and no matter how inconvenienced she might be, always strives to do the right thing.

When her first husband passed away, she had the courage to sell her home in New York and move to Florida in search of a new life. Roz eventually met, fell in love and married Gil, a terrific man. I hadn't seen them in many years and was excited about the visit.

Roz insisted on taking us to their club for dinner. Gil was having trouble walking, and as we entered the club, took a nasty fall. Immediately I knew that before we left, I would give him a gift of my own - a healing. After an excellent meal, we returned to their home, and I asked Roz and Gil if I could perform a healing on his legs.

Gil sat in a chair, removed his shoes, and placed his legs, one at a time, on my lap. Knowing his left leg was particularly bad I focused on the area that was swollen and felt hard to the touch. There was very little strength in this leg and almost no energy from his knee to his ankle, so I ran channels of energy up his legs and through his knees and hips. Any place I sensed a weakness, I filled with green energy, creating a healing environment. My intention was to reduce the swelling, soften the tissues and strengthen his legs. I felt there was a good connection between my guides, Gil's spirit, and the healing energies. I was confident the healing was successful.

After finishing, I asked Gil if he felt anything during the healing and he said no. But when he stood up, Gil was stunned. The pain was gone and he felt lighter on his feet. He proceeded to try and convince everyone the pain was really gone. I was elated to leave my friends with a little thank you for their hospitality.

Then we were off to Miami where we had a great time at the wedding. It was fun to reminisce with all the relatives. I told my sister-in-law, JoAnn, that I was a healer and shared some of my experiences, including the recent healing on Gil. JoAnn is a counselor and involved in meditation, so she had an understanding of what I was talking about.

Later, at the reception, JoAnn asked for my help. She explained that a guest had been suffering with a sinus headache for two days. The pain was so excruciating she could no longer tolerate it, and was going to leave early.

JoAnn introduced us, and the woman gave her permission for the healing. Standing behind her chair, I placed my hands on her head and immediately saw colors in my mind's eye which confirmed there was a great connection and healing taking place. Although the music was blasting, people were talking and laughing, and there was the normal hustle and bustle you would expect at a wedding, I had only one thought in my mind, to have her sinuses completely clear and pain free. I wanted the best outcome for her and was both thankful and confident her needs would be met. The entire procedure probably lasted all of ten minutes. When I opened my eyes, I noticed people staring at us, and a few asked what I was doing.

When I removed my hands she proclaimed, "It's gone, the pain is gone!" She hugged and thanked me while her husband shook my hand and patted my shoulder. They were able to enjoy the entire reception and when I saw them the next day, she was still pain free.

I met Marjie Kern at Patricia Higgins' home while attending a dinner party. Marjie told us the story of how she injured her leg when she tripped over a wire and took a terrible fall. Although nothing had been broken, she was still in a lot of pain. Patricia has a healing room in her home and asked me to do a healing on her friend. Marjie explained what happened:

I landed so hard it knocked the wind out of me. I am not one to visit a doctor, but this pain was worse than delivering a baby. My right leg was black and blue from my ankle to my knee. The doctor examined my leg but nothing was broken. At the time of Wayne's healing, it was slowly improving but was still very painful.

Although I agreed to the healing, I had no expectations because, in the past, people have tried to hypnotize me with no results. Therefore, I expected this to turn out the same way.

Wayne asked me to lie face down on the massage table. As soon as he touched my back, I felt my stomach go into a wave that went from my waist to my chest. It was like an ocean. I was embarrassed! I couldn't stop it. I hoped Wayne wouldn't see it.

Then Wayne asked me to turn over on my back. While he was at my feet, I had the distinct sensation that there were many hands all over me. It was very odd, as I knew there was no one else in the room. Suddenly, I felt the presence of my deceased father, Fred Malina, and even saw a vague image of him. I was in awe. As Wayne worked up my injured right leg I felt two darts of pain come out of the knee and leave my body. Immediately the pain was gone. Throughout the healing there was a continuous movement of energy within my body that was different from anything I had ever experienced.

When the healing was over, I felt an elevated sense of happiness and relief, and the pain in my knee was completely gone! I was embarrassed about the stomach wave, which I couldn't control, but Wayne said that he never saw it.

I never observed Marjie's wave, however, wherever I placed my hands, I could feel energy jumping and moving throughout her body. My intention was to eliminate the pain and heal her knee. Throughout the healing, I had a very good feeling my intention was being fulfilled. It was confirmed when Marjie sat up, eased herself off the table into a standing position, and declared all of her pains were gone and she felt reenergized.

Another positive, yet unexpected, outcome was that Marjie was fully breathing, perhaps for the first time in her life. She realized that prior to the healing, she had been taking little shallow breaths, but now, she was taking big, deep, breaths, and her breathing seemed easier and smoother. Even the color tone of her skin seemed to improve from the increased oxygenation. These conditions indicated that her breath had been blocked as a result of tensions and pressures, accumulated over time, which were stored in her body. It was evident that a massive shift in Marjie had taken place.

COMMENTS BY KATHY: The healer always makes a difference in the outcome of the healing. Although Wayne began with the thought of healing a specific pain, his gratitude and thankfulness for the complete healing of the person, was, as always, his primary intention. In this healing, in addition to healing the pain, it was breath.

There is nothing more important than breath. If you think your job, or a relationship, or even money is the most important thing, try going without air for 3 minutes.

Once Marjie's breath was able to flow more freely, it was amazing how quickly she began to heal. Our breath brings oxygen to our organs. Take a moment right now and just notice your own breath. Are you holding it? Can you feel it going into your lungs? Have you shut off parts of your body because you don't want to feel the sadness or hurt that is stored in a particular area? It may seem difficult to conceive at first, but we actually have the ability to bring breath into every part of our bodies. When we can really breathe, our whole body feels alive.

I highly recommend reading and practicing the breathing exercises in the book called: The 12 Stages of Healing by Donald M. Epstein, D.C.[18].

---

18   Donald M. Epstein, D.C., *The 12 Stages of Healing*, (California: Co-published by Amber-Allen Publishing and New World Library, 1994)

CHAPTER 14

Extended Family

Energy healings are not reserved solely for humans. Our animal friends are great receivers of healings and almost always show an immediate, positive response and increase in energy. Unencumbered by human fears or programming, their natural instinct allows them to receive unconditionally.

KATHY:

It was just after Thanksgiving while visiting friends in Michigan that I performed a hands-on healing on Janice. I felt the structural difference between her two ankles and afterwards, asked her about the injury. She told me it happened many years ago while riding her horse, Pony. During the healing, she became acutely aware that she needed to do something to help her horse, but was unsure of what to do.

Pony was a Morgan, a breed known for its high intelligence, reliability, loyalty, stamina, and versatility. Janice raised Pony from the time she was a baby. When Pony was two months old, she and her mother, came to live with Janice.

When Pony was old enough to be weaned, Pony's mother returned to her original farm alone.

For the next eight years, Janice cared for and trained her. As she grew up, Pony was like an overgrown dog, a pet. Eventually it was time to ride her. During one of their rides Janice was thrown and her ankle badly injured. There was a long recovery period and because so much time had passed, her fear of getting back on Pony was overwhelming. She was no longer able to ride and without enough exercise, Pony was becoming too high spirited for Janice to handle. Sadly, Janice decided it would be best for Pony to have a new home, which she found with a friend who owned a small ranch. It was the hardest decision Janice ever made. She was heartbroken at the loss of Pony and unable to even visit her. It was just too painful. It was like letting her baby go, over and over again.

Although she did not visit Pony, she did keep tabs on her and knew that Pony was unhappy in her new surroundings. Horses are herd animals and she was not accepted by the other mares. This stress caused Pony to take up the unhealthy and destructive habit of cribbing. Pony would grab hold of a fence rail with her teeth, curve her neck, and suck in air, causing damage to her teeth, her digestive system, and the rail. Janice did not know what to do. She only knew she loved Pony and did not want her suffering.

After feeling the benefits of our healing session, she asked if I would do a healing on Pony. I was leaving for the airport in the morning, and there was no time to drive to the ranch and do a hands-on healing. I offered to do a distance healing and contact her later that day with my findings. Janice didn't understand how a healing could occur without touching, but was open to the possibility.

When I focused on Pony an image of depression came to my mind's eye. I saw a woman on a park bench, hunched over, covered with rags, such sadness, no place to go, no purpose in life, totally despondent. I had never envisioned such a devastating image before. It broke my heart and instilled in me a tremendous compassion for Pony who was obviously in a deep state of depression. She felt unwelcomed, unloved, unwanted and unappreciated in her new surroundings. She was a horse with no purpose, alone and forgotten.

Her energy levels were depleted. I replenished Pony's charkas and felt her eagerly accepting the incoming energy. However, I knew it would not be long before she would sink back into deep depression unless an action step was taken. The message was loud and clear. Pony had to be moved and quickly.

Relaying this information to Janice, I recommended she immediately find Pony a new home. Janice decided to bring Pony back to her farm. This was a good start, but ultimately, not a good plan. Pony needed more than just a place to live: she needed a purpose in life; she needed to be active and feel wanted.

Janice updated me a few months later on Pony's journey:

Around the same time that you did the healings on Pony and me I spoke to a psychic friend of mine and shared my concerns about Pony. She referred me to a psychic who specializes in animals who subsequently did a reading on Pony. The psychic said that usually an animal will channel just a few lines, however, when she connected with Pony, she received 3 pages of information. The bottom line was that Pony was very unhappy.

Shortly after the healing, my daughter, Jessica, came home from college and visited Pony. What she found was so upsetting that she immediately demanded we bring Pony home.

My husband, Kevin, was not willing to do this for many reasons, three of which would be the added financial expense of wintering a horse, having a large animal on the property again and the time required to care for her properly.

Exasperated, Jessica took matters into her own hands and declared, "I'm bringing Pony home!"

A friend drove Jessica to the farm where Pony was living. It took a long time to walk the seven miles, but as soon as Pony arrived home, her spirits immediately perked up. The vet came by to evaluate her condition. Pony was severely emaciated, nothing but skin and bones. She had shared a field with an aggressive, dominant horse who regularly ate Pony's allotment of feed. In her depressed state, Pony did not fight back. With no one paying attention, Pony's health rapidly deteriorated and she would not have made it through the winter. In addition to love and attention, the vet recommended a high fat feed diet.

In her dispirited, down trodden, head hanging low state, Pony was submissive and easily managed. I was the Alpha female. It took about two weeks for her to start putting on weight. Now that she was receiving high quality feed and loving attention, her health and spirit were returning. By springtime, she looked great! Her coat was shiny, her eyes were bright, and her spirit was back! Also back was her desire to be the Alpha. The good news was she was well. The bad news was I could no longer handle her.

With the undivided attention she was receiving from Janice and Kevin, Pony stopped the cribbing habit, and was once again the healthy, vibrant, feisty, horse they loved. Not bad for a horse that a short while ago was dying from depression and starvation. In fact, with all this newfound energy, she was becoming too spirited.

As Pony improved, the attention started to lessen. The children were grown, and Janice and Kevin were away for most of the day. Frustrated and alone, with no one to work off the excess energy, Pony became aggressive, even chasing the dogs out of her corral. Janice knew Pony was not happy and suggested they seek a new home where she would have more company and exercise. However, Kevin had become attached and did not want to give her up. Pony had other ideas and when she kicked him in the groin, Kevin began to rethink his decision. This time they would make sure it was a perfect match. In addition to good care, Pony needed a purpose.

Janice and Kevin did their homework. They located a breeder of Morgan horses who, after researching Pony's bloodlines was very interested, made the two-hour trip and adopted her on the spot.

Pony now lives on an active Morgan breeding farm, close enough for Janice to visit. Accepted by the herd, her new owners report she is very happy and content.

On June 22, 2008, Pony delivered her first foal, a beautiful filly named Honey. I guess you could say Pony found her purpose. How much sweeter can life possibly get for this rejuvenated mare?

In retrospect, as Janice says:

In God's plan, in spite of all the suffering, in the end, it all works out.

Susie found Harley, her beloved eleven-year-old golden lab, on the floor, unable to stand. She immediately took him to the veterinarian who diagnosed an infection in his anal gland, causing a fever. The vet prescribed antibiotics, but they were not working. The fever did not reduce and upon further examination, the vet discovered a blockage. Concerned that the blockage was poisoning his entire system, surgery was recommended to remove it.

Susie is familiar with the power of healings, and because they were out of state, she called to request a distance healing.

I began the healing immediately and found Harley was extremely tired and moving toward crossing over. He had recently undergone surgery for his throat and it took a toll on him. In my mind's eye, I could see Harley off to my right - young, happy, playing with his toys, wagging his tail, and chasing deer. He was ready to enjoy himself. To my left, I could see old Harley - tired, yet loyal. He knew how much he was loved and still needed here by Susie and her husband. I sent as much energy to Harley as he could absorb.

I told Susie what I had seen.

She saw Harley before the surgery and told him that she needed him to stay, but also did not want him to suffer. Lynn, Wayne, and I were sending healings but the ultimate decision was his. Would he go to the right or the left?

We continued to send healings throughout the day, getting a sense that Harley was releasing the desire to go off and play in favor of staying with Susie a while longer. Susie called me later that day to tell me the surgery went well, that Harley was in recovery, and to please continue sending him energy.

It has been over a year now and Harley is doing great. His health has much improved, and he is enjoying his time with Susie.

WAYNE:

I have also had my share of healing pets. Ellen Krakower, a long-time co-worker, asked me to assist her two beloved pets, Nathan and Douglas.

Nathan is Ellen's 12 year-old dachshund who suffered a series of debilitating illnesses over the last few years. Just before his tenth birthday, he ate tainted dog food and was hospitalized with kidney failure. This occurred during the brief period when animals across the country were poisoned because of an ingredient in many popular brands of dog food. In Nathan's case, he ingested this during a two-week period when Ellen switched from canned to pouch food, something she had never done before. Ellen noticed Nathan drinking excessive amounts of water. She checked the lot numbers on the back of the food pouch, and realized she had purchased the poisoned food. Nathan survived the incident, but a year or so later he was acting strangely again.

He was drinking excessive amounts of water which caused Ellen much concern for she feared his kidneys were shutting down. He became paranoid, staying upstairs for days and hiding under the bed. He would not let her near him and seemed to be exhibiting signs of delusion. When she was able to get him outside, he would run in circles and seemed confused and unsure of his surroundings. Ellen took him to the vet, and he was diagnosed with Cushing's disease. She was told that since he was in the first stages of the disease, the treatment would be more detrimental to his health than the disease itself. It was at this point she turned to me for a healing.

Wayne performed the healing telepathically and soon thereafter, all of Nathan's symptoms disappeared. He is the sweet and friendly dog he always was and the only reason he goes to the vet now is for his yearly checkup. Although the vet indicated that his disease would worsen over time, this does not seem to be the case and Nathan celebrated his 12th birthday in March.

As Nathan got older, another hurdle was thrown into his path. He lost the use of his hind legs. Although it was a struggle, he still managed to get around by pulling himself along using his front legs. Ellen took him to the vet who felt that he would never regain use of his hind legs. Disheartened, she contemplated the use of a harness. But then remembered the power of the healings and asked me to send one to Nathan.

Wayne sent a telepathic healing and Nathan began to show immediate improvement. After a few more healings, Nathan regained complete use of his hind legs! On behalf of Nathan and me, we are forever grateful.

In addition to Nathan, I performed a healing on Ellen's cat Douglas. At two-months-old, Douglas became a member of her family and since Ellen had no specific knowledge of his medical history, assumed he was a sickly cat from birth. Rescued from euthanasia, he was a scraggly kitten who suffered from continuous eye infections. Although she administered several tubes of medicine over the years, nothing seemed to work. Now, at 4-years-old, the vet mentioned the infections could be caused by stress. That's when Ellen called me.

After the success of Nathan's healing, I again turned to Wayne to see if there was something he could do for Douglas. Wayne administered a telepathic healing and when I arrived home that evening I noticed that Douglas' eyes were dry and exhibited no signs of infection. This has been the case for about a week and I will continue to monitor Douglas' condition. So far, Wayne is four for four, and I will continue to seek his help at the first sign of any future symptoms.

INSTRUCTIONS: If your pet is suffering from any ailment or injury, you can help them. Using your mind (your thoughts):

- Close your eyes. Take a few deep breaths. Focus in on the animal.

- Notice your thoughts.

- Take your focus off "what is" and put your focus on "what you want" and "the perfect outcome".

- Instead of hope, have faith it will happen.

- Imagine you are channeling loving, healing energy into the area or injury or concern.

- Visualize perfection. Imagine your pet healthy and happy.

- If you get distracted, bring yourself back to focus.

- Trust yourself.

- "Listen" for any guidance. There may be an action step that needs to be taken. Relax, you have "freedom of choice" to do it or not.

As a beginner, limit the time to no more than 10 minutes.
Pay attention to the reaction the animal is having.
One healing grows upon the other. Repeat as desired.

Option: Gently place your hands on or over the area you are focusing on. Follow the steps above.

CHAPTER 15

Healing of the Putnam Valley Market

WAYNE

Nestled in the upstate New York community of Putnam Valley resides a favorite local market owned and operated by two brothers, Domenic and Nino Santucci. More than a market, it has become a hub of social activity because of the warm and friendly environment these two brothers have created.

When the birds excitedly greet the new day with their melodious chirpings these brothers are already hard at work preparing their store for the usual customers. In addition to supplying all the amenities of a small market, they cook breakfast, lunch, dinner and some of the best pizza you will ever eat.

To run an A-one establishment requires dedication, thus long after the birds have finished their tunes, Domenic and Nino are still hard at work. Although they often work sixteen-hour days and close for very few holidays during the year, they never complain. Rightfully proud of the Putnam Valley Market, this is how they provide for their families. As small business owners, Domenic and Nino represent the backbone of the American economy.

Domenic Santucci

Nino Santucci

Even though they are young, when you work as hard as they do ailments are apt to develop. Moving or standing on a hard concrete floor day after day creates strain on the entire body. Not having time to eat properly causes a lack of nutrition. Insufficient restful sleep creates exhaustion. Working long hours and worrying about bills creates stress. Do any of these sound familiar? Too many people in our society fall into one or more of these categories.

Through the years Domenic and Nino have benefited from my journey into wellness. At first it was magnets for their feet resulting in more energy and less leg fatigue. Then it was better nutrition through vitamin supplements. As my health improved, their health improved. Domenic, particularly, was a willing participant. We would discuss his state of health, and I would recommend the appropriate supplements. Overall, his health improved, his mind was clearer, he was able to focus better, and he almost never got sick. He was feeling revitalized. These newfound products were enhancing his immune system and his health. Through these successes I had built up credibility.

During this time I began learning about energy healings and what I learned, they heard about. Domenic was the first person at the Putnam Valley Market to volunteer for a healing. His main complaints were exhaustion and tired legs. I had no massage table with me so we proceeded to the kitchen where there was a stainless steel table large enough to accommodate his prone body. Domenic lay on his back and we began the healing. As soon as I placed my hands on his body I could feel the energy rocketing through him. Throughout the healing, everywhere I placed my hands, I had the same sensation.

When the healing was complete, Domenic questioned, "What was that? What happened to me?" He felt energy flowing through him, saw magnificent colors, and had the sensation of many hands touching his body simultaneously, a common phenomenon. When he stood up he was completely rejuvenated. The pain in his legs was gone, he was reenergized, and all his fears and worries had disappeared! He did not understand what happened to him but was in awe with the results. This was the beginning of the healing of the Putnam Valley Market.

As time went on, Domenic wanted more. Due to my busy work schedule, I advised Domenic to visit Kathy for a healing.

KATHY

When I first met Domenic, he seemed quiet and timid. Soft spoken, his energetic presence was like a whisper in the wind, so soft, he was almost transparent. In fact, it felt as though he was "not really here". He had no specific physical problems or pains, but knew that he wanted to experience the rejuvenation of a healing.

Instinctively, I knew he needed more play, which was definitely lacking in his life. Domenic is a talented musician and loves to play the accordion, but between the long hours at the Market and raising his family, he has little time to do the things he loves. He was living a life dominated by business, pressure, and tension.

I began the healing at his feet. It was here that I felt he lacked balance, and his life force was working at minimal capacity, which explained the sensation of "not really here". I channeled energy through his body, balancing it on both his right and left sides. When he felt balanced and energized, I was guided to his ankles.

With my hands resting gently in place, I immediately knew he had suffered a severe ankle injury earlier in his life. I sent rebuilding energy to restructure the ankle and repair the damage done long ago.

After the healing we spoke about the injury I perceived. Domenic shared his memory of hurting his ankle as a child while playing with friends, and then being punished for getting hurt. This incident took the play out of his life, and put fear in, afraid to play because if he got hurt, he would once again be punished. Thus, he associated play with punishment.

I advised Domenic to take his family and accordion to the park for a picnic. He needed to be away from all the responsibilities of the Market and his home. It was imperative for him to relearn how to play with the people he loved and trusted. Domenic took my suggestion to heart and set aside a day with his family where he rekindled his joy of playing music for them. When he told me about the picnic, he was smiling and very excited that he had taken a major step forward. Domenic's experience:

The healings I received from Wayne and Kathy were a great benefit to me. I heard Wayne speak about them but until you experience one for yourself, you really cannot understand how amazing they are. These healings were life altering for me. I was hoping to experience something that would make me feel a little better and more relaxed but what I got exceeded anything that I had hoped for - an indescribable sense of peace!

At first, I did not know what was happening but with each healing there was a sensation of energy moving through my body. It was weird, as I had never felt anything like it before. There were many colors but I particularly remember beautiful blue lights. They were small and almost like a fireworks display. They would light up like an explosive firework in the sky and then dissipate just as quickly from my vision. How was I seeing this? My eyes were closed. I have no explanation, but I loved the show. I wanted it to keep coming.

Just as with Wayne, during the healing with Kathy, as the healing progressed the movement of energy increased. It seemed as if Kathy had more than two hands on me at one time, but logic told me that was not possible. I was enjoying the sensations that were happening within me. I observed people; some were relatives, but I can't recall who they were. I cannot put a name on any of them. This was a great experience. The hour went by in what appeared to be minutes, and I did not want it to end.

This was the most relaxed that I have ever been. I could not get up and did not want to get off the table after the healing. The pain that had been bothering my neck was completely gone. I was very thirsty and Kathy explained that I had to drink a lot of water because of the high vibration level that had taken place in my body. Astonishingly, all my worries were gone. I no longer fretted about the little or big things that had, prior to this healing, seemed so important. Forget the bills, they don't matter. None of the things that stress me on a daily basis matter anymore.

I do not understand what happened to me but I know it was great. I visit Kathy whenever I can and each experience is different and beneficial to me. Whatever this is and however weird it sounds, it works.

Play is an essential part of life. In today's society, most people work so hard and under such duress they have forgotten how to play, resulting in a very hollow existence. A balanced life needs to include play and when we have fun, we naturally laugh. We have all heard the expression "Laughter is the best medicine". Domenic now understands the full meaning of that phrase.

WAYNE

Domenic could not help but talk about his healing experiences and many people were starting to hear about them. He wanted his 15-year-old son, Mario to receive the same benefits he had. I was shopping at the Market one afternoon when Domenic asked me to do a healing on his son. This quiet man had an emphatic determination that I'd never seen before, and I knew I was not leaving that store without doing the healing.

We went to the kitchen and Mario stretched out on the same stainless steel table where I had performed a healing on his father. As hard and cold as that table was, I knew it wasn't comfortable, but from the moment I touched him there was such a rush of energy that I felt like he was floating. I perceived energy moving up his legs and torso. Mario saw colors and so did I. There was a balancing of energy taking place in his brain and throughout his body.

After the healing, Mario said, "I feel great! What was that?" He had felt energy coursing through his body and had never before experienced anything remotely similar. Now, Mario was calmer and more relaxed then he had ever been in all of his life.

A 15-year-old smiling and raving about his experience attracted a fair amount of attention. As a result, Domenic asked me to do a healing on Julio who also worked at the Market.

Skilled in Karate, Julio was injured the previous day when he pulled a hamstring muscle during practice. He was walking with a distinct limp and in severe pain that ran down the back of his leg. Hamstring injuries are very painful, usually taking several weeks of rest to fully heal. I believe the only reason Julio agreed to let me touch him was because he saw and heard Mario relating his experience in a very animated manner.

I placed both hands directly on his injury and felt tremendous heat spread over the surrounding area. Moving one hand behind the knee and the other to the top of the hamstring, I ran a channel of glowing golden energy between both hands which expanded, filled and balanced the area. I then directed green and indigo energy into the back of the hamstring to complete the healing. The entire process took about ten minutes.

As I removed my hands, Julio began to gingerly flex his leg. He gradually expanded the stretching and started walking around. At first he moved slowly and then picked up the pace. Julio was astonished. The limp and pain were completely gone! Several days later Nino gave me an update: the pain never returned.

Nino was the next to be healed. I went to the Market one evening to pick up some hamburger buns, and he looked exhausted. The bags under his eyes reflected the duress he was under. He had been working sixteen-hour days for five months with only two days off. I told him he needed a healing, but he said he was too busy. Domenic, Mario and Julio were all abuzz about their healing experiences and Nino knew about them, but everything he had ever been taught refuted the possibility of such happenings. Nino is a smart and logical fellow. He knew and trusted me, but told me that to touch people and heal them was reserved for a group of people who were written about in the bible thousands of years ago. I was defying the only logic he had ever known. So, he challenged me.

"Do you see that woman in front of the store? If you can heal her, I will believe. She had surgery on her back, and it is worse than ever. She is in pain all the time."

I accepted his challenge.

Nino led the way out of the store and we approached the woman who was sitting at a picnic table in front of the Market. "Toni Ann, this is Wayne Gabari. He is a healer and would like to see if he can help with your back." She said that long ago she had been to a healer and would try anything. "I am much worse since the operation. The surgeon ruined my back. I am in agony all the time." She looked at me and said, "You look good." The more we chatted the more comfortable Toni Ann appeared. I asked her if she wanted to lie face down on the picnic table or stand." She elected to stand.

My intention was on healing her entire spine. I asked Toni Ann to lean back into my hands as I began to do a spinal cleansing which rebuilds the spine using all the major chakra colors. This is performed by envisioning energy as a color, pooling it at the base of the spine, then moving upward, wrapping it around each vertebra, from the tailbone all the way up to the base of the skull. This is done for each chakra color, first wrapping it in red, then orange, then yellow, then green, then blue, then indigo and finally gold.

Toni Ann began to wobble and then cry. I asked her if she was all right. She replied, "I am seeing such beautiful colors." In a comforting tone, I reminded her to lean back into my hands. I was concerned that she might lose her balance and fall forward. While all this was going on, cars were driving by and people were entering and leaving the Market. I guess we put on quite a show. People may have commented, but Toni Ann and I never noticed. When you work on a securities trading floor there are all kinds of noises and distractions. It takes a lot to disrupt me, and I never lost my focus.

As the healing gradually wound down, I had a good feeling Toni Ann was going to have a major improvement in her back. Before I could ask her how she felt, she exclaimed, "My back feels so much better. I can't believe it! Who are you? Where do you live?"

I told her if she had any other problems she could reach me through Nino. I had to go; there were some burning hamburgers I had left on the grill that needed rescuing. By helping Toni Ann feel so much better, I enjoyed the best-burnt burger I ever ate.

A few days later I was back in the Market and before I could get a word out, Nino said, "I believe! After you left the other night Toni Ann came into the store with a spring in her step. The pain and grimacing were gone, replaced with a new vibrancy. She said you were a saint."

I responded, "I'm very happy I was able to help her but thank God you didn't tell her where I live."

Because of what he had seen through others experiences, Nino was now a believer and ready to receive his first healing. We proceeded to the famous stainless steel table.

It was the height of the Friday evening rush. The kitchen area was extremely noisy with people talking, phones ringing, pots clanging and pizzas going in and out of the oven.

As Nino reclined on the table, I raised my vibration level and immediately knew what he needed. I focused on peace and serenity as I touched his feet. From the moment I made contact with Nino, he was out like a light. It was as if years of aggravation and disturbance were being peeled away from this wonderful selfless man. There was a gentle soothing wave of energy that slowly traveled up through his body touching every cell in a relaxing, rejuvenating fashion.

There was a mirror effect and I was feeling the same relaxation that was processing through Nino, visualizing all kinds of exquisite colors, and it was as peaceful as could be. Cradling his head in my hands I duplicated the same intent in a brain balancing sending peace, love, and serenity back and forth between his heart and head. When I finished, he was still out cold and there was a deep sense of calmness throughout his body.

We had a captivated audience as a few of the Market's employees were intensely watching, but Nino was in another world. They probably couldn't understand how he could be asleep on such a hard table with all the hustle and bustle going on around him.

Gradually Nino's consciousness returned and he awakened. This is what he had to say:

Boy, do I feel good! The whole healing seemed as if it only took a few minutes (although it was actually about an hour). I felt as if I were asleep but not sleeping. There was energy and tremendous warmth shooting through my body. I saw spots of beautiful assorted colors. The purple and red shades were particularly beautiful. It was such a relaxing energy, and I felt it moving throughout me. Everything feels better. The pain in my legs and lower back are all gone. The fatigue that I had been feeling is completely gone. I feel great! I'm RE-ENERGIZED from what was the most stressful time of my life. The heartburn that I was suffering from has disappeared. This was a truly amazing experience and no amount of talk can do it justice. You have to experience one to fully understand the power of these healings.

Nino was now a big believer. He trusted me and knew that these healings were able to do wonderful things. A short time later he showed his trust when he called asking if I could come to the Market that night and do a healing on his wife, Maria. With her many responsibilities bringing up three active young children and Nino working long hours, she was stressed to the max. Everyone in the family was feeling the pressure and Nino thought I could help. I agreed and we met that evening.

I knew Maria, but hadn't seen her in a few years. We went to the Market's upstairs office, sat on the sofa, and spoke for several minutes. I explained how I became a healer and what we were going to do. She expressed her concerns about the daily pressures that were affecting her health.

I understood she was suffering from a feeling of hopelessness and was angry because she had a lack of control. I wanted Maria to see the fears and limitations she was living with, release them and create a new life of joy and possibility.

When I perform a healing, I always set my intention for the complete healing of the person's physical, emotional, mental, and spiritual being. Then the result is whatever happens. I can never predict the outcome.

I raised my vibration to an extraordinarily high level. Like going into a deep meditation, I closed my eyes and focused my intention on having my entire being vibrate at a level higher than the vibration of dis-ease (lack of ease). This is because no abnormality can exist in an environment where the vibration level is higher than that of its own.

I called in all my guides, and Maria's guides, to join me in performing this healing. Throughout most of it, I felt as if we were in another dimension, as if time stood still. We were totally in the *now*. It was a terrific feeling, and I knew that only good could come from it.

Each cell in Maria's body was filled with the glowing energy of existence. It was a peaceful energy that reflected her love and importance of her family. Energy was moving everywhere, from the tips of her toes to the top of her head, and in all the fields surrounding her body. When I reached Maria's head and cradled it in my hands, I filled every cell in her body with love.

Then a spectacular thing happened, something I never experienced before or since. The whole room was filled with angels. I couldn't believe it. They were all over us, and I felt as if I were bumping into them every time I moved. Their love was everywhere, going right to the core of Maria's existence. It was exhilarating, and I sensed that I was in another dimension reserved for special times in a person's life. I was visualizing all spectrums of beautiful colors but these magnificent angels stole the show. They were there for Maria, and I knew she was undergoing a life-altering experience.

My instincts led me to work on Maria's energy fields far outside the body. There were imbalances that were corrected and filled with energy. With the team I had, there was nothing but the best coming out of this healing. I did a final sprinkling of golden energy dust on Maria from head to toe and balanced it throughout her body and fields.

My vibration level gradually slowed and as the healing ended I could not wait to see what Maria felt. She was in a deep state of processing, and after allowing her system about ten minutes to absorb this new energetic state, I touched her right shoulder, told her to take her time but we were finished.

As she lay quietly, with her eyes closed, she said, "I feel so good, I don't want to come back." Little by little she started to come around. "This is the best that I have ever felt." I knew we both needed water from the high vibration level so we drank and she shared her experience:

I felt as if I were lifted into another world. My body was here, but my spirit wasn't. I was seeing a beautiful bright light. I never wanted this vision to end. I felt so tranquil. This was more peaceful than I had been in a long time. It was like a whoosh of wind passing through me with no explanation. I wanted to stay in this state and never come back.

Maria flew down the stairs proclaiming, "This is the best I have ever felt in my life!" Nino was ecstatic because he knew that both he and his family's life had just changed for the better. He thanked me profusely and so did Maria. "Take dinner home! Take drinks! Take anything you want!" exclaimed a grateful Nino.

Helping my friends was reward enough for me. There are not enough adjectives in the dictionary to describe the elation that permeated within me as I left the Market. I was very thankful to have been blessed at being selected to serve as the conduit for such a magnificent healing.

For Maria, the stress never came back. In the days that followed she felt better and better and life continued to look brighter. The daily trials were easily managed. She never had even a small relapse. A huge weight had been lifted from Maria. She is now optimistic and relishes every minute of her life and family.

On Sundays, Kathy and I send distance healings at 9 pm, and the Santucci families receive theirs. Maria commented how well her children are now doing in school. I thought to myself, "I wonder how many of those angels are still with her?"

COMMENTS BY KATHY: I also have experienced the room filling up with Angels during a healing. My client was in an extreme state of hopelessness and like Wayne, I found myself saying "excuse me, pardon me" as I was guided through the healing. The depth of love, compassion, support, and healing energy they bring is breathtaking. It was an experience I will never forget.

Although Maria had a huge breakthrough in healing and a profound experience that she will never forget, she will need to practice and strengthen this new way of feeling or her old thought patterns may slowly seep back in. If someone goes back to talking about their old ailments or upsets, instead of touting their newfound health, they will be a magnet to whatever they are speaking. It is the law of the Universe: like attracts like. We've all heard the expression "misery loves company?" Well it is also true for "well-being loves well-being."

The weekly distance healings support and promote well-being and health. Whether in-person or long distance, the consistent influx of energy keeps the body, mind, emotions, and spirit balanced and charged. When parents do better their kids do better and vice versa.

KATHY

Nino's belief in our energy healings took off and he wanted to help everyone he knew. When his longtime friend, Sal Ferrara, shared that he was suffering with some difficult ailments, Nino knew exactly how to help him and gave him the gift of a healing.

When Sal came for the healing, I knew this healthy-looking young man was very close to shattering. It was unmistakable. There's a saying, "When the student is ready, the teacher will appear." Sal was ready!

Although skeptical at first, Sal was also excited with anticipation. He had been feeling lost and confused for a long time. Something he could not identify was holding him back and draining his energy. Sal had suffered with carpel tunnel in both wrists and now the pain in his left shoulder escalated to where he feared he would be unable to continue working. All this pain in addition to a diagnosis of ADD was exhausting him. He felt depleted of energy. The medical community offered medication or surgery, but he wanted no part of either. Not knowing where to turn, he listened to his friend Nino and decided to give energy healing a try. This was outside the spectrum of his beliefs, yet at his gut level it felt right to him.

It had become increasingly hard for Sal to be with people. If someone touched him, even gently, it was irritating and made him extremely uncomfortable. I explained that his system was overloaded and once his energy centers were rebalanced and recharged, he would not feel like that anymore. However, if he was not comfortable with me touching him, I could perform the healing without placing my hands on his body. Sal said he was becoming much more relaxed just speaking with me and thought he would be okay being touched.

We spoke about the parts of his body that were hurting and what they represented in his life. For instance, the right shoulder is where we hold our beliefs. He was happy to show me the tattoo of a cross on his right shoulder, the symbol of his religious beliefs. He then asked, "What is the left shoulder?" I said, "Trust." He showed me the tattoo on his left shoulder – a lion's head. Sal's birth sign is Leo, the lion. I suggested this might be a reminder to trust in himself and his own inner guidance regardless of what other people think.

Next was a warrior tattoo on the right side of his upper back. I asked him, "Why put a tattoo on your back where you cannot view it?"

"Because my knowing it's there gives me strength to go forward."

We spoke of his wrists and the carpel tunnel which is "anger and frustration at life's seeming injustices."[19] He confirmed this was what he was feeling.

At this point, Sal was ready for the physical hands-on healing.

I took a reading of his chakras and then began the healing by welcoming his support team as well as my own. I often receive visions of clients past lives. Sal was one of those clients. It's not so much like a movie, but more like a knowing, a story being told to me, or a snapshot in time.

As soon as I placed my hands on his ankles, and closed my eyes, I immediately received an image of him nailed to a cross. After repairing and healing the holes left by the nails that had been driven through his feet, I was then guided to repair his hands. When I opened my eyes to move around the table, I was astonished to see Sal with his arms extended and spread wide open. Most clients lie with their arms by their sides. As I began working on his hands, I was drawn to his wrists. It was here that the nails had ripped through Sal's flesh and bones leaving ghastly wounds in both.

After the healing, I told Sal what I saw. He was not surprised, explaining that many times he had experienced the feeling someone was trying to "crucify him"

---

19   Louise L. Hay, *You Can Heal Your Life*, (California: Hay House Inc., 1999)

and used those exact words to describe the sensation. He also said that during the healing session he felt his aching shoulder pop back into place. In that moment, much of the pain that plagued him dissipated.

The next vision I shared was another past life. Sal was shackled to the oar of an ancient ship where the slaves were chained in the bottom of the boat and brutally forced to row until exhaustion or death.

The questions we addressed were:

- Where in this lifetime do you feel like a slave?

- Where are you shackled now?

- Why do you not free yourself?

Sal explained he had grown to detest his previous job but felt forced to stay because of the substantial money he was earning. Eventually, both of his wrists gave out and he could no longer perform that job. He moved to another position that evolved into again, what he felt was "slave labor". Feeling trapped again, his lower back deteriorated to the point where he had to switch careers.

Currently, he works on a computer, in a small cubicle, nine hours a day. Because of the intensive pain in his shoulder and wrists, he is unable to perform his duties. He feels trapped and afraid. Sal is now "chained" to his desk for hours on end, similar to the way he was chained to the slave ship. This is a recurring pattern. He is recreating his past life as a slave in his current existence.

I asked him, "What do you really want to do?"

"I want to help people. I want to make a difference in people's lives."

I shared a premonition that came to me during the healing. I saw him as a spiritual preacher, teacher or guide of some kind, making a difference in people's lives. He was standing in front of a large group, but it was definitely not in a church and it was not a religious type of event. It was more of a spiritual outdoors type church.

It was then I remembered a gathering place I had seen while walking the trails behind a church in a neighboring town. I told him of this place and asked him to search it out.

He knew the church I was talking about because a few years earlier he had been drawn there while driving a delivery truck. He drove into the parking lot feeling like there was something there for him but couldn't figure out what it was. Eventually he left but had a strong sense there was something he needed to do or see at that place.

I suggested he go to the church, drive to the rear parking lot near the cemetery, get out of the car, and follow the trail down the hill into the wooded area where he would find what he was looking for. He agreed to do this in the near future.

Sal left the office feeling peaceful and re-energized. He had arrived irritated and uncomfortable with being touched before the healing, but gave me a big hug and thank you when he left. I spoke with him a few days later, and he said he felt like he had found home. I believe he has - inside of himself.

This work is transformational. There is no going back. Why would you want to? Make a little course correction in the direction your life is going, even a little baby step, and you can end up in a much more glorious place. Sal took an action step by coming for a healing, which cleared the energy of his past lives. He is no longer "chained" to his desk and is free. His intuition was validated, leaving him with a renewed trust in himself.

——— ———

Jenny Felippelli came to see me after much urging from Nino, her mother's cousin. A beautiful twenty-five year-old woman, you would never guess from her outer appearance the turmoil and suffering that was going on inside her.

When we met, Jenny shared her concerns and history of pain and chronic illnesses: sinusitis, acid reflux, arthritis, asthma, allergies, back pain, the ever present stomach problems, and most recently, the surgery for her sinus polyps. She spoke of her attempts to find relief from the pain, symptoms, and illnesses that plagued her since she was twelve years old. The list was astounding! Years of antibiotics, inhalers, decongestants, and a myriad of other drugs, some over-the-counter and some by prescription, many of which she had been on since childhood.

It was no wonder she was feeling poorly. Her body was exhausted from this onslaught.

The perpetual cycle Jenny was caught in was taking a toll on her view of life as well as her body. Through her eyes, life seemed very unfair. Always sick and hurting, she seemed resigned to this fate and sad, thinking, "This is how my life will always be." Although the path she followed for so long was in some ways helping, it was not leading her to optimal health. She did not really believe a healing would help, but in spite of her skepticism, maintained a slim glimmer of hope and agreed to receive one.

Why was she unable to internally heal when everything outside seemed great? She was beautiful, athletic, engaged to a wonderful guy and enjoyed her job. I asked about her childhood as many of these illnesses originated in her youth.

Jenny explained that her father was prone to drinking and as a result, would often fly off the handle for no reason. This was especially true at the dinner table when the family was gathered together. During dinner the children were discouraged from making any noise or movements for fear of setting him off, creating a strained and stressful environment. A time when these children should have been nourishing their bodies with food became a time when they held their breath and maintained silence.

Over a prolonged period, this behavior can put a severe strain on the digestive system. Most of us have had moments in our lives when we walked on eggshells around someone or participated in a meal where someone at the table was uptight and looking for trouble. This kind of tense situation goes straight to the pit of your stomach, and you just want to rush through the meal. Whether it happens with someone we love or a complete stranger, the experience affects our body. If this was to happen once or twice and you were old enough to have a say, you would most likely not eat your meals with that person again. However, when you are a young child and the person creating this tension is your father, there is no option.

When a pattern like this continues, almost every day for years, it will definitely take a toll on the digestive system. In addition, holding your breath waiting for the other shoe to drop, over a prolonged period of time, will take its toll on the respiratory system in the form of asthma, allergies, and sinus problems. Shallow breathing cuts off oxygen to the vital organs.

Even when these behaviors stop, the systems can get locked into patterns of defense or constriction, and we cannot always release the patterns on our own.

Like holiday traditions, many family behaviors are also handed down. If these behaviors are negative they can create patterns of illness. Illness is an accepted condition. What if we never got sick? What would your life be like if you never got a headache or sore throat or cold or stomach virus? Did you ever use illness as an excuse to get out of doing something you didn't want to do? Or to get someone's attention? Or to stop someone's behavior towards you? Or to stop them from leaving you? Unconsciously, illness can bring attention, and even power, to a person's life.

For instance if a couple were fighting, and a child was upset by this, the child might come down with a cold (mental confusion). The illness of the child would be a great distraction inside the dynamics of a family, and may even bring loving attention toward the child. This could be a wonderful tool as a young child but as an adult, when one has the option to leave it no longer serves a purpose.

Healing - releasing an illness pattern - can happen in an instant or it can happen in small increments over time. For some, it may be more frightening to make a change in one's behavior than it is to be ill, and healing may never happen.

During the healing I balanced and recharged Jenny's chakras, repaired her sinuses as well as her immune, respiratory and digestive systems, and replenished her entire energetic blueprint. She was completely relaxed and internally peaceful after the healing. For the first time in a long time Jenny felt really good. She left the office elated and filled with hope!

Her asthma and allergies were much improved and she was able to stop taking the medications. Over the next few months, Jenny came occasionally for hands-on sessions, but also would call for distance healings when she was in severe pain and unable to leave her house. She always received much relief and most times the pain would disappear completely. As she is practicing her new awareness and makes changes in her life, she may revisit the old patterns from time to time. However, her overall health is much improved and wellness is the new possibility for her future.

Jenny's mother, Silvana, told me Jenny was much more relaxed after the healings and she was enjoying life more. Now that her daughter was doing so much better Silvana was less worried and ready to schedule her own healing session.

Silvana had experience with healing having attended several healing masses held by her local Catholic church which helped her enormously. She had been suffering from carpel tunnel syndrome and after one of the healing masses the pain completely went away and never returned. Thus Silvana avoided surgery.

Upon first meeting her I could tell she was ultra stressed by the goings on in her life. Silvana was suffering from asthma, nerves and insomnia. She was taking the same medication as Jenny for stomach upset, along with a list of others. In addition to the years of concern and stress associated with her daughter's many medical issues, she was also separated from her husband of 30 plus years and in the midst of a stressful divorce.

She was worried about the divorce, but even more so, her children's long history of health problems had taken a heavy toll on her. Now that Jenny was feeling so much better Silvana was ready to focus on her own well being.

Like her cousins Nino and Domenic, Silvana is a hard worker, committed to her family having a great life. To make ends meet she works long hours, six and more often than not seven days a week.

We spoke about her life and her conflicting emotions regarding the ending of her long-term marriage. She and her husband had been together since they were young teenagers. Silvana had been committed to her children being in a happy family and assumed the role of peacekeeper at all costs. After more than thirty years, she faced a life-altering decision. Going through divorce was awful but for her own sake necessary. This is what Silvana had to say:

During the healings, I cried a lot. There was a rush of energy through my body, and I felt tingling from the tips of my toes to the top of my head. It was so strong that it held me in awe. I could hear sounds around me, and although I was awake, I felt like I was someplace else. I saw rapid flashes of white circles of light which were surrounded by black stars that were also rapidly flashing. My body was numb, and I was floating. I felt as if I could not move anything yet I was awake. Eventually I went into a deep sleep. I don't know how long I was gone or where I went. It could have been a minute or it could have been an hour. I had no concept of time. As I started to come back, I could hear Kathy's voice, but I couldn't come back. It felt so good! I was a little scared, and I kept hearing Kathy's voice gently urging me to come back.

There is nothing like the feeling that I have after a healing with Kathy. I felt completely rested. All of my fears were gone. I felt so good. I felt so special, like a chosen one. I cannot even explain this feeling to a person who has not had that experience. I was so calm that I wanted to stay on the table forever.

These healings completely changed my life. More than ever, I am a true believer in God as a result of this experience. I now look at the world from a different point of view, how wonderful it is, and things cannot be that bad. You come out of that healing space and there is nothing, and no one, that can upset you. All fears are gone, including the fear of death. I now know where I will be going after death, and it is so wonderful.

My asthma is almost gone. The inhalers I used to take up to twelve times a day are now completely unnecessary! I was able to stop this medication. What I received was a soul healing. I was now released from the stress I had from my separation and divorce. You could say that I was lost and now, I'm found. The old Silvana is back!

I received additional healings, and each one was amazing. One grew upon the other and my level of relaxation was fantastic. I felt so good about mine and Jenny's healings with Kathy that I wanted my son to benefit as well.

Favian came after much persuasion from his mother and sister, and the differences he saw in them. He was perpetually tired because his snoring caused him to lose sleep. Like his mother and sister, he was also living on medications to control stomach acids. Coming from the same family, I had a pretty good idea of what was going on and proceeded with the healing.

Although I only saw Favian once, Silvana told me his stress levels were way down, he was much calmer, and was very well rested as opposed to always feeling tired.

Jenny, Silvana, and Favian benefited enormously from their healing experiences as individuals and as a family. Each one is feeling better, calmer, and more able to deal with their life experiences. Their interactions with each other are happier and more loving, and there is a healthy redistribution of responsibility and contribution within the family. They have new conversations, more energy, and are more supportive of each other than they were before the healings.

As Nino witnessed the miraculous changes in everyone he sent for healings, any lingering doubts were gone. Now that he had a proven access to help people there was no holding him back. Nino knew his long-time friend and hair stylist, Mauro Costa, was suffering through what can best be described as "hell on earth" and generously gifted him a healing. That gift turned out to be the best Mauro ever received.

Mauro was happy to accept Nino's gift and came to my office for the healing. He filled out my client profile form and wrote, "I'm going crazy!" Many symptoms and fears plagued him. He was scared and had no idea what to do. He had seen psychiatrists, medical doctors, and recently been hospitalized. He was losing his vision and afraid he was losing his mind. Driving was becoming increasingly difficult with anxiety attacks so severe he would have to pull over on the side of the road to scream and cry. He prayed to God for help. Fortunately for Mauro, God answered his prayers and sent Nino.

Mauro was leaving for Brazil in a few days and was extremely frightened. His cultural background included black magic and voodoo, and he was afraid that he was being taken over by something evil and didn't want any part of it. He thought that something was trying to possess him.

After Mauro expressed his fears I had a metaphysical understanding of the areas that needed attention. I knew he was running scared and trying to escape from life. His life force energy was moving out of his body which creates intense suffering. My intent was that Mauro would see the circumstances that created this condition and would have the courage to overcome.

He reclined on the table for the hands on part of the session. In order to evaluate the overall energy flow throughout his body, I performed a chakra reading. This reading provided me with a visual assessment of constrictions and blockages in his main energy centers. Using a crystal pendulum suspended from a chain, I held it over each of the chakras, front and back, to determine the flow of energy to and through each area.

Every chakra but one was shut down. It was no wonder Mauro felt so diminished. He was running on sheer willpower alone. It is hard enough to be in your own skin when your life force is blocked or misdirected but with Mauro, everything was shutting down.

Inviting our angels and guides into the healing, I set my intention to be the vessel for this man's needs. I was guided to replenish and recharge each and every chakra. I did this, first on his back, connecting each one to the next, restoring, recharging, and revitalizing each energy center followed by the replenishing of his immune system with a spinal cleansing. When this felt complete, I asked Mauro to turn over on his back.

Placing my hands on his ankles I waited for guidance. The answer was immediate. Remove any and all attachments that were feeding from his energy. Mauro is a very generous and loving man, but was being energetically abused by some, who took advantage of his good nature.

Have you ever been in the company of someone for a period of time and after they leave you feel absolutely exhausted or drained? That person was energetically feeding from you. Many people do not realize this is happening, but it happens all the time. Those who are actually taking the energy may not realize that they are tapping into the other person's life force. This is an unconscious act for most people. An alternative to this behavior would be to replenish one's energy by sitting or walking in nature, swimming or playing in the water, or just being around plants and trees. The earth will replenish our energy. We do not need to take it from each other. In addition, there can also be a healthy exchange of energy between people, a mutual sharing back and forth. Have you ever been with someone and both of you leave feeling really good? That was a positive, or mutual, exchange of energy.

With this awareness, I connected at Mauro's feet to perform a "cutting of the ties". This healing technique is done through intention. Gently disconnecting the feeding tubes of the other people's connections, I asked that they be guided to replenish themselves from their own source energies. Using healing green energy, I closed all openings left by these disconnected tubes. Without all these "suckers" feeding off of him, Mauro was now able to replenish himself.

Aware that his fears were created from an absence of love, I intended he be filled with light and love from the tips of his toes to the top of his head and beyond, that every cell in his body vibrate at the level of pure love, and that he create only health and well being in his life. That each and every field around him be restored and repaired to reflect the magnificent being he is and he remember his own magnificence.

I proceeded from chakra to chakra and created a flow of energy from one to the next, grounding him to the earth and to his magnificent connection to all that is. When this was complete I returned to his feet, grounded him to his physical body, closed the healing, and gave thanks.

Mauro experienced a deep inner peace. Relaxed yet energized, he could not remember feeling so good. All the demons that had been chasing him seemed to be gone. He could not wait to thank Nino for this extraordinary gift.

During the healing I saw beautiful colors. I saw yellow, green, orange, mixes of green and orange, blue, and lines of purple. They held me in awe.

This healing had such a profound effect on Mauro that he scheduled another appointment to see me after his return from Brazil. At the second session, he shared how his life had been evolving. Each day he felt stronger and began to have visions of his childhood. He remembered what happened to him when he was five years old while living in Brazil.

Mauro had been sexually abused. The impact the abuse had on his life took a toll on him. He was thirty-nine and, only now, after all these years, was able to remember. This secret had been driving him crazy and his body finally said, "No more - enough!"

While sitting in my living room, I had a vision. I saw myself as a young boy, little Mauro, and me, big Mauro, holding that little boy close and crying with him, telling him that no one would ever hurt him like that again. Little Mauro was sitting on my lap and crying, and I remembered the horrible sexual abuse that happened to me, and the pact I made over 30 years ago. "If anyone abuses me again, I will go crazy!" When I was a child, I would become uncontrollable and bang myself into walls. Unknowingly, I suffered with this silent torment for all these years. Now that I remembered, I vowed to little Mauro that big Mauro would protect him. I made a new pact with myself. "No one will do that to me ever again!"

I realized that many people in my life were taking advantage of me and I was being abused over and over again in many different ways. People took advantage of my home, my friendship, my money, and I let this happen. No more. The people in my life would respect me or they would not be in my life. I realized I created a prison in my mind and locked myself in it. I was the one with the keys to unlock the door and set myself free. Kathy, I am free!

And so it was. The people who had been taking advantage of Mauro have since moved on, thus creating openings for new and healthier relationships based on mutual respect.

When Mauro returned from Brazil, his finances were in a shambles. He had ten cents to his name, and $800 in credit card debt and bank overcharge fees. He realized the man he had been dating was no longer a good match for him and the relationship ended.

Eventually, someone new came into his life and helped Mauro deal with his finances. The bank refunded the overcharge fees, he got a debt consolidation loan, and took control of his home. His business, although always good, increased even more, which quickly improved his financial situation. Many great things were happening including a trip to Bermuda to be the personal hairstylist for a wedding party – all expenses paid, plus a generous fee.

There have also been new opportunities for Mauro to practice standing up for himself. Such an opportunity arose when Mauro went for a medical test and the person who gave the results tried to intimidate and sexually accost him. Mauro had the courage to say, "No!"

He declared, "I am a victim no more!" and filed sexual harassment charges against this man.

A representative from the clinic, where I went for the medical test, met with me as they wanted to stop any further abuse by their employee. I now have a new future to live into.

Another opportunity to exhibit his new way of being came about as the result of a fender-bender in a parking garage. Both men got out of their cars and the driver of the other car, who was much bigger than Mauro, demanded $500 to pay for his bumper. Mauro stood his ground and said, "No! You hit me when you backed up. I'm not paying you anything."

This was a new way of being for Mauro. No longer a victim, he is now in the driver's seat of his own life. Mauro now knows he has choice.

Mauro's health, finances, friendships, and his life in general, continue to get better and better. Even though he realizes it is not always easy, he knows that in the process of being true to himself people may leave but, this creates new space for healthier relationships to emerge and evolve. The things Mauro was attracting before are not what he attracts now. As Mauro feels better, he attracts better. He is no longer afraid. He is happy.

During my last session with Kathy, little Mauro was again sitting on my lap but this time he was smiling and happy. Right before my eyes he started to grow until he was an adult. The adult was me! My emotions were now elevated, and I am stronger than I have ever been. I am a real man. I am my own man!

Mauro often calls Nino and Maria Santucci to thank them for saving his life. He doesn't just say "Thank you." He tells them how much he loves them and their family. He says, "You saved my life. You gave me back my life." Nino keeps telling him, "All I did was send you to the healer."

Mauro's first healing was on March 3, 2008, and he received a total of five healings over the next two months. Once he realized his hidden fears, Mauro courageously turned and confronted his demons. Although the abuse stopped thirty years ago, the self-punishment and self-imprisonment continued. Over this incredibly short period of time, he not only uncovered this horrific experience from his past, but through his courage, brought it to resolution.

On April 26th, with forgiveness and love in his heart, he confronted the person who sexually abused him when he was a little boy. Mauro called me with great joy and happiness in his voice. The truth had been spoken and apologies had been made. A huge darkness had been lifted from him and the other person as well. No more "dirty little secrets". No more shame. There was only freedom, peace, love, and a new future to be created. This sequence of healings opened his eyes to things that had long been suppressed, and supported him throughout his journey from victim to victory.

This new awareness enabled Mauro to change his life from the negatives that were costing him his health, love, peace and dreams for his future, to a new positive outlook. Mauro is now successful at setting boundaries for how people treat him. He says how his life goes. He stands up for himself and has a strong voice. And his greatest gift of all - He has forgiven the person who initially abused him, forgave himself, and in doing so, set them both free.

In place of the anger, which served to cover the pain, there is now only love. New possibilities are now available for their relationship and for all the relationships affected by this. Mauro has moved his focus from the wound of this experience, the absence of feeling loved, to the gift of this experience. The gift is his incredible depth of love that he brings to all of his relationships, to the lives of everyone that he touches. I have experienced this for myself, and I am honored to be in his presence.

I would like to acknowledge Mauro. It takes courage to be so real and share his experience with all of you that are reading this. His intention is to help others and encourage those who have similar demons chasing them to stop running, turn around and face them. Please, do not judge the person that did this to him for that person most likely also experienced something similar in their childhood and did not know how to stop the pattern of behavior. This is not meant to be an excuse for such behavior, just a point of view from a larger lens, or the bigger picture so to speak. We are all in this together. We all have our wounds. We can choose to see the wound or we can choose to see the gift from the wound. The fact is, we choose.

There is a saying, "Wherever you go – there you are!" We cannot escape ourselves. You are the only person that you will go through your entire life with.

Life is a journey, but the journey is within. We create our experience of the world through our thoughts. If we want to change our outside world we must change our inside thoughts.

If we look for the negative in the world, if we beat ourselves up with our thoughts, we will attract people and experiences to us that confirm these thoughts.

If we love and honor ourselves we will attract people and experiences to us that confirm these thoughts.

If we are not good to ourselves why would we expect others to be good to us? Say something new to yourself today, something nice that you have not said before. Begin a *Gratitude List* and add to it every day. Watch your world alter as your list grows.

When our thoughts are empowering, loving, and creative, we are comfortable inside our own skins and the experience of life unfolds joyfully.

How do we attract a better life?

1. Notice your thoughts.

2. Upgrade one thought at a time by thinking a better feeling thought.

At the end of this book there is a *Resource Guide* which lists books, movies, websites, and more. Use these resources to help you raise the vibration of your thoughts and ultimately your life!

Life is a journey, enjoy it! We are here to create heaven on earth. *Now* is the time to start. Take a step toward your heart's desire. The destination is limitless!

COMMENTS BY WAYNE: Toss a pebble into a pond and the ripple grows larger and larger.

The healing of the Putnam Valley Market started with one person. Domenic's courage to go against the grain and open an entrenched belief system, created a ripple effect and many lives were touched in a significant way. Some of these people had such afflictions that they were merely existing. The joy of life was simply gone.

The people who received the healings have a new awareness of their bodies, minds, and spirits. They now understand how good they can feel every day in spite of the difficulties that they face.

From being individual people with private concerns, they are now a community with new possibilities for health and well-being. They have new conversations about the joys of living and continue to share how these healings have improved their lives. As this community's outlook on life changed, and they are living from joy, they send out a new positive vibration and the ripple effect becomes exponential.

The healing of Mauro is truly an amazing story. For thirty five years he suppressed the negative feelings from the sexual abuse that happened to him as a young boy. Each time he felt abused, and suppressed more feelings, those feelings were stored, energetically one on top of the other. They compounded until eventually the energy erupted almost taking his sanity, vision, and ultimately his life.

Kathy's healing released the negative energy and opened a spiritual gateway that filled him with loving energy. The healing allowed the memories to surface. Mauro could have been plagued with anger and hatred. Instead, he chose — forgiveness, gratitude, and love. This has become the mantra for his life.

From the ripple that touched Mauro, he then created his own ripple and everyone who comes in contact with him notices the change and it alters their life for the better.

WAYNE

Standing quietly in the background, listening and observing, was thirty-two year old Cody Christiano, a long-time Market employee. A man of deep religious faith, he actively practices his Roman Catholic religion. Although skeptical of the healings, with all of the changes taking place for his employers, co-workers, and friends at the Market, his interest was aroused.

One day while I was shopping in the Market, Cody told me he was suffering with a bad back. Every morning, he woke up with extreme stiffness and struggled to get out of bed. It would take an hour for his muscles to loosen up and even then, he still could not bend over to tie his shoe laces. In addition to the stiffness, he was plagued with extremely painful muscle spasms that could come at any time. If he stayed in the same position for more than a few minutes the spasms would force him to shift. It was particularly bad in church when he had to kneel or stand for several minutes at a time, and participation in any athletics was impossible because if he jumped the spasms would be excruciating.

After listening to Cody, I knew he wanted a healing, but my instinct told me that he could heal himself. I gave him a recipe that would change his life and increase his spirituality.

- At night, when you lay down to sleep, picture a divine infant, with golden glowing light radiating from its core and surrounding its entire body.

- In your mind's eye, picture this divine infant just above your forehead, hovering over your sixth chakra.

- Visualize the perfection of this infant, knowing that it has perfect bone structure, perfect cardio vascular, and a perfect back. (or whatever the specific ailment area is for you) Know that this divine infant is you, in the image and likeness of the creator. Allow that perfection to radiate into your body.

- As you fall asleep, repeat the mantra: "I have a perfect back."

- Do this up to 10 times as you fall asleep and know that your divine infant has a perfect back.

I told Cody this combination of visual and thought affirmations will permeate through his entire body, and he will start to heal. His back can be as perfect as that of his divine infant. "It is the way you were meant to be." Cody heard my words and, despite his skepticism, decided to try it that night.

As I prepared for sleep, I pictured this beautiful golden infant and started the mantra: I will have no back pain in the morning. I think I fell asleep after repeating this eight times. When I woke up in the morning, I was about 50% better. I did not really believe that the procedure I had followed the night before was responsible, but rather attributed it to a "good day".

The second night, I followed the same routine, but probably fell asleep after repeating the mantra only five times. The next morning my back was about 70% better. I was excited and realized that there may be something to this.

On the third evening, I fell asleep after repeating the mantra only twice. When I awoke the next morning, I rolled out of bed, put on my clothes and bent over to tie my shoelaces. I was shocked! I haven't been able to do this in at least fifteen years! I was 100% pain free. Wow, this works!

Later that day, I used my back to pick up an object that weighed about fifty pounds. Usually I would have back spasms. Not this time! I even did it again as a test. I was so amazed this worked. It was a miracle. If I can do this, what else can I do?

My left shoulder had been hurting for about a month. If I put any pressure on it, I would have sharp shooting pains around my rotator cuff. The pain was killing me, and I planned to see a doctor.

On the fourth evening, I switched gears and focused on my left shoulder. I envisioned my beautiful divine infant, golden and glowing, and focused on the perfect shoulder, repeating this mantra as I fell asleep. The next morning, I woke up and started my day. At around 3pm, I realized that my shoulder had not hurt all day!

On day five, I followed this routine again and my shoulder has never hurt since.

Three weeks later, my back was a little stiff. I went back to the procedure. "I will not have back stiffness in the morning". I saw my infant. And when I awoke, the stiffness was gone and never returned.

I wondered about the next level? Could I do this for others? The whole experience has strengthened my faith, made me more spiritual, and I feel closer to the other side.

Not long after Cody healed himself, he and Nino were in the back of the store sharing their expanded points of view. They were discussing the feeling of negative energy that they'd been experiencing inside the Market recently. There were two customers up front and as Nino started to walk towards the front of the store, declaring he was done with negativity, the front doors flew open. Everyone was startled and one customer exclaimed, "What was that?"

No one was certain what created the force of energy that opened both doors, but the Putnam Valley Market felt clearer and lighter when the doors gently closed of their own accord.

CHAPTER 16

Forgiveness Heals a Broken Heart

WAYNE

One of the requirements for graduation from the two-year Transformational Energy Healing program was the presentation of a year-long case study. Each student was required to select a volunteer who would receive a minimum of ten healings. The experiences of both the healer and the volunteer were to be documented in detail and presented at the year-end retreat.

I knew exactly who my volunteer would be.

Angie and Tony Palmisano, two of my best friends, generously volunteer their money, time and energy for the betterment of the community. In addition to the innumerable hours raising funds and rehabbing the baseball field for the Cortlandt National Little League, they are active in the Elks Club, Italian American Club, and The Ladies of Mount Carmel Association. You would be hard pressed to find two more family oriented people. They are exemplary parents and deeply involved with the lives of their four children, Donna, Diana, David, and Derrick.

Their eldest son, David, a talented high school athlete who possessed great speed and power, starred on the football and lacrosse teams. He was a good student with a promising future and when David selected an upstate NY college, Angie and Tony were extremely happy that he would get a good education in addition to learning to be independent while living on his own.

It was in March of David's freshman year at college when fate dealt this loving family a devastating blow. The snow was piled high that year, obscuring visibility, as David and his three friends went for a drive. They went through a stop sign and were hit broadside by a car driven by another young man. David, who was a passenger, along with his three friends, was killed in the crash.

It was probably the worst call I ever received. It felt as if an arrow went through my heart. When unexpected tragedy of this magnitude strikes, it is impossible to believe. How could this happen? I cried my heart out, first for the shocking loss of this young man I loved, and then, for my friends. My God, how would they cope with such a loss? My sadness knew no bounds in dealing with this tragedy.

Prior to this disaster, Angie was one of the healthiest people I knew. She never had any physical problems until she lost her beloved son David, but since then, her health began to deteriorate. A gentle natured person, Angie rarely raised her voice and willingly sacrificed her own desires for family and community. As the years went by and Angie's father passed away, her mother, Mary, diagnosed with Alzheimer's, came to live with them. Angie left her career to care for her mother and in addition, now baby-sits throughout the week for her four grand-children. All this, plus her charity work, made for a very busy life. She never complained or asked anything for herself. As a result of her broken heart and quiet suffering, one ailment after another evolved over the years, her health diminished and she became heavily medicated.

COMMENTS BY KATHY: As a mother, I cannot imagine the impact Angie must have felt in her physical body when she learned of her son's death. The pain probably went through her like a shock wave. How hard it must have been to breathe. In addition to the mental and emotional anguish, the physical impact took its toll. When an event happens and we cannot be with the pain of it, we shallow breathe to avoid feeling and often fill our lives with busy work so at the end of the day we collapse, if we're lucky, into sleep. The guilt, self-incrimination, and resentments toward our self or another will result in illness and dis-ease. It is imperative to find forgiveness, love, and gratitude or one will continue to suffer right up to the moment of death, and sometimes, into our next life.

Angie agreed to be my case study volunteer and scheduled the first healing at her home. When I arrived she told me she was feeling so ill she almost called to cancel. I said, "I would have come anyway because that meant you needed my help even more."

As her friend, I knew she was suffering, but had no idea to what degree. When the body, mind and spirit are not in harmony, ailments will manifest in the physical body. Below is a list of ailments Angie was afflicted with at the time she began her series of healings, and the associated mental causes as per Louise Hay's book, *Heal Your Body*.

INTERNAL	MENTAL CAUSES FOR PHYSICAL ILLNESS
Diabetes	Longing for what might have been. A great control. Deep sorrow. No sweetness left.
High Blood Pressure	Long standing emotional problem not solved.
Extremely High Cholesterol	Clogging the channels of joy. Fear of accepting joy. Resistance, tension. Hardened narrow-mindedness. Refusing to see good.
Heart problems: Angie had open heart surgery	Heart represents the center of love and security. Heart Problems –Longstanding emotional problems. Lack of joy. Hardening of the heart. Belief in strain and stress.
Respiratory problems	Fear of taking in life fully.
Gastro - Intestinal Disorder	Prolonged uncertainty. A feeling of doom. Assimilation. Absorption. Elimination with ease. Inability to release the past.

STRUCTURAL/ PHYSICAL	MENTAL CAUSES FOR PHYSICAL ILLNESS
Neck pains – sharp pains and stiffness	Neck represents flexibility. The ability to see what's back there. Neck problems = Refusing to see other sides of a question. Stubbornness, inflexibility. Pain = guilt. Guilt always seeks punishment.
Shoulder pain and tightness	Represent our ability to carry our experiences in life joyously. We make life a burden by our attitude.
Lower back pain	Back represents the support of life. Lower = A lack of safety.
Sore hip	Hips carry the body in perfect balance. Major thrust in moving forward. Painful hips represent guilt in moving forward.
Sore calves	Legs carry us forward in life. Lower leg = fear of the future. Not wanting to move.
Both feet – pain Achilles Tendons	Feet represent our understanding of ourselves, of life, of others. Lower legs, ankles and feet receive brain communication through L-5 Lumbar vertebrae. L-5 represents: Insecurity. Difficulty in communicating. Anger. Inability to accept pleasure.
Left foot - Neuropathy	Left side of the body is the receiving side. Receptivity, taking in, feminine energy, women, the mother. Neuropathy causes pain and numbness in the foot. Burning or tingling.

THE HEALERS

And so it was that I began my first healing on Angie. It was an amazing sight to see her lying on her kitchen countertop with her mother, two daughters, and four grandchildren in skeptical observance. I took a reading on each of her chakras, and the crystal pendulum I dangled over Angie's body barely moved. Angie's chakras were either shut down or extremely low, indicating that energy was barely squeezing through her system. Lack of energy flow creates illness and dis-ease. Fully flowing energy is what keeps us alive, healthy, and vibrant. This would be the last time there were blockages of this magnitude for Angie.

I began the healing by raising my vibration level and gently placing my hands on her feet. Moving one hand to her knee, I concentrated on flushing every vein between the foot and the knee. After doing this on both lower legs, I moved my hands to her knee and hip, and followed the same procedure. Relocating my hands to her second and third chakras, I felt tremendous heat in her stomach area, a hot spot. I continued flushing the veins while filling her chakras with energy. Proceeding to the fourth chakra, located in the area of the heart, I was guided to work there for a longer time, because Angie had undergone bypass surgery. I continued to her head, flushing all the minute veins in that area. After completing the full cycle of healing the chakras, I returned to her stomach area which I felt needed more work. When I finished her physical body, I gently swept my hands through her auric fields, the energy fields around her body, creating a push to flush every vein. Angie then turned onto her stomach where I worked on her immune system and neck. Her pancreas, necessary for maintaining proper glucose levels, was the hot spot I had felt earlier. Placing one hand on top of the other over the pancreas area, I channeled extra energy into that organ to reset its function to optimization. After flushing her kidneys, I finished with gentle contact on her feet where I funneled energy up through her entire system.

When Angie sat up, she was excited to share her experience. Her stomachache was gone, but she felt heavy. She said that the first time I touched her stomach it hurt worse, but when I returned to that area, the pain went away. Her neck felt much better and had improved flexibility. She felt relaxed. During the healing, she felt weight on her legs as if I was holding them down, but she knew that my hands were somewhere else. Besides feeling much better, she saw how the dynamic circular movement of the crystal had increased so dramatically, from the slight movement, if any, when we began. Now, the crystal spun at a high rate of speed, in a clockwise direction, with a six-inch circumference indicating high energy levels in all chakras, thus reinforcing her feelings. Angie wanted to know when I was coming back again.

This healing took over an hour. By the time it ended, her daughters and grandchildren had gone home. However, when they called later, they were shocked when Angie told them she was feeling much better.

Over the next six months, I performed a sequence of ten healings on Angie. As one healing grows upon the other, and each was different, it proved to be a very enlightening experience for both of us. At each healing, I raised my vibration to an exceptionally high level and requested mine and Angie's guides help with the healing. Knowing the background and trusting my instincts, I requested the loving spirit of David be present to assist. He was active at every session, and I knew that at some point he would guide me to the true cause of Angie's ailments.

During one healing I discovered a blockage in Angie's throat and asked the guides for permission to remove it. Permission granted, Angie was now free to speak. Another time, I removed shackles from around her ankles in the area where she was having many of her problems. Once removed, she was free to be her own woman and walk in any direction she wanted.

There was massive tension in her shoulders, as if two thick rubber bands were pulling in opposite directions making it almost impossible for her to move her neck at all. It was extremely restrictive and painful for her to turn her head or shoulders. I sent accelerated vibrations down Angie's spine and across her back. As I came upon various problem areas, I would fill them with healing energy colors. After the first few healings, Angie's back was never that tight again. It felt new and rejuvenated.

Gradually, the walls came down. At each healing I always spent a significant amount of time on Angie's pancreas, filling it with the sweetness of life and envisioning it as pink, plush and in perfect working order. In addition to the waves of energy I sent through her feet and up her entire body, I also sent focused energy to her feet, ankles, and calves to support her in moving forward in life. During each healing I would fill every cell in her body with the beautiful glowing light of existence and abundance of love.

The presence of my higher self was very active in these healings. During one session I saw my Indian shaman self standing directly over Angie and knew he was assisting with the healing.

My favorite healing is the "Pillar of Intent". This is a mirror healing. Rather than channeling energy into her body, I envisioned the perfection of my body, fully healthy and vibrant, and held the space for Angie to absorb her own reflection of perfect health and vitality. The purpose was to strengthen her inner core, and empower her to self-heal and be true to herself.

With Angie lying face up I slid my hands underneath her lower back and cupped my fingertips around her spine. I focused on healing my own spine, restoring my immune system as well as every other area of my body, and could feel the healing taking place in both Angie and myself. Leaving my left hand on her spine, I moved my right hand lower to her tan t'ien, an area just below the bellybutton. The area became energized, and it felt as if a rebirth was taking place within Angie. Using my left hand, I proceeded to each hip and swept away all the pain she had in them. I then moved to the thymus and pituitary glands, spending a few minutes on each one, and creating a steady flow of energy between them, all the while mirroring the rebuilding that was taking place inside of me.

I finished each healing by sprinkling energy sparkles over her entire body. In addition, I placed a beautiful cloud of green and gold sparkles of energy over her head that would trickle down on her if she needed it.

As the healings progressed, Angie's aches and pains began to disappear. Some of her problems completely went away while others would disappear for hours, days, or weeks, and then gradually return, but with each healing, she was able to maintain some improvement. She felt much more relaxed, and her limp was almost gone.

During one of the healings, I noticed that Angie's left leg was quivering and a short while later there was a loud pop! I couldn't believe it! After the healing I asked her if she had heard it and what it felt like immediately after the pop.

"Yes! I heard it, too! I felt a heavy weight go down my leg and into my foot, creating excruciating pain which went out through my toes and was gone!"

At another healing, I swept away a dark cloud that was hovering over Angie's heart. Whenever I worked around Angie's heart, I always felt an overwhelming sense that the essence of David's spirit was with us. It was almost palpable. At these times, Angie would move into an even deeper state of relaxation. This deeper state was accompanied by what I call "small puff breaths". Sometimes, she would appear not to be breathing at all. These are levels of consciousness where core/soul/spirit healing takes place. At these levels, her spirit would leave her body and go with her loving son, David. I was amazed to see Angie's core leave her body to spend time with David and then return. Angie knew this was happening but could not remember anything about the journey. This was a spiritual experience that can happen during energy healings. My instincts told me that David was instilling in her core the feeling that he was fine, there was nothing to worry about and in fact, he was better than ever.

During one of the healings, I had a vision of a young man sitting in a beautiful garden, and I am certain it was David. The presence of his love was everywhere, and I knew that he would get to the cause of Angie's problems.

After the eighth healing, while driving home, I was still trying to uncover the deep rooted cause of Angie's ailments. Suddenly, I felt David's presence in the car with me. This was a feeling unlike anything I had ever experienced. I didn't see him, but knew he was there. His presence - peaceful, serene and loving - engulfed me. Before I could finish asking the question, the answer was already in my head. David enlightened me, "She's blaming someone or something for my death."

It was my responsibility to discuss this with her at our next session. David's message had to be revealed. At the beginning of our next healing, I asked Angie, "Are you blaming anyone for David's death?"

"I don't think so, but, I never went to see the place where he died. I wanted the best for him. I wanted him to go away and be able to do things for himself. I wonder how fast the driver of the other car was going. I don't know if I can ever forgive the driver of the other car."

All these years, Angie kept this blame and guilt within herself. We had a positive conversation where I stressed that no one was to blame. Nothing she could have done would have prevented the accident. The driver of the vehicle David was in accidentally went through a stop sign, and any car traveling on that road at that specific time would have hit their car.

I said, "It could have been me, you, or anyone driving down that road when the boys went through the stop sign. The driver of the other car also suffered broken bones and will have to live with the death of these four boys for the rest of his life. This was an unfortunate accident, and it was David's time to go. If you can begin to forgive, even a little each day, you will begin to heal. I know David is at each healing, reinforcing the knowledge that it was his time to leave. Hopefully, with his help, you will find peace and consolation."

During this ninth healing David's presence and love for his mother was electrifying. I felt her core filled with loving forgiveness and her cells bursting with glowing energy. For the first time, Angie visualized colors. While working at her feet, she saw a glowing white light which exploded into bursts of purple, a strong healing color. I believe Angie was "seeing the light".

At the end of the healing, there was an amazing validation when Angie and I saw the black and blue color of her injured toes return to a normal healthy pink, right before our eyes.

As one healing grew upon the other, Angie progressed into deepened levels of relaxation. Many fears and apprehensions disappeared. Her back and neck, once hard as a rock, are now soft and flexible. She feels like a completely different person from when we began this process. Angie's body is working significantly better internally and structurally, and if she continues to forgive, she will heal spiritually, emotionally, and physically. The greater the depth of her ability to forgive, the more her ailments will evaporate.

After the final healing I tested her energy centers with the crystal pendulum. Each one was spinning flat out like a fan, in a clockwise manner, indicating a maximum level of energy! This was an incredible turnaround from our first session. The transformation that took place in Angie was nothing short of incredible. She is a different person. And so am I.

Angie shared her own observations:

During the sequence of healings, I had some amazing experiences. One time, I had a foot cramp that completely dissipated. Another time, I felt pain shooting around in all areas of my left leg, as if the pain were trying to avoid the energy, but then it completely disappeared. In one healing, I felt as if I were drawn into a very dark black area, and immediately thereafter, felt very relaxed. At the beginning of another healing I was thinking silly thoughts and wanted to stay focused on them throughout the healing, however, when Wayne started to work above my hips, I went into the twilight zone and all these thoughts disappeared. There was one special healing when I observed a faint light. It was not bright and was at a far distance. The light was long and seemed to spread across the entire horizon. There was a person in the middle, and it was me.

As a result of these healings, I am much more relaxed, all the time, and have a substantial increase in my level of stamina. Even when exhausted, I have the energy to keep on going. My shoulders used to feel as if they were being pulled tight, like a rubber band being stretched to its limit. Now they are completely relaxed. My respiratory problem is gone and I now breathe deeply with no difficulty. The pain in my hip has completely disappeared. My knees are better and have much more flexibility. The annoying tingling in my left leg is gone and the cramping in my calves is barely noticeable. My sugar levels, when I test them in the mornings, are much better.

In addition to restoring much of my health, the greatest gift I received was when Wayne worked on my heart area. I knew that I checked-out with my son David, but have no recollection of where we went. However, after each of these experiences, I felt a greater sense of peace about the death of my son.

The sequence of healings was extremely beneficial to me also. To observe the improvement in my friend as the benefits of each healing compounded was a rewarding experience. It was during these healings I discovered a new awareness of death. Throughout my life, I had been indoctrinated with conceptions of fear surrounding death and the passing of the spirits of loved ones. That fear is now gone. The constant presence of David's spirit at these healings gave me a new-found awareness. There are countless spirits simply a fingertip away from each of us awaiting our invitation to help us on our journey. Knowing the spirits are far from gone has created a tremendous peace and comfort within me.

COMMENTS BY KATHY: Sooner or later we will all be affected by the death of a loved one. It is comforting to know that although these people have died and are no longer available to us in this physical realm, they are not actually gone at all. They are simply freed from their physical bodies, and their spirits are alive and well. Having had the experience of more than one person who has crossed over, I know that the sense of peace will continue to expand for both Angie and Wayne. I agree with Wayne, as Angie continues to forgive, her illnesses will fade away.

CHAPTER 17

Touchdown Mike Spinelli

KATHY

Mike Spinelli is an accountant for a major corporation. In addition, he prepares income tax filings for a large clientele and is the proprietor of "The Brake Shop" located on Route 9 in Wappingers Falls, NY. He is a facts-and-figures man who lives within the realities of a conventional executive.

For most of his life, Mike suffered with migraines and traditional medications were not working. When Mike first came to see me he was skeptical, apprehensive, and unsure what he had gotten himself into, but also hopeful and willing to try something different and new. We spoke a bit about his life and then proceeded to the hands-on part of the healing.

As I placed my hands on Mike's ankles I sent a stream of energy up his body to scout out any blockages that were initially apparent. When the stream reached his head, there was some darkness there, like a heavy cloud. I asked his angels to escort it out and it disappeared. I was then guided to Mike's head to balance the energy in his brain. With my hands cradling his head I imagined filling it with liquid gold and gently rocked his head slowly back and forth until the liquid was equally balanced in both hemispheres. There was a sense of peace, and I gently removed my hands as I instinctively knew a substantial amount of pressure had been removed and cleansed from the area. Moving from chakra to chakra I reenergized each one and balanced the energy throughout his body, closed the healing and gave thanks.

Each time Mike came for a visit, something new and exciting seemed to happen. As Mike continued to shift there were openings for new conversations and deeper levels of healing and experiences. One time, when I had my hands on the back of his head I sensed an injury he may have received as a young child. I inquired about it after the healing at which time he shared an experience from when he was just a little boy. While playing in a kiddy splash pool another child hit him on the back of the head with a hard toy which cut his head and made him bleed. It was a very traumatic experience and he had completely forgotten about the incident until I asked about the specific area. I believe this injury created a weakened place in Mike's head that was the developing point for the migraines.

Many times, when I finished the hands-on portion of the session, I sat quietly while Mike relaxed on the table and continued to process. With his eyes open, he would stare at the white ceiling and later share the visions he saw; colors, faces, waves, people he knew. I always looked there too, but unfortunately, I was never able to see those extraordinary things. Perhaps one day.

Mike was such a gift to this work because he really didn't believe in any of it, yet he was the one experiencing the unexplainable phenomena such as kidney stones that passed without pain, migraines that ceased without medication, and visions of dead relatives on the ceiling tiles.

When a person is altered on the inside, their world tends to alter on the outside so it is beneficial to do this work in small, manageable increments. If you want something in your world to be different, the change must begin inside of yourself. He is now comfortable telling others about his experiences:

I had been listening to Wayne tell about his experiences with healings and thought maybe they would help with my migraine headaches. I have suffered with them for decades and they come very frequently. When I do get a migraine, I take strong prescription medications to help alleviate the pain so that I can be somewhat functional. Anyone who suffers from migraines knows how excruciating the pain can be. Even though I heard what Wayne was saying, I was extremely apprehensive about receiving an energy healing. How could something that has plagued me for so many years be eliminated by someone's touch? It seemed unfathomable.

One evening, my wife, Diane, and I were at dinner with a friend, who was an orthopedic surgeon. I began to relate some of the things that Wayne had told me about the energy colors he envisioned and about his core leaving his body. I was talking kind of jokingly, commenting about what Wayne had said. To my utter surprise the doctor remarked, "Don't mock it," and he was serious. His girlfriend, Mary, has a doctorate in nursing, and as part of her studies learned about a form of Asian healing techniques that use energy. If this surgeon, who I had great respect for, didn't think that it was a joke, then I would follow up on it.

Mary told me that this was something Buddhists do, and if I could find someone who is good, it might very well help me with my headaches. I valued her expertise and after hearing Wayne's comments, decided to make an appointment with Kathy. I was a skeptic but would try anything to get rid of the migraines.

It just so happened that I was coming down with a migraine as my first meeting with Kathy approached. I elected not to take any medication, and this way it would be easy to see if these healings could do anything.

After about a half-hour interview with Kathy, the healing began. While lying on the table, I started to have some very unusual feelings. I did not know what the norm was for a healing but these feelings were very peculiar for me. I felt as if I were floating in water. When Kathy was touching my left leg, it felt as though her hands were on both of my legs. So I sneaked a peak and saw she was really only touching the left one.

To my astonishment, when the healing ended the migraine was gone. I couldn't believe it! How could this be? Kathy said she saw a lot of dark energy which she was trying to release. Somehow this energy was stored within me, and whatever she did released something because the pain was no longer there.

That night, I awoke at about 3 AM with an excruciating migraine. It was so bad that it forced me to take the medication. So at this point, I knew that the healing worked for several hours but then the pain returned.

The next morning I was feeling exceptionally good and in a great mood. Off to work I went and everything seemed so enjoyable to me. I volunteered to help a colleague from the United Kingdom with a PowerPoint presentation to about twenty people. It was a very dull subject and not something I thought would keep the audience attentive. About halfway through the presentation, my colleague stopped. Right in front of the group he asked me what I thought was so funny. I said I didn't think anything he was describing was funny; I was just in a good mood. It was here I realized that I was feeling so elated from the healing that I had a glow about me, and people thought I was laughing at nothing. The mood persisted all week long, and everyone was asking me why I was smiling all the time. It was evident that something happened at the healing, and everyone around me was aware of the transformation. It was great to feel this good.

I made another appointment with Kathy and two weeks later received my second healing. Because I fell asleep during the first session, Kathy recommended that I try staying awake to feel the full impact of the healing. Again, I felt as if I was floating in water and something was flowing from my head down through my toes. Even though my hands were at my side, it felt as if they were elevated and somehow I was cupping a ball in each hand. I looked at the ceiling, and it started to wave. It was as if I was looking at a tarred road on a hot day and the heat was creating a mirage. It was then I saw dark shadows floating across the ceiling. I didn't know it at that moment, but this was another release of dark energy taking place.

That night, again at about 3 AM, I awoke to excruciating back pain. It felt like a kidney stone, and I had to take pain medication to sleep. The next day I spoke to Mary, and she surmised that it had to do with the healing. She felt my body had identified the kidney stone and was now rejecting it. Whatever was happening to me after these healings was somehow being reflected in painful 3 AM wake-up calls.

So off I went to the urologist for tests. Sure enough, the results came back showing I had a 3mm kidney stone floating around. This sounded like a lot more pain to me, which the urologist confirmed by saying, "When you pass this stone it is going to be very painful." In preparation for what I knew was going to be hell, he gave me a prescription for Percocet and instructed me to start taking it as soon as the pain started to provide some relief. I was not very excited about the prospect of having to pass such a large stone, and to add insult to injury, I had to carry around a little strainer to urinate through and catch the stone for analysis.

At my third appointment with Kathy, I could not help but tell her my bad news. She told me she would either pulverize or coat the stone so it would pass easily. I listened but was skeptical that she could somehow help with such a large object going through such a small canal. To my astonishment, two days later I passed the stone without any pain whatsoever. I never had to take the Percocet. I caught the stone in the strainer and could not believe how pointy and sharp it was. WOW, how did she do that? I was quickly becoming a believer!

During that third healing, something new and very shocking happened. I saw three faces as I looked up at the ceiling. One large and two smaller, but could not make out any real facial features. I was amazed. What was going on here?

As soon as the healing ended and before I could say a word, Kathy said that she saw my father in the room along with two angels. This blew my mind! I freaked out! I said, "What the f… am I getting into here. I'm here for my migraines, not the supernatural." Kathy said that part of this work can be about getting into another dimension and you can never predict what might happen at a healing but the client's best interest is always at the forefront.

I began to notice that my headaches were not as strong as they had been. When they did come, taking Aleve would finish them off. I did not have to take the prescription medication and was very happy with these results.

During my next healing, I saw the faces again. At first, I did not know what they were, but then I clearly identified the larger face of my father centered between two smaller faces. My father had been deceased for three years. I know what I saw.

At the time, I was having difficulty with my eighty-plus-year-old mother. She missed my father, was lonely, and suffered bouts of depression. No matter what I tried to do to help her and please her, it was never right. This put a tremendous strain on me and my family. I felt that these difficult times were contributing to my migraines. Kathy told *me that if my father appears again, I should speak to him and ask for his help with my mother. I did not know what to expect at the next session, but sure enough, my father appeared. The ceiling was illuminated in blue, and sometimes pink, but because I was still in such awe, I just looked and never communicated with him.*

Later that night, I had a dream that felt painfully real. I was a football player. We were down near the goal line with short yardage to go for a touchdown. I was standing behind the quarterback and waiting to run the ball in for a score. The goal line was my mother's dining room table, and it was flanked by two large defensive linemen who were going to do everything they could to stop me. I had to score this touchdown. There's the snap. The quarterback pitches the ball to me, I go air-born, crossing the goal line and scoring the touchdown! I immediately woke up in pain. I had slammed into my nightstand, catapulted over it and crashed into my dresser which was located against the wall. Everything on the dresser was knocked all over the place. I also dented the wall. I created some commotion! My wife jumped out of bed wanting to know what was going on. I must have been some sight sprawled on the floor, wreathing in pain and things from my dresser strewn all over the place.

I have never sleepwalked in my life. I have never fallen out of bed in my life. After everything settled down, the question that kept popping into my head was how did I fly over the nightstand and knock everything off the dresser? It was amazing that all these things always happened on evenings when I returned home from healings.

During the next session my father appeared, and this time I talked to him. I asked him to turn his face so I could view his profile. He smiled and did as I requested. I asked him to go to my mom and help her with the depression she was plagued with. I had no idea what to expect but the following morning I got a response. My mother called and said she saw my father sitting at the foot of her bed and it was the first time she had seen him since his death. She smelled his musk oil, the cologne he always wore. I don't know exactly what transpired between them but something happened.

My mother was suffering with terrible pains in her feet. She had been to see at least six doctors for the problem who all said nothing could be done. They each had different explanations, but ultimately attributed it to old age. For months, she had been trying to remember the name of the doctor who had helped her with her feet over twenty years ago. Immediately after the vision, she remembered the doctor's name. She went for treatment, the doctor made some adjustments to her shoes and the pain completely disappeared. She felt that somehow my dad had reminded her of this doctor.

COMMENTS BY WAYNE: There is no coincidence here. When Mike scored that touchdown over his mother's dining room table, it was the first time in a long time that he was able to do anything right in the eyes of his mother. Or maybe the real touchdown was Mike asking and then receiving the help from his dad.

WAYNE

One night while at an Elks Club dinner dance, Mike confirmed his belief in energy healings. He had been dancing to every song when all of a sudden he strained both thigh muscles, just above his knees. He was standing by the table in a lot of pain, and in front of a large group, asked me if I could do a healing on the muscles. Although he was not comfortable receiving a healing in such a public place, because of the extreme pain, he insisted on it. When I put my hands on his legs, he commented about the tremendous heat he was feeling in his lower thighs. The procedure continued for about ten minutes. As soon as I removed my hands, he flexed his legs exclaiming, "The pain is totally gone." He reiterated this several times for the whole group to hear and then danced the night away with no reoccurrence. This prompted Mike to request that I do a healing on his mother at a future date.

One evening when Mike's mom, Margie, was visiting, I offered to do a healing on her. It was a very emotional event. She saw all kinds of colors, and she could feel energy moving through her body. My intention was to fill her with love so that she could be more forgiving and appreciative. Margie cried and admitted she did things that hurt people, but could not seem to stop herself. The healing was a start, and so was the visit from her husband, but she would have to take this new beginning and change her actions. Time would tell, but at that moment she was pain and worry free. We laughed as I told her to throw her cane in Mike's pool, she wouldn't need it anymore.

KATHY

For Mother's Day, Wayne and I offered a complimentary special group distance healing for mothers. Some signed up on their own while others were signed up by their loved ones. Normally, we do weekly group distance healings on Sunday mornings at 9 AM and Sunday evenings at 9 PM. However, this special healing was to be sent at 10 o'clock. Wayne thought it was 10 AM and I thought it was 10 PM. The result was the mothers received two separate healings within a 12 hour interval. Mike's mother was one of the recipients although neither Mike nor his mom knew it at the time.

Three days after Mother's Day, at Mike's healing session, I told him that Wayne and I had included his mom and wondered how she was feeling.

After speaking to his mother later that evening, Mike called to relate her story. In addition to feeling both physically and emotionally better, she had a high level of energy that had been missing for several years. Margie was doing things she previously did not have the strength or ambition to do. She tirelessly cleaned her entire house, went out shopping, ran errands and was still not tired at the end of the day. Mike was floored! He told her about the healings and she was so excited, and felt so good, she wanted to buy us a bottle of champagne. These healings gave Margie an improved quality of life!

WAYNE

About a month after Mother's Day, Mike invited me to his home and asked me to perform a healing on his mom, and his mother-in-law, Mary. Mary is on the north side of ninety and does very well for herself. I knew it was going to be fun and could not wait to get started.

Mary went first. Suffering from a long standing eye problem, she must put drops in her eyes several times a day. With this in mind, I began the healing. Energy was moving rapidly throughout her body and when I reached the head area, I focused my intention on her eyes. Placing both hands over them, I saw glowing, healing, green light enter both eyes. When the healing ended, Mary remarked, "I feel very good but I don't really notice anything different." I told her to take notice over the next few days as healings can be very subtle and results often appear days later.

Margie went next. Since she had previously experienced the effects of hands-on and long-distance healings, as well as the ripple effect from Mike's healings, Margie was looking forward with excited anticipation. Before we started, she explained that her lower back was hurting her almost all the time, and the energy burst she had received from the Mother's Day healing was gone.

During the healing, I felt a significant amount of energy going up her legs and balancing throughout her body. I focused on her lower back and pictured the entire area completely healed. When we finished, Margie commented how hot my hands were and that her back did not hurt at all, yet she did not feel as energized as she had after the Mother's Day distance healing.

As with Mary, I told Margie to see what happens, which proved to be very prophetic when a few days later I received an excited call from Mike:

> *My mother-in-law does not have to use the drops for her eyes anymore. She has taken them for years and doesn't need them anymore since the healing you did on her! And, you're not going to believe what happened to my mother. The day after the healing, Diane was driving her home and Margie was looking at her and said that she saw her deceased husband, my dad Tony, driving the car and smiling. She did a double take and said that it was as real and clear as if she were watching TV. She knew that Diane was driving but saw her husband. She wanted to reach out and touch him but she knew that Diane was driving.*

Belief systems are amazing. When people are entrenched in a belief, they are not easily swayed to another way of thinking. It is exciting to observe the change in the Spinelli family. Mike had the courage to go forth and try something different. As his belief system completely changed during the process, he felt that healings could benefit everyone and so brought this whole new healing modality to the senior members of his family with great success. Not only did Mike score a big touchdown, he won the game for his family.

CHAPTER 18

Mama's Boy

WAYNE

My mother, Doris, is a very active 82 year-old woman. She was only twenty when she married my father and assumed the responsibility of raising his two daughters, Janet and Eleanor. This was no small feat as she was only ten years older than them. Their mother had passed away at a young age from lung cancer, and my father had been raising the girls on his own. Prior to this, Doris had sung in the chorus of the Metropolitan Opera. She relinquished her singing career to marry Ed Gabari, raise his two daughters, and eventually gave birth to three sons and a daughter of her own.

For many years, mom managed the office for the Children's Institute in Westchester County where she was highly valued by the patients and doctors alike. She loves to travel and in any given year will go on at least five excursions. She has an exceptional zest for life, loves to dance and party, and will always take a stand for the underdog, even to her own detriment. Some would call her a rebel, I call her mom. A few years ago, she was cited by the owners of her apartment complex for feeding squirrels around her building. Doris fed them peanuts, and the shell remnants were left as evidence of her kindness to the animals. Though many referred to her as the Saint Francis of Assisi of Riverdale, a few tenants did not appreciate her cause. She eventually went to court to defend her position but lost, and had to sign an agreement to stop or be evicted. It amazes me that the squirrels around her apartment complex are still looking pretty hefty.

Through most of her life my mother has been blessed with excellent health, however, in her later years, she developed osteoarthritis in her left hip and right knee. Both degenerated to the point where they had to be replaced. The two separate operations took place within a three-month period followed by extensive rehab to restore flexibility and learn how to use her new body parts.

Soon after, I started her on nutritional products which have maintained her general health very well. At 79, she retired to pursue her passion for travel and I began attending the Transformational Energy Healing program.

In the summer of 2006, my mother started feeling a terrible pain in her right hip, "the good one". She gradually developed a pronounced limp which continued to worsen each day, but because of her memories of the long and painful rehab, and fearing the worst, she delayed seeing the doctor as long as possible. By November, it was so painful she scheduled an appointment with the orthopedic surgeon who had performed her previous hip replacement.

The surgeon examined mom and determined her condition warranted an MRI to assess the status of her hip. He wanted it done right away, but my mom did not want it to interfere with the upcoming holidays and scheduled it for January, 2007.

My mother's fears became reality! The doctor told her that the cartilage in her hip was completely gone and the area was loaded with arthritis. There was no getting around it; Doris would need another hip replacement. She was becoming a bionic woman.

COMMENTS BY KATHY: Just as Doris experienced, I also have experienced in my own life, and in observance of others: **what we think about becomes our reality.** How many times in your life have you worried and focused your attention on your biggest fears, which then came true? That is the Universal Law of Attraction! Like attracts like and you get to be right. For example, if you focus on how great your relationship is, or how bad your relationship is, you can change the outcome by simply changing your thoughts. Choose an area of your life. Become aware of your thoughts. It is the way you think it is. Now change your thoughts about that area. Think of how you would like it to be. How will you feel when it is like you want it to be? Focus on that. Do this for about three weeks, and watch it change.

If you think you can, you can. If you think you can't, you can't.

The doctor wanted to schedule hip replacement surgery as soon as possible. Adding to my mother's fears, the doctor's assistant told Doris that it was so bad, "You will not last a month. The pain will continue to worsen and you will not be able to stand it." Finality!

With the results of the MRI and the verbal commentary, plus the pain that she was in, Doris felt cornered with only one option, but still, she delayed making the appointment.

It was around this time that I was evolving into a healer and my skills were growing by leaps and bounds. I thirsted for every morsel of information I could get my hands on and anyone willing to be my guinea pig would receive a healing. My healings were getting better and better with some amazing results. But now we were talking about my mother and an MRI that indicated a replacement operation was a must.

After raising six children – including three fairly wild boys, and a girl just as tough - my mother is not one to mince words or keep her opinions silent. Yet, when it came to her own suffering, she kept it to herself. The day I discovered she was in pain, I sent a distance healing without her knowing. The next day she called, "Did you send me something?" She suspected I might have sent her a healing, explaining she had felt significant relief. Sherlock "Doris" Holmes was on the case, and nobody was going to fool her. I confirmed her suspicions and told her I had sent a distance healing the previous afternoon. Although she was still limping and in pain, there was substantial improvement. We would meet on the weekend, and I would perform a physical healing. By now it was early March and mom was still trying to avoid surgery.

As always, I set my intention for total healing. My confidence was high because her pain had been reduced from the distance healing. If the pain reduced, even for a short time, then I knew it could disappear forever. I didn't tell my mother, but my goal was set - complete cure.

I started at her feet and ran a channel of energy throughout her body. As I began to work up my mother's legs, her muscles started to twitch. I opened my eyes to look for signs of any distress or indications of pain, but there were none. She was lying calmly, with a facial expression of total relaxation and peace. The twitching continued throughout the entire healing. I wish that I had filmed the process because she looked like a Mexican jumping bean. Every time I moved to a different area it would start to twitch. It really became quite humorous when my hands were approximately a foot above her body and I was sprinkling energy over her. Her eyes were closed, and she could not possibly have known where my hands were and yet every area I went over jumped and twitched. I thought to myself, "This energy healing is great stuff. You have to see this to believe it." I attributed this phenomenon to her body absorbing new energy into her cells, releasing the old, and the exchange generated the twitching. Ultimately, a feeling of euphoria is experienced. For my mother, this is a common occurrence and she has an awareness this is happening because we have discussed it in the past.

After working over her entire body, I performed a Pillar of Intent healing. With my left hand under the base of the spine and right hand on the area just below the bellybutton (the tan t'ien) I ran a powerful channel of energy between the two. Moving my left hand to the degenerative hip, I felt a glowing stream of energy flowing back and forth. There was a tremendous level of vibration taking place within my mother's body as, in my mind, I proceeded to scrape the hip clean of arthritis and any loose debris. This is called a Psychic Surgery healing. With one hand on each side of the damage, I filled the entire hip area with a beautiful deep blue, the color I was guided to use. I envisioned the hip being pink and working perfectly, as when my mother was in her 20's. Lastly, I requested my guides cover her hip with a beautiful healing green.

Throughout the healing, the vibration level remained extremely high. In my mind's eye, I saw many different colors and there seemed to be an organization to them. Each color was like liquid in motion. The spectrum began with multiple shades of red, in an oval shape, but not really defined. Shades of blue then floated in from all directions, and surrounded the red, causing the red to shrink and then disappear into the middle of the oval, leaving only the blue in complete view, which then became the center color. Then greens, then reds, and the pattern repeated. My eyes burned with desire to see more. They actually felt strained from the intensity of watching this show. The deepest feeling of love enveloped me and rocked my inner core, permeating every cell in my body, and I knew that my mother's hip was healed. In giving my mother a healing, I also received a healing, and felt as if I was on cloud nine.

Mom's body stopped twitching and jumping and was now completely relaxed. I gently touched her right shoulder and told her the healing was over. She said that she felt good while she was lying there, however, I was eager to see how she felt when she arose.

Doris Gabari had a miracle that day. When she stood up, there was no limp and no pain. It had all disappeared. She had gone from walking with a horrible limp to a completely normal, pain free stride. All flexibility had returned. All other aches and pains she had were also gone. She kept repeating, "I can't believe it, all the pain is gone!" This was music to my ears.

When Mom regained her composure and understood the reality of what had happened, she had a serious question for me. She looked me right in the eye and asked, "Wayne, is God in you?"

"Of course He is because without His power and the perfect universe that He created, none of this would be possible. He has always been within me."

The only difference between the Wayne now and the Wayne before is that I now know how to use the gifts that He has bestowed upon me. I cannot describe my gratitude to Him and my Guides for their granting my request for Mom's healing.

It has been years since I did that healing on my mom. Although there have been minor setbacks, whenever something comes up we do another healing. Mom continues to walk perfectly with no limp or pain and considering the surgeon's scalpel was only an inch away, it is truly a miracle. Doris' new motto is, "No pain, no cane."

COMMENTS BY KATHY:

Scientific evidence: When I see it, I'll believe it.

Hope: "Wanting"- to believe or have faith - that something will happen, somewhere in the future, but not necessarily today. Wishful thinking.

Faith: Believing regardless of evidence.

Most people move back and forth between hope and faith. This confuses the Universe.

Unwavering Faith; I Believe: The Universal Law of Attraction says, "When you believe it, you will see it."[20], [21]

Doris had "Faith" in Wayne, and Wayne had "Unwavering Faith".

Mother Theresa said, "Life is a promise, fulfill it." When we are able to recognize the gifts and talents that we have been given, and have the courage to use them to their fullest potential, we are living the promise. Wayne has that courage and the results are miraculous.

My mother related her experience to the doctor she worked for during much of her career. The doctor said she would only believe it if my mother had an MRI confirming that the hip was not deteriorated. I have to wonder where the doctor thinks the pronounced limp and horrible pain went. To her credit, Doris said, "Why should I pay for an expensive MRI when my hip feels perfect?"

Over the next few months, I continued sending distance healings, as well as doing hands-on when the opportunity arose. It was Memorial Day weekend when my mom arrived for her healing accompanied by her best friend, Mary Janos. After her healing, mom asked if I would do a healing on Mary's eyes. Being a mama's boy, of course I said yes.

---

20   Ester and Jerry Hicks, *The Law of Attraction*, (Hay House, Inc. USA – http://hayhouse.com, 2006)

21   Florence Scovel Shinn, *The Wisdom of Florence Scovel, Four Complete Books*, (New York: A Fireside Book, Simon & Schuster, 1989)

Suffering with allergies is a way of life for many people and Mary was one of them. She could not stop her eyes from running. For almost a year, the tears ran like rivers morning, noon, and night. She spoke to her ophthalmologist who said, "Better wet than dry", implying there was nothing he could do for her. This constant tearing was very uncomfortable, and often times embarrassing. "My mascara would run down my face at any time during the day." Being a businesswoman, this created many awkward situations.

Mary chose to sit in a chair for her healing. Standing behind her and placing my hands on the top of her head, I began by running a steady flow of energy through her body filling every cell with a magnificent glowing gold. Focusing in on her eyes and covering them with my hands, I gently imbued them with loving green energy. When the area felt full and protected, I was guided to lift my hands off her face and move directly in front of her. I turned my fingertips toward her and rapidly fired healing green energy deep into both eyes. I could see every cell, fiber and blood vessel eagerly absorbing as fast as I could send. When that felt complete, I then began to work on her immune system to ward off allergies that were affecting her. Placing one hand on top of the other at the base of her spine, I channeled in as much energy to the immune system as she could handle. My hands were so hot it caused Mary to comment that she felt as if hot towels were touching her. I proceeded to the thymus gland above the heart, placed both hands on that area and filled it with healing green energy.

When the healing ended, Mary immediately noticed that her eyes were not running and exclaimed, "I cannot believe this!" Once she recovered from her astonishment, she realized that everything felt better!

It's been years since I performed that healing on Mary and her tearing eyes have never returned. One simple healing eliminated the discomfort Mary thought she would endure for the rest of her life.

In September of 2007, a new series of ailments showed up in Mary's life. She was suffering from continuous acid reflux and a very painful knee. What message was her body trying to tell her through these physical communications? I offered to do a healing on her.

I placed my hands on her knee which felt creaky, like an old rusty hinge. After filling the area with liquid energy to soften it up, the feeling of corrosion dissipated. As soon as I finished with the knee, I was guided to place my hands on her chest between her heart and throat. Immediately, I received a vision of an open, used can of "Drain-o" situated in the center of her chest and knew that the wall of her esophagus had been badly compromised. Before I could ask her spirit for permission to remove it, another vision showed her entire canal had a lining of rust. This issue had been around her for a long time and was surfacing through the acid reflux in her esophagus, or so I thought. I asked permission to remove the "Drain-o" can and permission was granted. Once removed, I healed the shredded wall of her esophagus with silver and blue and sealed the entire wound with a large bandage.

After the healing was complete, Mary was absolutely parched and I gave her water to drink. She was amazed that the acid reflux was gone. I asked Mary what had been eating away at her to cause such pain in an area of her body that brings her nourishment, but she could not recollect anything at the time. As she stood up she realized that her knee didn't hurt either.

COMMENTS BY KATHY: As Wayne said, in every healing, it is always our intention to set our goal with un-wavering faith for a complete cure. Many times, a complete healing will take place and the pain will never return again. I believe that this happens because whatever was causing the pain to appear in the first place has been cleared from the person's life and is no longer an issue. The pain is just an old stuck pattern, or energy block, and once the energy is freed up, the pain is gone. Other times, the pain is relieved, only to return again after a period of time. For me, this is an indicator that the body is trying to communicate to the person that there is some "action step" that needs to be taken, or "behavior" that needs to be altered, or "pattern" that needs to be broken. Many times it is a "thought pattern." It could be as simple as, "I can't believe the pain is completely gone" spoken over and over again until "voila!" the pain is no longer completely gone.

What if the person repeated over and over "Thank you for my healing, my body is now healthy and healed, I am so blessed!" until the pain becomes a forgotten memory?

After a blissful three weeks, the acid reflux returned, but Mary's knee remained pain-free for approximately six weeks before it started aching again.

A few months later, Mary told me that at one time she had a bone density problem. Her doctor prescribed the new wonder drug, Fosamax, which she faithfully took for over two years. One day, Mary had a terrible pain in her chest and rushed to the emergency room at her local hospital thinking she was having a heart attack. Fortunately, she was not, but her doctor never knew exactly what caused the pain. Mary thought that it might be a side effect from her medications and asked her doctor. He agreed there were side effects associated with Fosamax and immediately changed her medication. Shortly thereafter her bone density improved, and she was taken off the drugs. After stopping the Fosamax she was never bothered with the chest pains again.

Yet, the pain that Mary thought was acid reflux continued. I believe the "Drain-o" vision I saw was actually a symbol of the Fosamax, and that the lining of rust I envisioned throughout her esophagus was damage caused by being on this drug for such a long period of time. As "Drain-o" has the power to burn through even the toughest clogs, I believe that the long-term use of Fosamax burned the lining of Mary's esophagus.

To verify my intuitive interpretation, I went online to check for patients reporting the side effects of Fosamax. Sure enough, I found that there were many negative side effects relating to the use of this drug, including damage to the esophagus. Here is a quote from the website[22] written by a daughter regarding her mother:

> *My mother was taking Fosamax from 1995 until 2005 for osteoporosis. I believe she was part of a clinical trial. Her osteoporosis improved. However, her medical records say she was barely tolerating the drug and that she had severe esophageal ulcerations, nausea, jawbone loss, and vertigo from the inner ear. She was told to continue the drug. In October 2005, she began to have trouble swallowing. She was initially told it was anxiety but was then diagnosed with esophageal cancer and died nine months later.*

Mary believed that the damage caused by this medication was at the root of her problems with digestion. We started a new sequence of healings to rejuvenate her esophagus and repair the damage. The first was a distance healing where I focused on her esophagus sending a glowing, spiraling, light energy from the top to the bottom. Like a Roto-Rooter servicing, I envisioned all debris and ulcerations being scraped off the lining. I then coated the entire area with green liquid energy, filling every nook and cranny. My final vision was of her esophagus - pink, plush, and normal. It was a beautiful sight.

Mary called a week later and excitedly exclaimed that she had stopped using the acid reflux medication. She had not had an attack since the distance healing. There was one moment when she feared she was going to have an attack, but as I had instructed, she viewed her esophagus as working perfectly, and the feeling went away. She had broken the cycle of negative thinking that was induced by fear of the expectation of pain. In its place, she created a new thought process to go with her new esophagus.

22　http://www.askapatient.com

COMMENTS BY KATHY: I believe the side effects of the medication Mary took for osteoporosis caused real internal damage to her esophagus. In addition, the second medication she took to stop the acid reflux pain, caused by the first medication, was also hurting her. The esophagus is the area between what we swallow and what we can stomach. Once Wayne did the healing and Mary changed her thoughts, her esophagus became just as he declared - pink, plush, and normal. As Mary continues to digest new ideas and create new thoughts that empower her life, she will continue to experience this new way of living life without fear. She will be enjoying a life of well-being, health, and vitality! She will be telling a new story about how great she feels.

Doris was just getting started with helping her friends. Her limp was gone, and everyone she knew noticed and wanted to know what happened. After seeing Mom and hearing her stories about the healings they were amazed at her results. The Reay family was the first to take action and made an appointment with me.

In today's society, people suffer from all kinds of emotional traumas. What could be more frightening to a person than losing their power to think, reason, understand, communicate or recognize their loved ones? This was the future confronting Mary Reay, then 79 years-old, and her daughters, Tara and Michele. In recent years, Mary was stricken with vascular dementia. In addition, she also suffered with a painful knee.

I was optimistic that Mary could be helped and chose to perform an energy brain balancing, which in many cases can bring about a complete change in the effected person.

We began the healing. Raising my vibration level, I set my intention for Mary's complete recovery, called in all of her guides, as well as my own, and expressed grateful thanks for the healing they were about to perform.

My first vision was a petrified forest with stunted deteriorating branches and Mary's brain turning to stone. My intention was clear. I immediately eliminated this vision from my mind and replaced it with a botanical garden where the branches were growing and expanding. Cradling her head in my hands, I began to balance her brain's energy. My energy elevated to a new level and it felt as if I were in another dimension, completely serene and requesting the best for Mary. I envisioned her brain being pink and plush and working perfectly. It almost felt as if I could reach out and touch this blossoming garden. New roots for communication were working in perfect harmony with the nerve endings in her spine and would return Mary to normalcy. In my mind's eye I saw her brain being able to communicate through her spine to send out clear messages to the rest of her body. This was how I saw it and that was my intention for this wonderful woman.

When I felt the brain balancing was complete I proceeded on to the rest of her body. I continued in the same higher vibration level throughout the healing which ran so high I felt a buzzing sensation throughout my whole being. Placing my hands on the front of her upper torso just below each of her shoulders, I funneled energy into the area sending her life force down through each chakra, ultimately grounding her to the planet. As each of the energy centers opened, there was a distinct balanced flow being restored. I spent a significant amount of time working on her legs and feet to anchor her completely into her body.

Upon completion, I touched Mary on the shoulder and she gradually began to return. She sat up on the edge of the bed and we spoke about her experience. She didn't have a lot to say, but as soon as she stood up she reached down and touched her toes. There was no loss of balance. She had not been able to do anything like this for quite some time, and became very excited about this accomplishment. She then exclaimed that there was no more pain in her knee. At this point, she kept repeating, over and over, "When are you coming to give me another healing?" Mary could not articulate what she had experienced, but knew that her spirit and body had benefited from the healing and wanted more.

Mary was being cared for by a woman named Jasmin who lived with her and took care of her needs. Previously, Jasmin had told my mother, "Mary never smiles and almost always has a blank look on her face. When she does communicate, she's oftentimes quite nasty and easily irritated." This time, when my mother returned Mary to her home, there was an amazing difference. The next day Jasmin exclaimed to my mother, "This was a divine healing. Mary has not smiled in the four months that I have lived with her, and now she smiles all the time!"

Mary had three completely lucid days after the healing and frequently asked Jasmin, "When am I getting my next healing from Wayne?" During that time, she became active and interested in life again. She held meaningful conversations and wanted to go shopping. After the three days, she gradually began to slip back into the old patterns associated with vascular dementia.

COMMENTS BY KATHY: Because patterns of behavior become habitual, it can often take more than one healing to reset. Wayne's healing reset Mary's health. She knew the positive impact this single healing had on her overall well-being and was living in joy again. Being able to live an active, interested life and having meaningful conversations is so important. Jasmin could see the difference and was enjoying being with a smiling, happy woman. Unfortunately, Mary was not able to maintain this new energy level on her own, and knew she needed more sessions. Ideally, Mary would benefit most from a consistent visitation schedule or series of distance healings to maintain her energy level until this new pattern of health becomes habitual.

Mary's daughter, Tara, was the next to receive a healing. An attractive 38 year-old woman, she suffered with a terrible case of acid reflux. It was so debilitating that she could not eat and as a result was thin as a rail. She had lost so much weight that her cheeks had sunken in which caused her cheekbones to protrude from her face. Tara told me her doctor said she was starving to death.

My perception was that many of her energy fields were blocked and that she was under such intense stress that even eating small morsels of food was impossible. I felt there was something in her life that was bothering her that she could not digest.

I began at her feet sending wave after wave of healing energy shooting through her body, regenerating every cell. Placing my hands on her stomach, I instilled the intention that her stomach would sweeten and that she would once again enjoy the little things in life.

I ran a stream of glowing energy, like a golden light, from her stomach just under the rib cage to the upper part of her torso just under her neck, covering the whole digestive area. I followed with a full body healing and afterward Tara felt completely relaxed, more-so than she had been in a long time. Her mouth was dry from the extremely high vibration level and she was able to drink water. She was very peaceful.

The final healing of the day was on Michele, a corporate executive and mother of two children. At 40 years of age she was constantly under pressure from both areas of her life, as well as her mother's illness. Michele was hoping for a healing that would bring about relaxation.

As soon as I began the healing I sent a high level of energy pulsing through her body. In addition to increasing her energy levels, there was also a very serene balancing of the energy taking place within her. When we finished, Michelle noticed that many of the petty concerns of daily life that had bothered her were gone. She said this was the best and most relaxed she had felt in a very long time:

I am usually very fidgety and continued to be fidgety throughout the healing. I did not know what to expect and thus was anxious. I was conscious and completely aware of everything that happened during the healing. Even though I was alert, I could not control the flow of energy that I felt going through my body. My left leg was quivering, and I knew it, but could not stop it. My breathing is usually very intense but now I realized that it was different. It was deep, calm and relaxed. I saw beautiful colors, mainly yellow and green and they appeared circular in form. I began laughing hysterically and thought, "This is not real!" It was an amazing experience, and when it was over, I felt very relaxed.

After I had finished all of the healings we had a barbeque and Tara was able to eat. I have checked on her several times and each time she stated that she has not been bothered by the acid reflux since the healing. She is now eating, has put weight back on, and has resumed a normal life.

Several months later, my mother called and asked me to do a distance healing on Mary Reay. Mary was experiencing agonizing pain in both legs and was unable to get out of bed. I sent the healing and an hour later my mother called to share her excitement. Mary was out of bed, walking perfectly and pain free!

It was very satisfying to be able to help my mother walk pain free and avoid a serious operation; help her friend Mary Janos by improving her eyes as well as her digestive problems; and improve the quality of life for her close friends, the Reay Family. After all, what more can you expect from a Mama's Boy?

CHAPTER 19

Egg Shells from Heaven

KATHY

My sister, Lynn Esposito Raymond was a gifted healer. She had a spectacular zest for life and was always ready to help anyone with her skills. Lynn performed healings for many years with superb results. Her intuition was second to none and she knew that the dregs of human emotion, when fully inhaled into every fiber of the body, will somehow be reflected in *dis-ease*. The worse the torment or trauma a person is confronted with, the more devastating the internal impact on that person.

Julie, a nurse, came to her for a healing. This was not a happy-go-lucky session to have her energy levels increased. This medical professional was diagnosed with uterine cancer and this was a final attempt to pull off a miracle. The surgery was already scheduled and time was not on Julie's side.

As they discussed the circumstances surrounding the development of the cancer, Lynn's intuition took over and before long the cause was uncovered. Julie was the younger of two sisters and as far back as she could remember, her older sister was considered the gifted artistic sibling. The theme that her sister was the crown jewel of artistry resounded throughout the family. No one wanted to see what Julie was capable of creating, thus she stuffed her feelings of inadequacy and disappointment deep inside for years only to have them develop into uterine cancer.

The uterus correlates to the second chakra[23] which supports creativity, feelings, emotional needs, boundaries, trust, warmth, intimacy, attachment and letting go, addictions, the organs that are located in that area and much more.

Over a lifetime, when a person feels emotionally hurt or wounded and doesn't process the experience fully, the emotion (energy in motion) gets stored in the body. Similar emotions get stored in the same area of the body each time. The energy begins to stack emotion on top of emotion. For instance, sadness stacks on top of sadness. Anger stacks on top of anger. Then, because we don't want to feel all these stored feelings we start taking shallow breaths, which ultimately stops oxygen and blood supply from going to those areas. This compounding of emotion and lack of breath will eventually manifest into symptoms. If the symptoms are ignored and the feelings are further compressed, this will eventually cause dis-ease.

Lynn knew what had to be done. She instructed Julie to visualize her uterus perfectly formed with no abnormalities and no cancer. Being a nurse and an artist, Julie was able to visualize a healthy uterus. Lynn also set her intention for Julie's uterus to be completely healed. Being a powerful healer Lynn proceeded to perform the healing on Julie with great expectations. There was a tremendous flow of energy, and Lynn was able to generate an extremely high level of vibration within Julie. During the healing Lynn envisioned a magnificent purple flower. As purple is a healing color, things were looking good, and the message came through that Julie

---

23   Rainbow Chakra Centers chart #5, http://www.InnerLightResources.com

was on the mend. After the healing which they both felt was a complete success, Julie went home and painted a picture of a gorgeous purple flower for her daughter.

A few days later Julie went to the hospital for tests, and when the results came back there was a combination of shock and elation. The doctor was shocked and could not imagine what had happened. The tumor was gone, and everyone was elated. I wonder how many times the doctor went over the data to see where he might have misinterpreted something.

Lynn had uncovered the true cause of the cancer and when confronted with the stuffed emotions that had been festering for years, Julie was immediately willing to accept herself as the talented artistic person that she was. With this acceptance and the power of the healing, the cancer never had a chance.

———————

Healers are humans too, and even though Lynn was a master at what she did, she had a real life experience that brought her to a crossroads in her own life.

There was a time when Lynn was living her perfect life. Unfortunately, *"Shift Happens!"* and over the course of a seven-year period, what was once a beautiful, loving relationship deteriorated and took its toll.

LYNN'S STORY:

It was Sunday, and I was attending a picnic at my best friend Debbie Gancher's house when I started to have excruciating pains in my stomach. Unable to eat or drink anything that day, I knew I was in trouble. I left the picnic, went home, and later that night broke out in a cold sweat. With 15 years of emergency medical technician experience, I knew my symptoms were not good and I was going into shock. Lying there on the cold tile floor, I told myself "I'll feel better in the morning" but knew I was lying. I was dying. In that moment, a small spider crawled passed my face and I heard the words, "GET UP AND CREATE A NEW LIFE!" I had missed my "exit point."[24]

———————

24 Sylvia Brown with Lindsey Harrison, *Life on the Other Side,* (New York: New American Library, 2001)

184

I immediately called my sister, Kathy, who was out of town until Monday, and asked that she send me a distance healing. I was not ready to go to the hospital so she sent her son, Bryan, to bring me to their house so I would not be alone. After the healing I was comforted by sleep.

Kathy returned home and she, Debbie, and another sister, Patty, took care of me but I knew I had crossed the line. Over the next few days I continued to worsen. Because I was unable to shift my thought processes, the physical consequences manifested! I now needed medical intervention or I would certainly die. Since choosing to miss my exit point Sunday night, action had to be taken. These were my private thoughts.

Patty, highly intuitive and also a healer told me that if I was not better by tomorrow she was dragging me to the doctor.

It was Wednesday morning, three days had passed, and I was still indecisive of where I wanted to be treated. There was a hospital only a mile away, but I knew it was not the right place for me. Kathy did a healing on my belly, which was extremely tender, and the healing made it feel a little better. She asked if I was ready to go to the hospital and I told her no. We both knew I needed medical intervention, but I was not ready to admit it. Kathy and Wayne sent a steady stream of healing energy. I was resting and feeling somewhat better when Kathy left for work at 1 PM knowing Patty would be arriving shortly.

COMMENTS BY KATHY: When I first got the call from Lynn, I knew she was in bad shape. We spoke of her symptoms, the spider which symbolizes creativity, her missed exit point, and what she wanted. I also knew she had chosen to live, so I was not concerned that she would die.

When I arrived home, we discussed her options. She was not yet ready to receive medical intervention, even though we both knew it would most likely be necessary if she was going to live. She had thought the negative, hurtful, thoughts for too long and had now manifested the physical consequences. However, she was still undecided about her next step. We spoke of the resentments and angers she was harboring, of her inability to digest the sequence of events that had led to this point in her life, and the lack of self-forgiveness for being a fool. She no longer trusted her ability to make good choices and was beating herself up. She literally could not stomach the choices she had made.

We discussed her physical symptoms. Since she was not on any medications that would mask the symptoms or pain, and was feeling somewhat better after her physical healing with me, I honored her request to stay where she was and rest. We both knew she would not be alone as she had the amazing support of her angels. I would continue to send her energy while she worked her way through the mental process of coming to terms with what was ahead. She never had surgery before, and it was not her first choice. However, because of the deterioration of her physical condition, my concern was that Lynn would not be able to do the mental processing necessary for the energy healing to be completely effective. She was not yet ready to forgive.

I knew Patty would be arriving shortly and be the force Lynn needed to make a decision on the hospital of choice, and until her arrival, our friend and neighbor, Kathy Pepe who lived downstairs, was just a phone call away.

When Patty arrived I heard the doorbell, but did not have the strength to get out of bed and open the door. Instead, I fell back to sleep. Patty went home to get her key. When she returned and entered the room, she stood at the end of the bed and said, "Are you walking to the car or am I calling an ambulance?"

I now knew what I wanted. "Take me to Danbury Hospital! They are far more advanced and they incorporate holistic medicine." I walked to the car.

Thirty minutes later, we arrived at the emergency room. Upon examination, the doctor confirmed what I already knew: I was in serious shape and in need of surgery. Shortly thereafter, the surgeon arrived and said, "I think you and I are going to have a date tonight."

I agreed, "I think you're right!" We had bonded.

He then said, "If you had waited until tomorrow you would be dead."

I calmly replied, "I know, that's why I'm here today."

The emergency surgery was scheduled to take place that evening. It was estimated to last over three hours, after which I would be moved to the intensive care unit for recovery and remain in the hospital for at least two weeks.

My intestines had burst. My surgeon, Dr. John, removed five quarts of feces, one quart of puss, and a foot of intestines from my abdominal cavity. Obviously, I was very fortunate to be alive. Dr. John gave me a temporary colostomy so that my body would have time to heal internally from the infection and recover from the invasiveness of the surgery. The plan was to keep the bag in place four to six months before reconnecting the intestine.

I knew I needed the surgery, but I had my own plan for recovery. Kathy and Wayne intensified their healings. My family was there for me with all their love and support. Patty, Kathy, my son Jesse, and his girlfriend Tiffany, remained at the hospital throughout the whole surgical procedure.

In reality, the surgery lasted only two and a half hours, I never had to go to intensive care, and I was released from the hospital after only six days.

On the sixth day at around three in the afternoon my awesome surgeon came to remove the staples, discuss follow-up treatment and say goodbye. He appeared to be distressed and had a sullen look on his face as he gave me *his* horrific news.

"It was cancerous. And worse than that, it has spread to your lymph nodes. We did not know it at the time of the emergency surgery, but the lab reports just came back and you need to start chemo immediately. I can recommend some really good people in your area."

I looked at him and said, *"Chemo?"* Every cell in my body screamed, *"Not even an option!"*

He implored, "But it has spread to the lymph nodes, and you need to start treatment right away." Again the words came freely from my lips as I attempted to reassure him that I was all right and encouraged him to calm down.

"I totally understand where you are coming from, and I don't expect you to comprehend my way of life, but I am already fine. In my world, it is now up to me."

I asked him not to say anything to anyone. He urgently stressed that I discuss it with my adult children. Again my reply was, "Not even an option. I don't want anyone to know who does not share my point of view and would not understand how I feel." When he left the room I really felt bad for him. After all, he thought I was going to die.

Alone in my hospital bed, I reverberated to myself, *"Chemo?"* And again, every cell in my body said, *"Not even an option."* I knew I was on the right track. My first stage of treatment was to get up and out of the hospital. There was nothing more they could do for me. The medical world had saved my life, and now it was up to me to free myself from this dis-ease.

As I lay there in the hospital bed, reviewing my life, it was very clear as to how I had evolved to this point of despair.

Where it all began…

It was in March of 2000, when my perfect life began. I was out with a group of friends, one of whom was celebrating the completion of her divorce. This gala event took place at a quaint little establishment in the Litchfield Hills of Connecticut. As the evening drew to a close and my mother and I were preparing to leave, I came face to face with "Prince Charming"!

He was a distinguished looking man with big blue eyes, gray hair, and a captivating political smile. Clad in a black leather jacket, blue shirt, tight jeans and cowboy boots, he oozed charisma. His energy was incredible and best of all he was right in front of me.

A woman standing next to me noticed my reaction and sarcastically inquired, "Do you know what this man does for a living?"

I said, "Gee, let's see, captain of his ship?"

To which she quipped, "How did you guess that?"

This man obviously took orders from no one. He was in charge of every situation. He looked into my eyes and asked, "Can I buy you a drink?"

"Not unless you want to drive to my town of Southbury, about 20 miles from here," never really expecting him to say yes.

"I can do that," he replied.

There was something mesmerizing about this man. As I began to leave, the woman standing next to me cautioned, "I love him dearly, but you have been warned!"

We had a few drinks, a lot of laughs, and fell deeply in love. A man who never took a day off from his job spent the next three years learning how to play. We had met in March and by Christmas, the following year, were engaged.

We were in love. People were envious. Dining was one of our favorite festivities and on many occasions, strangers sent drinks to our table. We were really happy and it showed. Once, at a restaurant in Providence, Rhode Island, the patrons were taking bets that we were having an affair because we were just too happy to be a real couple. As we were leaving, one of them came over to ask, in order to see who won the bet.

By this time I had quit my job, and we were spending all our time together. We decided to remodel my house and had a lot of fun doing it. We would work for a few hours and go eat for a few hours.

One year, on my birthday, he took me to lunch and we came back three days later. Life was great. We were on a three-year vacation!

Suddenly, things began to change. The demands of his job increased so he started to work more and more. Then his staff was reduced, and he had to spend even more hours making up for the shortfall. After all, he was the captain of the ship, and the work had to get done.

Although his job required he travel to many different locations and handle a multitude of situations, he was always available to me via cell phone or his private office number. I trusted him completely. The world was wide open to my prince, and because he had his own airplane, he could literally be anywhere.

We went from spending all of our time together to rarely seeing each other. As his workload continued to increase, I became lonely and depressed. I had no job while his job was 24/7. This left me a lot of time to think, and think I did.

I remembered a time when we were with our friends at a local club, a place we frequented on Friday nights. He loved to dance and usually danced all night long. There was one guy that he was compelled to compete with, to see who could get their body closest to the dance floor and then who could endure that dance position the longest. This playful competition was a weekly event.

However, on that evening, he just stood in the doorway. At the time, I brushed it off thinking he must be tired and just let it go, but there was a woman who insisted on dancing with him. It didn't feel right, and he was acting really weird. Now, when I look back, I can see that this was when our perfect relationship began to deteriorate.

He started coming home less and less, explaining that he slept in his chair at work where he had efficiency living quarters adjacent to his office. I totally trusted this man and really missed him. I tried to be understanding, feeling bad because I knew he had to work, and I was just being selfish. After all, he was a workaholic before I met him, so I could understand him working those long hours. Even so, I became more and more depressed and more and more lonely. It got so bad that I didn't even want to be around myself. Because of the sporadic and minimal amount of time we were spending together I never mentioned my depression and loneliness to him. Instead, *I STUFFED IT!*

People began to report sightings of him with other women. He would always have an explanation of who they were and what they were doing together. His job required significant interaction with many different kinds of people and situations, and as I trusted him completely, I wanted to believe him. However, as these sightings continued to increase I began to question his behavior more often and in a more accusatory fashion. He continued to use his job as an excuse. My doubt continued to fester. I made my own excuse. I was in love with him and was planning to marry him, and since he would be retiring soon I hoped our life would return to the perfect conditions that we had. I could be patient a little longer.

Eventually, I reached a breaking point and returned the engagement ring telling him to keep it until he was sure that I was what he wanted. He claimed he didn't understand but said, "Okay."

He continued to call me and finally, in May, I agreed to go away with him to celebrate my birthday. He gave me an awesome card and in it was my engagement ring. He spent the rest of the trip telling me how great it was to have someone you really love to sit and talk with. I was so relieved that he was ready to go back to the way we were. After all, I loved this man and was concerned about him working all those hours. He was both physically and mentally exhausted.

Unfortunately, when we returned home the old pattern resumed, and eventually, once again I broke the engagement. He continued to call in an attempt to convince me of his love and his desire to get back together.

I was on an emotional roller coaster and more often than not, I forced myself to believe what I knew were lies because I wanted it to be true. Now, not only was he lying to me, but I was also lying to myself. We were no longer living together or even engaged; yet we continued this unhealthy pattern, and it was taking a physical and emotional toll on me.

On Father's Day, 2003, Prince Charming came to my house. He spent 45 minutes convincing me that he was sincere in his love for me and wanted us back together. We went to dinner to celebrate our reunion. The hostess commented, "Wow, you two really look happy. It's nice to see people who enjoy each other's company."

It felt like old times again. We ordered dinner. I excused myself and went to the ladies room. I returned just in time to overhear a phone conversation he was having. *"I'm in Hartford with Joe and Mike. I love you too."*

My heart sank to the floor! This man who just convinced me again of how much he loved me and wanted it to work for us, was now telling lies to someone else and telling them how much he loved them.

At that instant every cell in my body was activated. The angst and upset that had been festering inside of me anchored into my cells. This was the exact moment when the cancer began and from then on, every thought I felt, and hurt I experienced, fed it.

Our whole relationship was built on nothing but lies. I could not believe how many thoughts I was thinking at the same time. It was overwhelming. All the times he wasn't with me, all the gifts, cards, things we exchanged in what I thought was a sacred relationship with the man I planned to marry raced through my mind. All the times I was alone and feeling guilty about him having to work came back in that instant, and I realized that lying came naturally to him.

When he saw the expression on my face he immediately went into a lie. "That was my granddaughter. I was supposed to go there for dinner, but I wanted to be with you instead. You have it all wrong."

I was speechless.

I could not get out of there fast enough. I left immediately but was forced to wait for him because my purse and cell phone were in his car and I had no other ride home. It all seemed surreal. I screamed and cried hysterically the whole ride home. When we got to the house I began to smash everything that reminded me of our relationship.

Nothing seemed to matter anymore. Was this really happening? My whole life changed in one quick second. I was in shock! I found myself in the bathroom beating on him, crying, "How could you do this to me? Why didn't you just tell me? Get your stuff and get out!" As he proceeded to leave he kept repeating, "It was my son and granddaughter! You have it all wrong!"

I was devastated! I cried for days. My mind was working overtime remembering every occasion he claimed he had to work. I no longer believed anything he said. My friends and family were also shocked. They knew how much we enjoyed and loved each other. The next few days I spent putting his things in garbage bags; his stuffed animal that played *Fly Me to the Moon*, the cowboy boots he was wearing the night we met, all of our pictures and mementos, and his clothes. Everywhere I looked reminded me of him. The piano I got him for Valentine's Day, all the furniture we picked out together, and our bed, our sacred bed. I was left alone with all of it. Everything in there was now a painful memory.

He continued to call trying to convince me I had it all wrong, even going so far as to say, "I swear on my mother's grave." I said "your mother is already dead, what else do you have?" He then said, "I swear on ...!" The impact of what he swore on was so strong that I immediately started to think maybe I did misunderstand. Maybe all this was finally getting to me, and I'm just depressed and paranoid. No one would ever swear on something like that if it wasn't true.

And so began the next four years of not honoring my own gut instinct.

Although I allowed myself to be talked into seeing him again, things were never the same. I never really trusted him again. In my mind I questioned everything he said. We were together less and less, but for some reason we could never completely separate. Hence, shift happens. We were no longer a couple, we were now an addiction.

I kept ignoring his actions and continued to fall victim to his words.

I proceeded to sell myself out, contradicting my personal beliefs in order to feed my addiction, which in turn, fueled my dis-ease. During this time he had a stroke, and I thought he was going to die. When someone you love is in this situation it puts a new light on life in general. Is all the other stuff that important, or is it ego? Is this just who he is? Is this who he'd been for the 59 years of his life before I met him? Do I expect him to be someone he really can't be? It didn't matter anymore. Once again, I told myself I loved him. His life was much different than the sheltered life I had lived before meeting him. Why is my way right? This man was worldly. He had seen and done it all. Was I just being shallow? I questioned all my beliefs. He was still alive and came out of it with minimal damage, barely missing a day of work. So again I would see him and continued to convince myself he will retire soon and then our relationship will return to the good old days.

In June of 2007, he finally retired. We spent the afternoon together and had an early dinner before he went to the final meeting of his career. He dropped me off, we kissed good night, and he said he would call me later.

But he didn't call. Another expectation went up in smoke.

Months passed before I saw him again. In November, two days before Thanksgiving I attended a self-help meeting. The topic was gratitude, focusing on all the things we are grateful for. I left thinking about how Prince Charming was one of the greatest gifts of my life.

So I called him to see if he would like to take me to lunch.

"Absolutely! When and where?" Over the next two weeks we spent quite a bit of time together. Again we kissed goodnight and he said, "I'll call you."

And he did, three months later on Valentine's Day, to tell me that he loves and misses me.

"You love me? You love me?"

"Heck Yeah!"

I was flabbergasted! This, too, was part of his normal behavior pattern. I would not hear from him for months, but he would call me every Valentine's Day and on my birthday. I hung up on him and returned to my shopping wondering how many more women will he call today?

In March of 2008, I decided to move to my home in Florida and start a new life. I called him to say goodbye, and we arranged a time to meet. We said our goodbyes in the parking lot, and he said he would fly down soon to check out the situation. We both said I love you, kissed, hugged, and cried. I climbed into the huge moving van and drove off to start my new life. Or so I thought.

About a week after I arrived in Florida, Prince Charming called from Connecticut, extremely upset because his brother was very sick. He asked if I would send some distance healings and of course I agreed. Again, he started with how I've always been there for him, and how he treated me badly, and he loves me, and now he's going to fly to Florida to see me. But he never did come.

Finally, the truth...

Months later, I was back in Connecticut. Thinking I could handle my addiction, I invited Prince Charming to stop by for a visit with Kathy and me. After a few glasses of wine combined with the effects of the stroke (which made it much harder for him to remember the lies from way back) I asked him, "Was the girl at the restaurant who had insisted on dancing with you that night so long ago, the same one you have always denied you are with?" He answered, "Yes."

That simple one word answer "yes" confirmed years of suspicions when I had constantly second-guessed myself. Finally the truth! The validation that I had been lying to myself, when deep down in my gut I had always known the truth, was shocking. All the excuses I had made, all the times I lied to myself pretending it was okay, everything I knew in my gut to be true, yet dishonoring myself so many times, was devastating. I had been living one big lie and inside of me was the dis-ease to prove it! The stomach pains and blood in my stools for the past three years was the physical manifestation of all the upset I had stuffed down not wanting to feel. In that moment, every memory I had suppressed came crushing in on me and I felt something inside of me pop.

About a week later at Debbie Gancher's picnic I started to get severe stomach pains and knew I had passed the point of being able to self-heal.

COMMENTS BY KATHY: It is said that people come into our lives for a reason, a season, or a lifetime. It is our attachment to them that sometimes causes our greatest sufferings. In this case, Lynn's attachment was extreme. Unfortunately, even with all of her skills, knowledge, and wisdom, she was unable to break her thought processes and addiction to this man. Even though she knew the damage that was being done within her physical body she was not able to stop the downward spiral.

Although the results of having to have surgery may look like a healing failure I have no doubt that the outcome from this experience will one day be recognized as one of the greatest gifts Lynn will ever receive.

So here I am - still alive - thanks to the miracles of modern day medicine!

I knew I was fortunate. The bag that was glued to the outside of my body and the intestine protruding from the side of my stomach, which emptied into it, was my constant reminder. Once my body had time to heal from the surgery the bag would be removed and my intestine would be reattached. For me, the cancer diagnosis was irrelevant.

As I left the hospital I knew it was now up to me. I had my own plan of action. There were only three people who I knew shared my beliefs: Kathy, Wayne, and another healer/friend, Lisa Venn, and they continued to send healing energy to my cells. These three people would give me their honest professional opinions which I totally trusted and respected, and I knew they would honor any decision I made. I did not tell anyone else because I did not want to draw any negative energy or worry towards me. Instead, I would share only positive aspects with others. I knew that I was on the track to recovery. It was a beautiful day and the sun peaked through the trees and warmed me inside and out. There was a slight breeze and the conversation was light. As I breathed in life I planned my future; sunshine, good food, good times, good friends, a loving family, and most of all, an attitude adjustment.

As we headed home I realized life as I knew it was over. I needed to be aware of my food and drink intake, but most of all I needed to be aware of the thoughts in my mind and the words that came out of my mouth. I had to stay positive and listen to my brand spankin' new gut instinct. As I sat there quietly, I breathed in sunlight from the top of my head out through my toes. This, to me, was the best medicine in the world.

Personally, at this point I already felt healed.

I was going to rehabilitate at the home of my eldest son, Frankie, and his wife, Robyn. On the way a huge rainbow arched across the skyline in front of us. Just another sign I had made the right decision.

Because no one else knew of the cancer diagnosis, the conversations were all positive and focused on my recovering from the surgery and getting back to normal life. The energetic environment was great. During the day I would sit out on the deck to soak up the sun, and I was surrounded with family who treated me with tender loving care. As I was recuperating in the main area of the house my grandchildren were constantly running in and out of the room, and I enjoyed watching them play. It was very comforting, and their laughter was extremely healing to me.

At my request, Wayne visited to perform a hands-on healing. He confirmed what I already knew. I was totally clean inside.

COMMENTS BY WAYNE: When I performed the healing on Lynnie, I filled every cell in her body with golden healing energy. Rather than resisting, or fighting against the cancer, I thanked it for the lessons it had taught her and hoped that she had learned from this experience and was willing to take the action steps necessary to maintain great health. I requested that any cancerous cells be elevated slightly above her physical presence so that they could be swept away and recycled into new positive energy. Moving my hands above her entire body, there appeared to be very little in the way of cancerous debris. My intention was for every cell in Lynn's body to be completely healthy and to create an environment where no abnormal cell could exist. My intuition told me that her stomach was totally clean. As I finished the healing I encapsulated her body and the energy fields around her in glowing, golden healing energy.

The main lesson here was that she be true to herself and create a positive lifestyle where forgiveness, gratitude and love would be her new focus.

My second healer, Lisa, was scheduled to visit me a few days after Wayne. In the meantime she was sending distance healings and sent one the day after Wayne's visit. When I went to receive it I was greeted with the message, "You are a perfect child of God. You are whole and complete." I was fine and there was nothing to receive. Lisa called me later that day and said there was a complete shift, and she no longer felt the need to make the trip to provide a hands-on healing.

In addition, Kathy was continually performing healings. With all these amazing people working on me and my change in attitude, I felt completely healed. I knew that the cancer was gone.

COMMENTS BY KATHY: It was clear to me that no matter how many healings were done, if Lynn did not change her patterns of thought and behavior she was destined to repeat this process and the cancer would return. She knew this too. She had to find a way to release the upset and sadness around her relationship with Prince Charming and recognize the gift in all of this.

When we are able to see the other side of the wound, the benefits can be amazing. During the first few years of their lives together, her prince brought her an unbelievably loving relationship, something only dreamed about in fairy tales. However, Cinderella wanted more than a Prince Charming, she wanted a man who would walk beside her and create a life together.

Ultimately, he was not the man she thought he was, and the disappointment was overwhelming.

In reality, it was Lynn's desire for more than her Prince could provide that destroyed their relationship. If Lynn could see the gifts and create a new relationship, using the contrast of what she does not want as guidance for what she does want, she could begin to manifest a new, healthier relationship, both with herself and with a new man.

She would be empowered to shift from victim to creator!

I left the hospital on June 18th, and five days later Debbie drove me to my first follow-up visit with Dr. John. While waiting in the exam room the attending nurse asked why I was there.

I explained, "I had emergency surgery two weeks ago and am here for a checkup."

She looked shocked. "No really, why are you here?"

"I'm not kidding."

"Oh my God, you look fantastic!"

I was feeling pretty good about myself when Dr. John arrived.

He asked if I had discussed the cancer with my children. "Please reconsider chemo", he implored. "I can give you some really good choices in your area."

I looked into his eyes and saw the fear and pain.

I told him, "I totally understand your point of view and concern, but, in my world, chemo is not an option. I know the exact moment I got the cancer. It was four years ago when I returned to the dinner table only to overhear my fiancé lie to the person he was talking to on his cell phone, saying he was "at a meeting in Hartford with two men" and "I love you too". In my world cancer is deep, deep hurt and that I had. I felt it in every cell in my body, but now, four years later, I was able to change that. I was able to confront him about the lie I knew in my heart we had been living. Everything fell into place, and my addiction to this man is finally over. You can fix my body but only I can fix my mind and spirit. The complete healing has to come from within me, and all the medicine in the world cannot do that.

The cancer was created in an instant and went away in the blink of an eye. I know the moment it ended. As soon as I let go of resentment and replaced it with forgiveness of both Prince Charming and myself, it was gone.

I truly believe that night when you operated on me I was full of cancer. You made me brand spankin' new from the medical perspective, and now it is up to me on the spiritual side. So I know you can't understand this anymore than I can understand chemo. I promise you that I am already okay. I am just weak but this too shall pass."

He took a blood test which was more painful than the stitches from my surgery or the bag hanging at my side. I asked him to hug me goodbye, promised that I was fine and would see him in six weeks.

Debbie, an intuitive healer, was the fourth and final person I confided in, telling her as we left the office I had been diagnosed with cancer. She confirmed what my other healers had stated, "You don't have cancer. Your eyes are clearer than they have been in years. You're actually in the present, you look ten years younger, and I'm not getting cancer at all." So off we went to find something good to eat and swim in her pool. Water therapy - another one of my meds.

The reason I chose to tell these four people was because they knew me well. They are all extraordinary at what they do and are honest if they disagree with me. They can tell if I am hiding anything from them and give me love and guidance at all times. I can call them anytime day or night and they will come in an instant. These are the professionals I have chosen and have nothing but love and respect for each of them. I am so blessed.

The reason I chose not to tell the rest is because they would not understand. They would be so afraid of losing me that through their worry and fear, without even knowing it, they would bring constant negativity to me energetically. They would be focused on my cancer, while I am focused on my well-being. They would also worry needlessly, pulling themselves away from their own well-being. Two of my sons are police officers and need to be focused on their jobs, not worrying about their mother. My third son Jason would probably understand my way, but why even tell him? He sees how well I am doing.

I have seen how people react when someone tells them they have been diagnosed with cancer. People feel sorry for you, apologize, look at you pathetically and spend their energy feeling bad for you. Then they tell you how sick they are, plus each and every friend and family member that they can recall, and every horrible detail they can remember. They say, "You are crazy and if you don't follow your doctor's instructions you will die!" Or they can't be with what you have or are afraid it's contagious and disappear from your life. These are not the conversations I wanted to partake in.

As for chemo, first it kills both bad and good cells in your body and destroys your immune system. Then you are told "now we can rebuild you" when you haven't done anything about changing your thought patterns, and you are reminded 24/7 how sick you are.

Instead, I have only positive reinforcement. I hear *"how fantastic I look; and did I lose weight? Boy, you're tan! How are the kids? Congratulations, I heard you have a new grandchild. When is your Mom coming? Tell her I said "hi". And did I mention you look fantastic!"* These are my meds. So far we have sun (vitamin D), good food, water in the pool, and people I love and trust focusing on my well-being. Priceless! Can't get these at the drugstore!

By not sharing my cancer diagnosis, I recruited the positive energy (thoughts) of everyone I came in contact with. This, in conjunction with the four healers who were working on my physical body, promoted and helped me to visualize my body in a state of perfect health.

Within a few weeks, I was given the okay to drive and stopped by to visit my very dear friend Kathy Pepe, psychic and medical intuitive. She had seen me the day before I went to the hospital and confirmed I was very sick. Extremely concerned about my health, she visited me several times at the hospital. We also spoke regularly over the phone, and I assured her I was fine.

I wanted to surprise her so I knocked on her door. She was shocked to see me. She immediately hugged me and said, "You're gonna be okay kid. Your insides are so white and pure they look like the inside of an egg shell!" She just confirmed what I already knew – my insides were brand spankin' new.

We sat and visited as she confided in me, "Before you left for the hospital, your insides were very dark and heavy, and I knew that you needed surgery." She told me the exact area where she had seen the mass and she could not believe how clean and white the same area was now. This was a tremendous validation for me because I valued her intuition, and no one had ever told her that I had been diagnosed with cancer.

For the next few weeks, author Louise Hay, became my new best friend, my mentor, and my guru. I listened to her tapes in my car, and repeated affirmations before I went to sleep. I paid close attention to my thoughts and the conversations that came out of my mouth. I did not let my mind wander where it did not need to go. Everything will work out just the way it is supposed to, so I *"Let go and let God."*

Every day I grew healthier and stronger. After six weeks, I was able to eat and drink anything I chose and lost 20 pounds of excess weight. I felt fantastic. I learned to manage my colostomy bag and was able to drive. This was so important to me because my freedom and independence are my way of life. I was even able to resume my own healing practice: Heals On Wheels.

This experience has been my *forced behavior modification*, and I realize that this has truly been a blessing in disguise. The ending of my addiction is now the beginning of my new life.

COMMENTS BY KATHY: I completely agree with Lynn's point of view. The typical conversation that people have when they find out that someone has been labeled with cancer, or diabetes, or chronic fatigue, or whatever… are what we call illness conversations.

They get caught up in the "ain't it awful" conversations and that just feeds negativity with negativity.

Every day, we get new cells. Every day our bodies are repairing the damage we do to ourselves or is done to us. Every day we have a new opportunity. What will you say today?

I prefer wellness conversations: "Wow, you look great!" "You're doing fantastic!" "Wow, what a speedy recovery!" "You look like you lost weight!" "I love your hair!" "Want to go with me to…..?"

Do you remember how it felt when someone said something loving or kind to you? If you know someone who is not feeling well, find something to compliment them on. And be authentic. Make it real. We know when someone is faking it.

When Lynn was able to pay attention to what she thought, and what she spoke, her life and health began to alter.

One of Lynn's prized possessions is a set of three ceramic monkeys …

See No Evil - Hear No Evil - Speak No Evil.

I never realized how profound they are until now.

Imagine how life would be if every one of us practiced THIS behavior?

In September, I went back to see Dr. John for another blood test. This time my sister, Kathy, accompanied me. When he came into the room, Dr. John was shocked that I looked so good. He could not fathom that I was healthy. He was adamant that I had cancer, needed chemo and was ignoring his medical advice. He went so far as to try to enroll my sister as an ally in his plan to convince me to receive chemo treatments. Kathy said, "Are you kidding? I am one of four. I don't believe in chemo either. How about if you spend the next week, while you are waiting for the blood test results, imagining Lynn's entire insides healthy, pure and clean? Are you willing to do that?"

"That's really outside my belief system, but I think I could give it a try."

A week later, Dr. John left a message in my phone. "Lynn, this is Dr. John. I just wanted to let you know that the results from the blood tests all came back in the normal range. That's encouraging. Hopefully that's good news for us, and I'll see you when it's time to get that colostomy closed."

On November 19, six months after my emergency surgery, Dr. John reattached my intestines, thus eliminating the colostomy bag. Six days later, more than a week ahead of schedule, as I was leaving the hospital he commented, "If all of my patients healed as fast as you, I would be out of business."

KATHY

The week before Lynn's reattachment surgery, she began a new relationship with a man we'll call her Knight-In-Shining-Armor. She had met him a year earlier at a local pub. They became good friends and since they were both looking for love and companionship they were a match (Law-of-Attraction).

Knight was kind, gentle, caring, and generous. Knowing of Lynn's condition and upcoming surgery, he offered his home and companionship. Lynn moved in and they began to build a life. Knight was retired and they spent all of their time together. Lynn was happy and content. Knight was a man who would take care of and not abandon her. He did all the housework, shopping, laundry, cooking and doted on her every need, including fires in the fireplace just because she loved them.

Lynn's recovery was fast and easy. She felt and looked great. She and Knight had many mutual friends and enjoyed the camaraderie of socializing with them. Lynn was back in her hometown, surrounded by friends and family. The connection that she longed for was fulfilled.

Things were really good between them as they moved into the summer months enjoying outdoor parties, picnics and fresh air; all the things Lynn valued. She had her sunshine and her freedom. Knight couldn't do enough for her. He was her anchor, which she thought she needed, and she enjoyed the strength and security he provided.

While all this was good, a sequence of events took place that did not support Lynn's well-being. It was time for her check-up. I suggested she not go, but she wanted to show Dr. John how well she was doing. Although I was not in alignment with her going back to see him, I went along to support her desires. As I feared, Dr. John pressured for chemo. He told her that even though her blood tests were good and showed no cancer, the type of cancer she had was very aggressive and would most likely come back without chemo treatments. She again refused chemo, but to my disappointment agreed to make another appointment.

I was not surprised when shortly after that visit, Lynn told me she could feel an area of hardness inside, mostly where the surgery and colostomy bag had been, and that her skin was extremely sensitive there. I told her that it was probably the severed nerved endings repairing themselves and scar tissue. I asked her to: do self-healings to dissolve and smooth it out; to imagine her body healthy; to stop drinking alcohol; to change her diet; to come back to Landmark seminars with me to create a new future of possibility; to come to the Network chiropractor; and to spend more time with her healer friends, away from the conversations of illness that permeated Knight's world.

Unfortunately, Lynn was spending more time with friends who spoke often of their surgeries and treatments for various ailments and illnesses as well as the prescriptions they were taking and the unhappiness of life. Initially, she tried to alter their thinking, but health problems and pain remained the crux of their conversations. Rather than leave, Lynn became a participant.

There's an ancient Indian proverb about Two Wolves:

An old Cherokee told his grandson of a battle that goes on inside each of us.

The battle is between two wolves.

One wolf is Evil. It has anger, envy, jealousy, sorrow, regret, greed, arrogance, self-pity, guilt, resentment, inferiority, lies, false pride, superiority and ego.

The other wolf is Good. It has joy, peace, love, hope, serenity, humility, kindness, benevolence, empathy, generosity, truth, compassion and faith.

The grandson thought about it for a minute and then asked his grandfather: "Which wolf wins?"

The old Cherokee simply replied, "The one you feed."

Eventually, it was time for the follow-up visit with Dr. John. I was out of town so Lynn invited Knight to her appointment and into the exam room. Once

Knight found out that she had been diagnosed with cancer and that her surgeon was trying to enroll her in having chemo and radiation, her universe jumped tracks. Knight was alive! This is what he did! He rescued damsels in distress! He knew all about surgery having had many himself. This was his world, and he was very good at taking care of sick people.

She now had to defend herself and her choices to Knight. They argued about her children's right to know versus her right to privacy and personal choice. He believed in the medical model and had little knowledge of her beliefs or skills. In short order, everyone heard of Lynn's history and diagnosis. She was now in constant defense. The questions became "How are you feeling? What did the surgeon say? Are you in a lot of pain?"

She felt pressured to bring her children to the next appointment. This time I was there. The declarations that the doctor made to her sons impacted my cells on such an intense level, I can only imagine the fear that ran through my nephew's minds and bodies. There was no mention of possibility or health. Only fear and death were presented.

Her sons wanted to support her and offered to accompany Lynn to the weekly chemo treatments. She stressed to them that she was not going to have any chemo and if they wanted to support her they would envision her as completely healthy and happy.

They understood her beliefs as much as they could, and they knew how important her freedom was to her. She was not one to stay inside or take medicine. They stopped imploring her and honored her wishes. The rest of the summer was spent talking about what was great in their lives, enjoying each other's company and visiting her grandchildren.

Lynn spent time at the pool with Debbie, a nutritionist, attempting to change her diet. She requested and received many healings and did her best to focus on what was healthy about her body. She was feeling pretty good throughout the summer.

Knight's house had a lot of dark wood, and Lynn took it upon herself to paint all the doors and trim bright white to lighten things up. She was revamping the upstairs so that she could be more comfortable. She was a "cloud dweller" and liked everything light and bright. Knight was a "cave dweller" and liked things dark and closed.

As the seasons changed, and the weather cooled, Lynn and Knight spent more time indoors. Lynn enjoyed her time painting and away from the conversations of illness. Knight enjoyed visiting with friends at the local pub or staying home and controlling his fortress. Lynn began to yearn for new adventures. As the days grew shorter and the nights longer she spent more time alone reminiscing about her past and contemplating the future.

As Lynn got healthier, she began to long for the sparkle in her life that she had with Prince Charming. This was not easy to recapture. Although Knight was a wonderful man and did everything for her, he was not the playmate she desired. As she got stronger it became more apparent to her that they were no longer a good match.

A knight-in-shining-armor rescues a damsel in distress. Once this damsel no longer needed rescuing, her desires reverted to looking for her Prince Charming and it wasn't long before her old playmate arrived on the scene.

Prince Charming was back and before long, Knight and Prince became friends. Thus, Prince Charming and all the memories of past adventures and upsets were ever present for Lynn. Knight was the anchor but Prince was the life of the party and the magnetism was still alive.

Throughout the autumn months, Lynn and Prince Charming had opportunities to discuss the past and recall the time they had spent together. She realized that the Prince's light had diminished. He was no longer the fearless adventurer she had known and loved. Somewhere along his journey, her Prince had turned into an old man and conformed to the fears of the aged. He was now resigned to a life of the common man. Her Prince was lost. And so was Lynn. There was no Prince Charming, and because she was now healthy and ready to move forward in her life, she did not need a Knight-In-Shining-Armor. She wanted a man who would be her partner, someone to create a new life with.

One of Lynn's greatest gifts was her ability to teach people to play and she made a great playmate. But Knight was not looking for a playmate. Knight was a caretaker of sick people and he and his circle were committed to suffering.

Although Lynn wanted to end her relationship with Knight, she did not want him to suffer the experience of abandonment that she had gone through. Depression ultimately had her hanging out at home and not interested in much of anything but watching TV. Since Knight took care of everything there was nothing for her to do except sit and think.

She was back in her old pattern of "Lady-In-Waiting". As her resentments built, they began to argue more, he began to drink more, and the old pattern played out – he abandoned her at home and spent more time at the pub. She was the abandoned victim again!

She could have created a new life for herself but didn't. A great life is generated and Lynn was not willing to do the work for herself and there was no one around to latch on to, to ride the coat tail and rush off with, to make her life the diversion of adventure she seemed to need.

Lynn again began to stuff her emotions and feelings. Old patterns of behavior had her reacting in old ways. She lost her joy, lost interest in life, and could not see a joyful future to live into. She told me she was more concerned with protecting Knight's feelings than in honoring her own. So she stayed and became resentful and lonely. I can't tell you how many times I heard Knight 'kiddingly' say, "Women are bitches" and that's exactly what Lynn was becoming. She was now living into Knight's belief system and he was living into hers. Men abandon her. I watched the disintegration of their relationship knowing they were both playing out old patterns, unable to stop the process.

Because of what the doctor said, she constantly had her hands on her abdomen where the surgery had been and as she fed the area with negative energy it kept growing. She was now taking pain medication, lying in bed watching TV, and had moved into a state of depression focusing only on what was not working.

Lynn, with all she had learned about creating a worthwhile future and embracing positivity and health, refused to do the work necessary to change her behavior.

It was easier to focus on what was wrong with her body and worry about the cancer returning and this became her pattern, her new addiction. She could not get herself to shift her thoughts. She had trapped herself, saw no way out, and became resigned. She said her relationship with Knight was pretty good, that it was enough, and that she didn't miss the exciting lifestyle she had had with the Prince.

I begged her to leave this environment and we discussed her going to Florida where she owned a home and our mother and eldest sister lived. She agreed it was a good idea but not wanting to hurt Knight, she decided to wait until after the holidays. I saw a glimmer of light in her eyes. She had hope!

She planned a wonderful holiday party, and her joy began to return. Everyone would be invited, including Prince Charming and his woman. This would be a black tie event. This is what she enjoyed. She loved being the princess, and everyone was coming to her ball!

Lynn told Knight she would be leaving after the holidays, but he refused to acknowledge her ending of the relationship, promising he would join her in Florida at a later date.

Lynn was trying to break out of this pattern, start a new life for herself and restore her diminished health. She saw what she had done, how she had created her present conditions, and was determined to make the course corrections necessary to heal. She was receiving daily distance healings from Wayne and me, as well as occasional hands-on healings.

She stopped drinking alcohol and hanging with the illness group. She spent more time alone or with me and family. She avoided being at Knight's home as much as possible but would not leave permanently until after the holidays. She changed her diet and focused on preparing the house for the party which was a great success.

In January, Lynn and I packed her car and left for Florida where she had a part-time, temporary job, working with me. For the next two months we would be working a two weeks on, two weeks off schedule as companions. We would be together and able to focus on her physical restoration. Every word that came out of her mouth, and every thought that she thought, was going to have to be monitored and corrected.

I had no idea how compromised her condition was until we were alone. The ride to Florida that used to take us 24 hours, took three days. She was not able to drive her own car because she was so uncomfortable she could not be in one position for more than a few minutes. Her skin was so sensitive we had to stop to buy pillows so she could place them under and around her body. She was eating little, if anything. She had kept up a façade for the party and her friends but once on the road, the truth of her condition was evident.

During our first two weeks together, like a broken record, I interrupted Lynn's conversations to help break her addictive thought and behavior patterns. She was going to have to find all the reasons for living that she could and visualize, pretending until it becomes real, her body as healed, with every cell in perfect working order and all systems fully functioning. I was quite insistent, demanding that she use her skills and knowledge to heal herself.

Suddenly, there was a ringing in my ear. I laughed and said, "Hold on, God is calling," which is what we learned in a seminar long ago and have paid attention to ever since. The thought was gentle but firm, and I heard loud and clear, "Let her be. Leave her alone. This is not for you to do. She has to find her own reasons to live." I was surprised, but understood. I thought back to the voice, making a static sound, "You're breaking up. I can't hear you."

But I did hear and told Lynn. I was there for support only. She would have to do this on her own.

After completing our first two weeks of work, we drove two hours to her house. She was no longer in constant pain and was able to stop taking the over-the-counter painkillers. She was starting to eat better, and we found a Chinese doctor/ herbalist/acupuncturist, who she trusted. He said the original blockage was never addressed and gave us herbs to brew into a medicinal tea to clean the colon and dissolve the blockage. But even with all of this she would not release the addictive pattern of needing to be rescued. Whenever I left her alone she continued to call Knight as well as Prince. Her addiction was that strong.

Although she seemed to be improving, she was not strong enough to return to work so Mom and Cricket came to care for her during my absence. The day after I left, her three sons and our nephew, Justin, arrived from Connecticut.

Three days after returning to work, while having breakfast, I saw a beautiful orange butterfly outside the window. My first thought was "Lynn, get back in your body!" Shortly after this, Cricket called to tell me that Lynn was in the hospital - on life support. My friend and co-worker, Eileen Giuliani, was with me when I received the call.

I was extremely upset and angry so we went outside and sat at the poolside table to talk. I could feel Lynn with us and kept gesturing toward an empty chair, pointing and speaking as if she were sitting there. I demanded she return to her body and heal it!

Within short order I left for the hospital which was two hours away. However, I wasn't alone. I was driving Lynn's car and she was with me the entire trip.

When we drove to Florida, the map light on the passenger side of her car would not work. Now, I could not shut it off and it lit up the passenger seat the entire time. I don't usually hear voices but there was clearly a conversation happening. I was speaking out loud to the empty lighted seat, and Lynn was answering in my mind.

When I arrived at the hospital, Mom, Cricket and her son Richard, Lynn's three sons, and Justin, were already there and waiting for my consent to take her off life support. I discovered I was her medical power of attorney, along with her three sons. I was told she was coherent and that I could speak to her but that she had already indicated she wanted the breathing tube out of her throat and they were waiting for my approval. Of course she wanted the tube out, who wouldn't?

On my ride to the hospital, I had spoken with Wayne who was sending continuous distance healings, and he reminded me that when Lynnie did her healings, she always recommended the family allow up to two days of life support to give the person the opportunity to choose life or death. I was determined that Lynn have that choice and told them so.

I spoke to Lynn and rephrased the question. With the doctor present, she nodded that she wanted the 48 hours and understood that the tube would remain in her throat during that time.

For the next 24 hours, the hospital did everything it could to support Lynn's physical body. During this time, she mostly slept but when she would wake up, she was coherent enough to listen to, and understand, the many calls she received from family members and friends. There was only love present.

Wayne continued to send distance healings.

WAYNE

When I focused on Lynnie in the hospital I saw her standing behind a purple veil and smiling, with a group of angels in front protecting her. Later, during this same healing, I saw Lynnie in a white dress, smiling and absolutely aglow. The vision was as clear as if I was watching TV. In each vision, Lynnie appeared happy and it felt as if things were going exactly the way they were meant to be. Even though she was showing me that she was happy and all was going well, my intent was still to heal her completely and have her stay with us.

I contacted Sheri Perbeck and requested her help. As well as being a fabulous healer, Sheri has amazing psychic abilities, and I was confident she would be able to connect to Lynnie's spirit. Because the information came to her in bits and pieces, I have provided excerpts from her reading which are most informative to our readers:

12:07 PM - Lynn is in the light, out of body. Family making the decision to pull plug. Lynn's waiting for them. They've known it's her time to go. Her father's waiting in the light for her. I see Lynn writing letters to family members explaining why she wanted to leave. They'll find them. She knew it was coming, almost like she had control for this time to come. She handed me an amethyst stone passing on healing abilities. More will come from this. Garden and white picket fence – wants to go "home" - feels she will be more helpful from there. Running stream there, very peaceful to her and beautiful. Tell her daughter-in-law she'll meet her there in Spirit when she sleeps and will explain things to her. Son trying to have a baby. Watch for rainbow. She lost her passion a long time ago, must go home. She felt she couldn't be herself, ever. Lynn is waiting for everyone to say their goodbyes and feels she can be more helpful from the other side. Lynn is standing before the light, waiting to cross. There is someone special there, waiting for her."

KATHY

Twenty-four hours later, there was absolutely no improvement in any of Lynn's bodily functions, and in fact, her condition was getting worse. There was nothing else the doctors could do so we chose to take her off life support. We were asked to leave the room while they gave her an injection of morphine and removed the breathing tube. After this procedure, we were allowed to return and found Lynn smiling and alert. When asked how she was feeling, Lynn replied, "I feel great!" It was a gift that she had the opportunity to speak with each of us before she left, including Wayne:

I was blessed to have Kathy hold her cell phone to Lynnie's ear so that I could speak to her. Aside from telling Lynnie how much I loved her, I tried to convince her to stay for everyone that loved her. However, my plea was for us and not what Lynnie wanted.

I then proceeded to send her the distance healing of my life. I saw colors that I cannot even describe. They were magnificent. Toward the end, I saw Lynnie through a beautiful forest green spectrum, and she was dancing. The long dress she was wearing was flying around as she swirled to the music that I could not hear. Shortly after this vision, I saw a beautiful orange monarch butterfly flutter through my vision. I realized later, after Kathy told me that she was gone, that this was Lynnie, telling me that she was free.

As she dosed off and her life forced diminished, she was extremely peaceful. When I asked her if she could see the light, she smiled and nodded. I told her to look for Daddy, that Sheri said he was there to meet her. She smiled again. I told her that we would all be fine and would take care of each other and that she could go home.

———

Lynn did not have a fear of dying or death.[25] We had spoken of this many times throughout our lives. In her early twenties Lynn had a miscarriage, hemorrhaged and almost died. She experienced the peace of dying, the absence of fear and the love that awaited her on the other side. She told me how surprised she had been at the lack of attachment she had felt to those she was leaving behind - not that she did not love and care for her children, husband and family - on the contrary, she felt only love for them. She explained that there was no suffering in dying; only light and love to move towards. She knew her loved ones would be fine without her.

However, she chose not to leave at that time. In fact, the experience brought a new awareness to her life and how she raised her children from that day forward. She allowed them, and herself, a greater freedom than she had prior to her

---

25   Anita Moorjani, *Dying To Be Me,* (Hay House, Inc., 2012)

near-death-experience. Instead, she encouraged them to embrace life fully, free from the fear of death.

Lynn had other close encounters with death throughout her years, including the exit point she bypassed when her intestine ruptured. Now, she had been given another exit opportunity, and this time she took it.

Some people live a hundred years in fear and never really live. For the fifty-seven years of this lifetime, Lynn really lived her life. She enjoyed each day and touched many lives. There is a saying we both loved and which describes her outlook on life:

"Life is not about arriving at the grave in a well preserved suit. Life is about sliding in sideways, wine in one hand, chocolate in the other, totally worn out, yelling holy shit, what a ride!"

Cricket and I stayed in the room for a while longer after everyone else left. It felt strange to just leave Lynn's body there and not have her going with us. We also knew that once we left the room we would never see her physical body again. After saying a prayer, we looked at each other and Cricket said, "She's gone. There's an empty space between us."

Lynn was the sister between us, the second born of seven children. There had never been a space between Cricket and me before. It felt very odd and empty, like something was missing. It also confirmed that Lynn was really gone and there was no point in sitting there any longer looking at the vehicle she had occupied. She was free.

Our family returned to Lynn's home to discuss funeral arrangements. It was strange to see all of her belongings left behind. Like her purse. What do you do with a person's purse? You just stare at it, that's what you do. Lynn came into this world with nothing and took nothing with her when she left. I wondered what all the attachment to stuff is really about. I wished she hadn't left.

Lynn's sons knew her wishes. Lynn would be cremated and a celebration of her life would be held in Connecticut three weeks later. All of Lynn's family, friends and fellow healers were notified.

A few days later I returned to work. Eileen and I were in the kitchen when Lynn's daughter-in-law, Robyn, called to discuss the details of the memorial service. Although Eileen and Lynn had met on several occasions, they barely knew each other, so it was somewhat shocking when Eileen started interjecting her opinions and comments about what we were discussing without the benefit of hearing what Robyn was saying.

Robyn suggested having the luncheon at the local pub that Lynn frequented with Knight. Eileen burst out, "No! No! It's too dark! She doesn't want it there!"

Eileen had no idea of what or where we were talking about because she was not on the phone with us, was not from Connecticut and has never been to the place we were discussing. She actually had no idea what was going on or why she was reacting. I looked at Eileen with surprise and said to Robyn, "I don't think that will work. What else do you have?" watching Eileen as I said it. Robyn said we could go to the restaurant down by the lake where we use to go for the fireworks. Although Eileen could not hear Robyn speaking, she burst out, "No! No! It's too far, plus she doesn't like it there!" Eileen continued to comment emphatically throughout the conversation, in spite of the fact that she could not hear what we were talking about. This behavior was extremely out of character for Eileen.

Laughingly, I said to Robyn, "Hold on. I think Lynn is here."

Eileen asked me, "What's happening? I don't know what I'm saying or why I'm saying this stuff, but I feel it. It's like I'm saying things that I'm not even thinking. I feel really strange. How do I know to say these things? I feel really agitated inside, adamant. I don't even know what I'm talking about, but I know it's too dark and too far."

I knew and explained, "Lynn is channeling through you. What you're feeling is the intensity of her emotions and what you're speaking are her thoughts. As long as she's here, would you mind if I ask her a few questions?"

Eileen responded, "I guess so." Then she said, "More space. Open."

I suggested, "How about having it at the Southbury Fire House?"

Eileen was quiet for a few seconds and then said it would be okay. I asked her how she knew this, and Eileen said because she felt calm so Lynn was obviously okay with it.

Robyn said she would check into the Fire House, adding that there would probably be 125 people, and her girlfriend would be catering the event.

Eileen burst out, "No! She wants Cathy to cater it. Cathy's her friend, and she wants to give back to her." Eileen then asked, "Who's Cathy?"

I relayed to Robyn what "Lynn" said, to which she replied as if she was speaking directly to Lynn, "Too bad, you're not here so you don't get to say. You shouldn't have left if you wanted any input."

Eileen yelled, "It's my funeral, and it's my money. I want who I want!"

Robyn stated, "I'm going to use who I want. Too bad."

Then Lynn jumped into me and I said to Robyn, in an extremely forceful voice, "It's my money! It's my funeral! I want it catered by Cathy!"

Robyn responded, "We'll let Frankie and Jesse decide." (Lynn's sons)

"Lynn" said, "Fine!"

Robyn said, "Fine!"

We both hung up. Lynn's energy left me.

Eileen looked bewildered, "What just happened?"

"Lynn's channeling through you, and me too, it seems. Is this your first time?" To which she replied, "Well, yes."

"Would you mind if I asked her a few more questions?"

"Sure, but this is very strange."

I asked specific questions regarding locations for the venue as well as what she would want there. Depending on Eileen's internal state, agitated or calm, I was able to write down specific details and forwarded them to Robyn.

The firehouse or some other place that has an open floor plan so that everyone can be together in the same room; close proximity to the funeral home; food; wine; music; dancing. "Lynn" was adamant about where *not* to have it and also that *her* friend should be the one to provide the catering services.

After a while, Eileen calmed inside and said, "I think she's gone."

We talked about what had happened, how it had felt and the fact that this was the first time anything like this had happened to her. She felt exhausted.

The next morning, Eileen entered the kitchen exclaiming, "So there I am, brushing my hair, and I start saying 'It's MY funeral, and I want it my way!' and she's [Lynn] feeling really upset!"

A couple of hours later, Eileen phoned me from her car in an agitated state. "Look, I don't know what you need to do, but you've got to convince people to do what I am saying because your sister is not leaving me alone! I feel her, and she's really angry about this. Do what you have to do, but just get them to listen. This is really uncomfortable!" It was clear that Lynn still wanted control. The battle of wills was underway.

A few days later, Robyn and I spoke again. She had found a completely different place, big enough to hold everyone in the same room, open, sunny, close to the funeral home, and the restaurant would provide the food so there was no need to have it catered. It was perfect. Everyone was in agreement and Eileen was left in peace, until the funeral, that is.

Lynn's body was cremated in Florida and the remains were being transported to Connecticut by Lynn's sons who were driving her car north. While on the road they called to see how I was doing. I asked them where their mother's ashes were and they said, "In the back." Eileen blurted out, "It's too dark." I then asked, "Where in the back." They laughed and said, "In the trunk." Eileen heard this and it was as if a switch had been turned on, "Get me out of there!" She yelled. "Tell them to put me in the front!"

Her sons had gotten used to the idea of Eileen channeling Lynn so they stopped the car, put the urn up front, and Eileen immediately calmed down. The rest of the journey was peaceful.

At the funeral home, photo boards of Lynn's life were displayed along the halls. The place was packed and there was a line out the door and around the building. About a half hour before the memorial service began, Eileen found her way in through a side entrance, bypassed the line of people waiting to pay their respects, came up to me where I was standing in the receiving line, and furiously whispered in my ear, "What the f--k is that picture doing there? Get rid of it!"

I was stunned. "What picture?"

"She doesn't want a photo of him there. Take it away. Get rid of it." Eileen knows how to conduct herself so this behavior was very unlike her.

I had no idea what she was talking about. I never even saw the pictures. There were so many people already talking to me when I arrived that I just headed to the front of the room where my family was. Unbeknownst to me, there was an additional photo of Lynn and Knight on the table at the front of the room where Lynn's memorial photo was.

Eileen [Lynn] was livid. "The one on the table right there," she hissed. "Get that damn thing out of here. Take it away!" Eileen sounded just like Lynn. "Now! Out!" Eileen had never seen Knight, had no idea what he looked like and wouldn't be able to pick him out of a crowd under any circumstances.

I looked at her as if she were crazy. "I can't. We're in the middle of your funeral!" There were people lined up, out the door with a forty-five minute wait, and the room was already full. "You [Lynn] left the impression that you two were still together. This is the result! The picture is going to have to stay. Now go sit down."

Eileen angrily spat out, "Go f—k yourself!" Then immediately added, snapping out of it, "Oh my God, would she talk to you this way? She's furious."

"I bet she is," I replied.

Following the memorial service, we attended the luncheon to celebrate Lynn's life. Eileen, who knew hardly anyone, went up to Heather, the girlfriend of Lynn's son, Jesse, and asked, "Are you pregnant?"

Heather was stunned that someone she had never set eyes on would ask such a thing.

"No." she replied.

Four months later, Heather and Jesse announced they were having a child. When I called to congratulate them, Heather told me that the day after the funeral she went for her regular check up and found out she was pregnant. She also told me about her strange encounter with Eileen whom she did not know. At the time Eileen had asked her, she had no idea that she was pregnant. The baby was due December 8, nine months after Lynn's crossing.

Eileen, who has the utmost respect for a person's privacy, has no recollection whatsoever of this incident and is appalled that she said it. Eileen's psychic connection to Lynn stopped after the luncheon. However, others continued to have experiences...

It was the family's desire to create a "Book of Lynn" for her grandchildren - the ones already born and the ones yet to be, so that they would know who she was. We asked people to send their stories of how Lynn touched their lives.

Lisa wrote: Lynn has blessed me with her laughter and also let me know that the work she will do from the other side is as important, if not more so than when she was here. Today when I was getting ready for the day, she told me turquoise will be the indicator to let me know she is around. Without even realizing it, about a half hour later I got dressed. It wasn't until later in the day when I was doing a healing on a client that I realized I had put on a turquoise shirt. Oh, how I love and miss my friend.

Michele wrote: I connected with her last night. I didn't see her in any form. It was more of a swirling of energy with different colors. It felt like she was waving her hands in front of my face while I was sleeping. It was so gentle and comforting. I am so thankful for that experience.

Robyn wrote: The night Lynn passed away I lay down and cried, for my husband, my children, my brothers-in-law, and for everyone who would no longer get the experience that was Lynn. That night I dreamt I was in a grocery store and was sitting on a bed in the middle of the aisle that was filled with miscellaneous merchandise. Lynn came around the corner with her friend Kathy Kukel and her sister Kathy close behind. Lynn sat down next to me on the bed and the following conversation ensued. (Lynn) "I don't have long, I can't stay" (Me) "I know, but I am sad." At this point I could feel my bottom lip protrude like a small child's, but I did not cry. (Lynn) "They have to let me go, they are keeping me earthbound, I need to just be free." While she said this she turned and looked at Kathy and Kathy. She then got up off the bed and, without look-ing back, walked away. Kathy, her sister, went running after her but couldn't catch her. And she was gone. --- Four months later, I was standing in my kitchen and I saw Lynn walk through my sitting room on the way to the living room. I knew it was her; she was wearing a long white dress, no shoes, and I could see her beautiful hair. I immediately text messaged Kathy, her sister, thinking Kathy's oldest son and his wife had given birth to their first child. I figured Lynn and Kathy were so close when Lynn had been alive that she would want to show her presence on this exciting day. Kathy texted me back saying that they had not had the baby. I thought maybe Lynn was just saying, "Hi." The next day I felt her again. I felt she was there but could not see her. That evening I found out that her youngest son had overdosed, but that he was okay and in the hospital. I now believe that she was earthbound to block her son from moving on.

When a person is alive, and we can see and feel them, that is their physical presence. When a person dies and their spirit leaves the body, their spirit and all of its associated energy exists forever. That person's energy can be felt if we remain still and allow it to be experienced. This extremely powerful energy, of the person who is no longer in physical form, can be shared by loved ones, thus greatly enhancing their lives.

COMMENTS BY WAYNE: Long before I knew anything about energy healings, my father, Edward Gabari, passed away. I was very sad. However, shortly thereafter, I could feel his energy just as if he was sitting on my left shoulder, the shoulder that represents trust. I felt more powerful, focused, and stronger, than I had ever felt in my life. I could feel his presence, and his energy has been with me ever since. It has made me a better person.

COMMENTS BY KATHY: I also experienced this type of phenomenon on more than one occasion. First with my friend, Tucker, who I wrote about earlier, and many years later, the brother of my friend Jack, who came to me through the channeling of my friend Phyllis. And there were other times that I did not write about. We really are all con-nected, regardless of which side of the veil one is on.

Since Lynn's death, I often talk to her as if she is still here. I know that she can hear me, even if there is no response. It was during one of these moments that I was telling her how much I missed her, and although I know she is with me, I still wished I could see her, except for that veil...

I immediately heard her in my head, "There's only a veil because you think there's a veil." We both laughed, and I thought back to her, "Yeah, I'm working on that!"

"... for life is eternal,
and love is immortal,
and death is only a horizon,
and a horizon is nothing save the limit of our sight."

– Rossiter W. Raymond

CHAPTER 20

Courage to Choose

There are many natural ways to heal even the most advanced of cancers. This story, told in her own words, is a profile in courage of a petite, 110-pound woman named Patt Dooley:

In 2001, while going through menopause, I started to bleed more heavily than usual and went to see my gynecologist. She examined me, found a lump in my left breast and suggested a mammogram. Since I have always had dense, lumpy breasts, this finding was not a concern for me. Right up front, I told her that if it was cancer I would be seeking alternative treatments.

Based on the findings of the mammogram I was sent to an oncologist who examined me and subsequently performed a needle biopsy. Using a local anesthetic, I remained fully awake the entire time. Before I let the doctor proceed, I asked her to please be careful taking samples so as not to spread any cells because if it turned out to be cancer, I had no intention of doing conventional treatments. During the biopsy five samples were taken from different areas of my breast. I told them to stop twisting the tool they were using for fear of spreading any cancer cells.

COMMENTS BY KATHY: Patt's 'lack of concern' versus the doctor's 'fearful concern' is of great interest to me. In quantum physics, there is a particle vs wave theory.[26] Experimenters revealed that the greater the amount of watching, the greater the observer's influence on what actually takes place.

The longer a person gives their focused attention to a thing, the greater the change to the thing. The thing can be cancer, a tumor, a fibroid, or the joy of money in your pocket or the lack of money in your pocket, or the love in your life, or the lack of love in your life. The law of attraction is activated and you get more of what you focus your attention, or energy, on.

What if a person, who is afraid of getting cancer, goes to their doctor for a check-up and that doctor goes looking for a cancer cell? However miniscule that cell may be, there is a pretty good chance that doctor will find a cancer cell. Now they are both focused on the one cancer cell and are fearful of it. What if that fear then grows the number of cancer cells?

What if cancer cells are actually "fear cells"?

I wonder how the results would have turned out had everyone been focused on the gazillion healthy cells and Patt was given those results instead? "You have a gazillion healthy cells — now go about your business, take care of yourself, forgive yourself and others, say wonderful and loving things to yourself and everyone you come in contact with." What if they said that to her instead?

---

26   *Quantum Physics Theory: Particle vs Wave*, (ScienceDaily, Feb. 27, 1998)
http://www.sciencedaily.com/releases/1998/02/980227055013.htm

On Friday, April 6th, the radiologist called.

"Is this Patricia Dooley?"

"Yes."

"I'm sorry. The biopsy revealed it was malignant. You do have cancer, and we have scheduled you for surgery on Monday."

"Thank you very much, but like I told you before, I am definitely not doing surgery or chemo. I am seeking alternative methods."

She then quoted statistics and told me that some of her patients had tried that route without success and had either died or returned for the traditional medical treatments.

Although I understood her concern, these fear tactics did not change my mind. In fact, I felt a strong voice inside me say, "Stick to your guns!"

I was alone when I received this dreaded news. I hung up the phone and sank to the floor in despair, where my six loving dogs rallied around me as I cried.

Upon further urging, I went back to the oncologist where he performed an examination and said, "Do you understand how serious this is? You have cancer in your breast that has spread to the lymph nodes. The tumor must be surgically removed and you must undergo chemo, followed by radiation. You have no chance of surviving without these treatments."

This was delivered as a death sentence.

It was during these weeks of testing that I had a flashback and remembered a seminar I attended two years earlier at our local library. The topic was *Alternative Healing Methods*. The doctor spoke about how our immune system can break down by eating unhealthy foods, stress, chemicals, and such. I was so impressed with her speech that I kept her name and all of her contact information.

I knew this was the way for me to go, so when the oncologist delivered his statement regarding the surgery, chemo and radiation, I emphatically said, "No way!"

When I finally pulled myself together, I scheduled an appointment with the natural MD to discuss my options. I was greeted with a big smile, a hug, and soft healing music. The atmosphere was more like a spa than a doctor's office, and I felt calm just being there. My husband, Tom, and I met with her for three hours reviewing all available natural treatments. It was during this meeting that the doctor asked me what had been going on in my life in the past few years. Were there any traumatic events? "Stress can play a big part in people getting a disease."

I told her, "I watched my mother develop Alzheimer's disease when she was only 51, and she spent the rest of her life in different nursing homes until she died at the age of 72. Also, just last year, I chose to close my hair salon that I had worked so hard to establish and which had flourished for 15 years. I was forced to close because my two best friends, who were my hairdressers, both moved out of state at the same time, and I was unable to find qualified replacements."

COMMENTS BY KATHY: *In addition to her mother moving further and further out of reach, the "feeling" of abandonment and betrayal by her two best friends and ultimately the loss of her business, took a toll on Patt and created a very deep hurt. She lost her connections. (Deep, long standing hurt and/or resentment = cancer)*

The doctor explained each option and said, "Like all treatments, nothing is guaranteed, however, if you follow this protocol, you have a very high chance of beating it." She explained that, "Cancer is not about surgically removing body parts. Cancer is nothing more than an immune system breakdown. When we physically and mentally change the chemistry of the body back to its natural state, the cancer will not survive in the body."

This was the first time that I had ever heard of an MD spending three hours with a patient and discussing potential treatments. I felt comfortable with this doctor and hopeful for a full recovery. The main reason was that she gave me *hope.* She was now going to help me build up my immune system to fight the cancer. This made complete sense, as opposed to my other options: surgery and poisoning by chemo and radiation, all of which would destroy my immune system.

I prayed to God to give me signs that I was doing the right thing.

Although there was a part of me that was fearful of not following doctor's orders, there was a much greater part of me that believed my body had the power to heal itself given the proper tools. Over the years, I had read many books, articles, and scanned the internet about information regarding nutritional supplements and herbs, as well as other healing modalities.

As a follow-up, the oncologist sent me a letter that explained what he had done, and that I was refusing all surgery and further treatments. The letter stated:

"I am writing with regards to your visit to my office on April 4, 2001. Due to the highly suspicious nature of the mass in your left breast, my recommendation was a core biopsy for a definitive diagnosis. This was done at the XYZ hospital with Dr. ABC that same day and the pathology report confirmed my suspicion of

a carcinoma. You were informed of the diagnosis. To my knowledge, you have opted to seek another type of treatment. I cannot stress to you the importance of surgery for the treatment of your disease. Please either follow-up with myself or another physician.

I started receiving phone calls from my gynecologist imploring me to have the surgery and follow-up treatments. I told her, "No." However, she did not take no for an answer and did everything she could to convince me to go for treatment. I eventually went to see her. She sat me down and asked when I was starting treatment. I told her I was seeing a natural MD and following her plan. She didn't even ask what treatments I would receive. Instead, she wanted the name of the natural MD so that she could report her. She kept repeating that I was being irrational and that conventional treatments were FDA approved and what I was pursuing was quackery. She stated that "alternative was not proven and was not real medicine." She convinced me to visit a cancer support group. The main focus of this visit was for me to see how people with cancer are living and healing after undergoing chemo and radiation treatments. As I left her office, I had a surge of energy and was determined to prove them wrong!

I started the alternative treatments at the doctor's office which required a few hours each day:

- Intravenous vitamin/nutritional supplements three times a week
- Neuro-Bio Feedback – geared to make the brain think more positively
- Energy healings to balance my body
- Sauna treatments to detox my body
- Lymph massage treatments to remove toxins

At home treatments:

- Numerous additional oral supplements and herbs
- Daily detox with coffee enemas
- Nightly self-hypnosis tapes to enhance the immune system
- Established controlled diet stressing:
  - Hormone and antibiotic free meats - no red meat (causes inflammation) and limited quantities of chicken
  - Abundance of organic vegetables and raw juices

- No shellfish. (Shellfish are scavengers/bottom feeders)
- Only wild caught fish (farm raised are given antibiotics and salmon are injected with color)
- No sugar (cancer thrives on sugar) limited organic fruits
- No sugar substitutes (toxic)
- Stevia was permitted (natural sweetener)

I went with a friend to visit the cancer support group. We had no idea what to expect. Upon entering the room and looking around, I immediately felt a wave of despair and sorrow permeating from everyone. I scanned the faces of these cancer survivors and was appalled at what I saw. Not one of them appeared healthy. In fact, each of them had one or more of the following illness traits: no eyebrows, yellow skin, or baldness, although some wore bandanas to hide this. To me, the majority of these survivors just looked plain sick.

I told the group that I too had been diagnosed with cancer but was not undergoing surgery. Instead, I was pursuing alternative medicine. Immediately, their heads turned to look at one another, and one person said, "Oh my God, don't risk your life like that. You're wasting precious time." It was clear by the looks on their faces that this group feared, did not understand, or was encouraged to avoid alternative treatments. As we left, with tears in my eyes, I told my friend, "This place is not for me. Even if I die, I will not die like this!" Right then and there, I made a pact with myself that even if it was my last treatment option on earth, I would not have chemo.

Now, more than ever, I was sure I had made the right choice.

Throughout my first few weeks of alternative treatments I was in awe. Never did I mentally or physically feel as if I had cancer. Instead, I was amazed at how much I was learning and was inspired by the levels of compassion and knowledge of my alternative doctor. I couldn't help but wonder how she possessed all this great information about treating the immune system while the other doctors were wearing blinders.

During the first week, the doctor performed a test by having me put my feet into a detox liquid. The results showed I had chemical toxicity in my body. I was not surprised as I had been a nail technician and salon owner and worked with chemicals every day for twenty years.

While I was receiving intravenous vitamin therapy, I would look around the room and observe the friendliness of the patients around me. We had to ask each other why we were here because none of us looked sick. I saw multiple sclerosis patients improving, someone with a large stomach tumor that was now shrinking, heart dis-ease patients who were told they needed bypass surgery were instead having their arteries naturally cleaned, and the list goes on. We all had our ups and downs in learning how to take the needed vitamins and adjusting our diets, but the feeling was unanimous - we would have a better outcome by participating in this natural healing process.

After the first month, my doctor sent me for a cancer blood test to see how the treatments were working. The results showed that the numbers were going down! We knew we were on the right track.

At the time I began the alternative treatments, I was reading a Chinese book about self healing. There was a chapter pertaining to the *female deer exercise* teaching how to rub the breasts to prevent tumors and cure breast cancer. While reading that chapter I had an overwhelming urge to look outside my window. I could not believe my eyes. Feeding on the grass was a doe covered from head to hoof with large tumors. My husband, Tom, and I could not understand how she could live with so many tumors. From that day on, we saw her every day.

I took this as a sign from God. If this deer could live with such massive tumors, then so could I. My prayers had been answered. I had asked for a sign that I had selected the right treatments. Now I felt completely confident with my choices.

Throughout this ordeal, one thing that brought me comfort was a heart-shaped crystal necklace that I cherished and wore every day. One morning, I dropped it and a large piece broke off the left side. I was very upset about this loss and did not realize what it symbolized. As I was driving to my doctor, I had an itch on my left breast and as I went to scratch it, I noticed the lump was gone! Upon arriving at the doctor's office, I was very excited and asked her to check it right away. She could not feel the tumor either.

On 9/11 of 2001, the day the World Trade Center was attacked, I went for blood work to confirm that the cancer was gone. The tests came back - negative!

I was cured! In less than six months, the cancer was gone!

Throughout the period that I was in treatment, my husband and I saw that deer every day and she had become a comfort to us. Amazingly, after receiving the report that I was cancer free, we never saw her again. As for the crystal, both my doctor and I believe that its breaking was a sign that the cancer was gone.

For the next six months, I continued the protocol to insure that everything stayed within the normal range. The alternative treatments were very expensive, but I was cancer free, and for me that was priceless!

When we tried to recoup our expenses from the insurance company, we were told they would pay only if I had chemo. "Since you are doing alternative, we will not pay."

I said, "Even if it worked, you won't pay?"

"No."

We even went so far as to call politicians, who were supposed to be representing our best interests, and they refused to call back. However, the end result was clear – I was cancer free.

A year later, I attended a cancer support meeting at the local hospital. One of the women in attendance was a recovering cancer patient from the original cancer support group meeting I visited. She immediately recognized me and said, "We all thought that you would be dead within a few months!" She was shocked at how healthy I looked. I told her that I maintained this healthy look throughout my treatments and although I had lost a few pounds because of the strict diet, I never lost my hair and never felt sick. She, on the other hand, was still undergoing chemo treatments, still had the same bandana around her head, had no hair, and looked terribly ill.

I told her that my alternative doctor tried calling the support group after I shared with her the experience of my visit. She wanted to give a talk on how nutritionals can be used along with chemo to minimize the side effects of medical treatments. No one from the group ever returned her calls.

Two years later, I received a return-receipt-requested letter from my gynecologist requesting that I make an appointment for a check-up. I believe she probably thought I was dead and if the letter came back she could close my file.

I made an appointment because I was excited with anticipation about seeing her reaction when she saw me alive. As she entered the room, she looked at me as if she had seen a ghost. She made no remark, and I was compelled to ask, "Don't you want to know what I've been doing?"

I told her that I had pursued alternative treatments and that the cancer was gone. She asked if she could examine me, and I agreed. Feeling an area of my left breast, she insisted that she could still feel something. To this I responded, "Doctor, you're not even feeling in the place where the tumors were."

I knew there was nothing there because I had recently completed a thermography test which can detect cancer years before a tumor appears. In addition, my blood work for all cancer tests came back normal. The doctor had little else to say and appeared very uneasy dealing with me. After all, she had insisted that I would be dead if I did not have my breast removed with follow-up treatments of chemo and radiation. I actually felt sorry for her because she was so closed-minded. Even though she saw me standing there as living proof that natural treatments can work, she never admitted that, based on everything she knew as a doctor, this was a miracle! She never showed any excitement or even expressed any elation about my being cured. It is my feeling that she was either confused by what she saw or disappointed at being wrong.

Four years after my original diagnosis, I had swelling under my left armpit. My alternative doctor was out of the country and I got frightened, so I went to a medical doctor who asked, "Why are you here?"

I told her about the swelling and about my previous history of having breast cancer and treating it through alternative medicine. She said, "This is impossible. You probably have cancer throughout your entire body. This is in your lymph nodes. I am calling a surgeon for you to see immediately!"

Shaking like a leaf, I drove the two miles to visit the surgeon.

I reiterated my medical history while he scratched his head, examined me, and read me the riot act about my choices. With my alternative doctor out of the country, I succumbed to the pressure and fear and agreed to have the swollen lymph nodes removed.

Before the surgery, I brought my mammograms to this surgeon so he could see the original large tumors in my breast and the report that had shown the few lymph nodes that were involved.

After the surgery, the lymph nodes were tested, and it showed a necrosis, which means "dead tissue" and in this case, dead cancer cells.

Upon completion of his final examination, I wanted his opinion on how the large tumor had disappeared, as he could see that I had never had surgery on the breast. Also, I wanted to know his opinion on what had killed the cancer in my lymph nodes. He believed that cancer doesn't disappear by itself. He had no explanation. He just shrugged his shoulders and smiled.

He then told me that his brother who lives in India practices alternative medicine and treats all diseases, including cancer, by natural methods, but he never believed that it could be done. I stood up, shook his hand, and said, "Well now you can tell him that you had a patient who received natural medicine and you took out lymph nodes that contained dead cancer cells. Then you can ask him to explain it to you." He said that he would.

He still insisted that I should take chemo because, "Once you have surgery, it is important to make sure that nothing is left behind."

I said, "No thank you. I'll take my chances." Again he smiled. He was a nice doctor. Ironically, the insurance company covered the entire surgery and associated tests. Even though the surgery proved to be unnecessary, the costs were covered without question because they fell within their model.

The intravenous, vitamin/nutritional therapy lasted for one year. I still maintain my controlled diet and take all the associated supplements. Ten years after being diagnosed with cancer, I remain cancer free!

My message to anyone diagnosed with cancer is that whether you choose chemo or natural methods make sure that it feels right for you. Don't go against your instinct. For me, this was obviously the right choice.

COMMENTS BY WAYNE: I remember when Patt was diagnosed with cancer and she refused to undergo the traditional medical treatments. I was amazed at her courage yet skeptical that she would survive on the path that she had chosen. At that time, I knew nothing about healings and only believed what the doctors said.

As fate would have it, I was watching TV and scanning the program guide when a show caught my eye. It was a documentary about gurus and yogis from the East and how they could spiritually transport themselves thousands of miles to where people were afflicted with various maladies and cure them.

They spoke about cancer and how they would envision a tumor in a person's body and completely encapsulate that tumor in a fortress. Thus, the blood flow to the tumor would be sealed off and the tumor would be starved to death.

I thought to myself that as powerful as these people are, that they are also human beings and if they can do it, then so can I. So I would lie in bed at night and envision my spirit going to Patt, and I could see the fortress encapsulating the tumors. I did this night after night and although I cannot swear that this ritual had any impact on Patt's recovery, knowing what I know now, I feel that it definitely contributed. For some reason, I was meant to watch that show and the healings that I performed were the inaugural version of what I do today.

Of course none of this would have been possible without the courage of Patt Dooley. She battled every obstacle and intimidation thrown at her from the medical profession and insurance companies. Even when she weakened and succumbed to the pressure of the surgeon, removing the lymph nodes for testing ended up validating that the choices she had made were right for her.

Although friends and family were happy with the results, most of the medical professionals were perplexed and never asked for her documentation or gave credit to the natural treatments and there was no media coverage to bring this story to the attention of the public.

I wonder how many more miracles could be accomplished if these two groups would be open to working side-by-side.

It is important to note that as healers, it makes no difference which modality a person uses and we would never advise a person in their choice other than to be true to him/her self. Our healings are independent of any other course of treatment and we can go to areas where no physical treatment can access.

It is my dream that people suffering with cancer or dis-ease will have all options available before deciding on a course of treatment and the insurance companies will pay for the treatments they choose. This shift will not take place until the people who experience these miracles and the people who witness them with their own eyes, are willing to share their excitement.

COMMENTS BY KATHY: I loved that the deer was present for Patt throughout her entire healing process. This deer just went about her business, everyday, in peace, enjoying the simple pleasures of having a meal and providing a sense of consistency for Patt and Tom. Regardless of the tumors that had taken over her physical body, life was still good.

Perhaps the breaking of the heart shaped crystal necklace was the completion of her love of the beauty salon, and the loss it represented. Her heart had been broken, but now it was time to create something new. She was free, with her whole future ahead of her.

If you are thinking that the alternative choice would be the one for you, please don't let cost stop you. Although there was much out-of-pocket expense involved, every day there are new natural, gentle, modalities available for altering the cellular structure in one's body. Much of the healing can occur before a penny is even spent if you can open your mind to new possibilities. Start with your thoughts. First become aware of what you are thinking. Then start telling a new story...of how good you feel, of how fast you are healing. A belief is only a thought that you think, over and over, for a really long time.

Our worlds are created in thought before they are ever manifested into physical form. Look around you. Everything you see was created from someone's thought. This is also how illness and dis-ease are created, from conversations that are handed down for generations. Cancers, bad backs, diabetes, everything! First we believe it, then we see it.

If you are suffering with cancer, or any other diagnosis, and you continue to tell the story of your suffering and fear, you will perpetuate the suffering and fear, and ultimately feed the diagnosis. Basically, whatever you give your attention to, you will get more of. That's good news if it is something you like, however, if it is something you do not like, you will still draw it to you. Just like learning a new sport, or game, this takes some practice to get the hang of. Although it may feel like a lie in the beginning, as you practice telling the new story, it will begin to come true and will no longer be a lie. Look for the evidence.

Start telling your story of the way you want it to be and watch your world change!

Patt Dooley was confronted with what she was told was a certain death sentence if she did not undergo recommended medical treatments. Patt had no interest in dying. She completely changed her patterns of life and has maintained this new, healthier lifestyle for over ten years. She is completely healthy, happy, and enjoying her life.

And if there is someone in your life who has tumors, why not try to encapsulate them in a fortress and dissolve them. Who knows what might happen. Perhaps you're the one they're waiting for.

WAYNE

Successful healings can be reflected in many different ways.

I was requested to perform a healing on a middle-aged woman who had been diagnosed with terminal cancer. She had gone through all of the traditional medical cancer treatments, yet her health was declining rapidly.

When I arrived at her home she was lying on the couch surrounded by all kinds of medical apparatus. We talked for a while, and looking her right in the eye I asked if she wanted to live. She told me she did but my instinct indicated otherwise. I performed a healing that I knew was very successful and at that point, she felt significantly better.

Approximately a month later I was notified that she was in the hospital, dying of cancer, so I went to visit. When I arrived, she was alone in her room and the nurses said that she had been incoherent for the last few days. As I touched her limbs I realized that the areas from her feet to mid calves and from her fingers to mid forearms were ice cold. To me, this was an indication that her spirit was starting to cross over and leave her body.

I began a physical healing and in short order these areas became very warm as she returned to her body. She then became very lucid and was capable of holding meaningful conversations. I sat in a chair several feet from her bed and began to do a distance healing on her internal organs envisioning her body being completely cancer free. After proceeding with this work for a period of time, she turned her head, looked directly at me, smiled and said, "Thank you very much but let me go." The voice that spoke to me was not her normal voice. It did not sound anything like her.

I felt her higher spirit was in direct contact with me during this statement because her voice was strong, her eyes were clear and direct, she looked angelic, radiant and completely at peace. I immediately changed directions and refocused my energies to comply with her wishes in helping her pass.

Four hours after arriving, I left her room an altered human being.

A few days later, she passed. She was a beloved person with many friends who were extremely sad to lose her. However, I believe that the lack of support and love she felt from her family gave her nothing to live into and no other way out so she took her exit point option. Her wishes were met and she was allowed to pass in accordance with her desires. I deem this healing to be just as successful as if I had totally healed a person riddled with cancer who was able to stand up and walk out the hospital.

Cancer is one of the most feared and deadly dis-eases.

Lynn Raymond was a tremendously talented healer. She created an environment which completely cured Julie of uterine cancer after one healing. As a result of the healing, Julie saw the changes that had to be made in her life, made them, and the cancer never returned. It could not exist in the new environment that she created.

Lynn also made the changes that were necessary and got a clean bill of health from the medical community. Unfortunately, she slipped back into the same addictive patterns that had created the original cancer. Once she fed that old pattern with fear and lost her zest for life, she decided it was not worth the amount of work it would have taken to change her thoughts, change her patterns, and create a life worth living. Dying became the easy way out, especially since she had no fear of it. She knew no one dies without their permission. She chose this exit point to go home.

Patt Dooley wanted to live and believed with her whole heart and soul that she could be cured by non-invasive natural methods. She confronted her fears and the fears of others and overcame all of them and in the end, graciously encouraged the non-believers to open their minds to new possibilities. She was committed to living and today, she lives her life true to herself and her whole and complete body is proof of her beliefs.

The middle-aged woman who was diagnosed with cancer was not happy with her life and saw no viable way to change her circumstances. In spite of Wayne's best efforts and intentions for a complete cure, she was no longer interested and her spirit asked him to stop.

We believe the ultimate lesson is that each of us controls our own destiny and there is no dis-ease that cannot be cured, if a person is willing and wanting.

CHAPTER 21

An Ancient Art

The ancient art of healing is not limited by distance. A distance healing means exactly that - wherever you are, it will reach you. Distance healings differ from hands-on-healings only by the physical touch of the healer. They are just as powerful, life altering and have the same capabilities as a hands-on session. Many people who have experienced both report that the result and experience feels the same, just the feeling of being touched is missing.

KATHY

Jessica has been a client of mine for many years. Her first healing was hands-on. She was in the process of a divorce and wanted balance, clarity, and peace. The healing had such an effect on her life that she has become a long-term client.

In addition to participating in our Sunday Night Group Distance Healings, Jessica travels extensively and has received distance healings in Switzerland, Germany, Holland, California, New York, Mexico, traveling on airplanes and trains, outside meeting rooms, in hotels, and so on. I have sent her healings from

New York, Connecticut, Michigan, Wisconsin, Colorado and Florida. Wherever she is, and wherever I am, when I send her a healing, she always receives the beneficial effect and positive results of the energy. Jessica says, "Whether I see Kathy in person or receive a distance healing the results are the same."

Jessica has been participating long enough to know how to prepare herself to receive the experience as well as the benefits. Whenever possible, she schedules a time when she will be alone, quiet and fully present, allowing herself to experience the full range of energy and emotional release that may happen during a healing.

One time while Jessica was flying from New York to Peru and I was traveling from Connecticut to Florida in a moving van, at our scheduled time, I sent Jessica a healing.

When she later communicated by e-mail, she wrote, "I felt the energy coming in and my body started to shake quite a bit. Realizing the person in the airplane seat next to me had no idea what was going on, I actually had to try to control my body from moving so he would not be concerned."

On another occasion, Jessica went to Switzerland and spent several days with her estranged husband. For the first time in a long time they were enjoying each other's company and Jessica began rekindling ideas about the possibility of getting back together. However, their old behaviors surfaced, things turned sour and any chance of reconciliation was lost. This was a devastating blow to her emotional well-being.

Jessica was distraught. She was so hurt, confused and depressed that she did not think she would be able to recover on her own.

I called Kathy for a telephone consultation and long distance healing. That healing was the most intense session I ever experienced. As I lay on my back, I felt a huge wave of energy throughout my body. My hands began hitting the bed. My body was jumping up and down. My lower body was bouncing. My upper chest was heaving and energy was shooting into my legs and hips. This continued for about twenty minutes.

Immediately after the healing, I was totally calm. I had a new rejuvenated energy and all emotional pain was gone. Instead of remaining in pain, I felt as if I had a course correction in my life.

The next morning I awoke with a new lease on life. I maintained this feeling until the next time I had an upset with my husband. I still loved him, but it was very difficult to go through the divorce and handle his mood swings.

Because of Jessica's previous experience with the healing energies, she allowed herself the freedom to emotionally and physically express the complete release of pent up energy that was trapped within her body.

From my perspective of the healing, and in my mind's eye, there was a masculine energy holding her down which I tried to forcefully peel off. It was as if there was a shadow form of energy lying on top of her weighing her down. It would not leave, and it would not release its hold on her. Forcefully removing it was not working so instead, I softened my energy and increased my level of vibration.

From this softer, higher vibration, I had a new perspective and realized the energy was trying to help her. I gently explained that she no longer needed the layer of protection it was providing and asked the masculine energy to release her and remove itself from her body to allow her the freedom she deserved. Through this request, it agreed, released, and dissolved. It just disappeared.

Now that she was free from the darkness that was engulfing her, Jessica was available and open for new energy to replenish her. I proceeded to strengthen her inner core and connection to her Source energy with a Pillar of Intent healing. Jessica welcomed this light and love with open arms and joy.

I have no doubt that Jessica's courage and willingness to experience the complete release of negative energy, followed by her welcome acceptance of revitalization energy, not only expanded and improved her relationship with her former husband, but, more importantly, with herself. As Jessica embraces the freedom to be her higher Self, free from her identity/ego, she leads by example. Her light will shine brighter and the ripple effect will benefit all those who come in contact with her.

Healing the wounds of our past, whether it is our personal wound, or our handed down through generations wound, highly impacts our families[27]. From generation to generation, in every family, there are good and bad stories and behaviors that are passed down. We hear these stories and then live into them. We make them happen. For instance, there was a story in my family: "People in our family have bad backs." Over the years, I saw evidence of this with my father, Lynn, and myself. My dad had a "bad back" and every now and then it would "go out". Lynn developed slipped discs and could hardly walk. I was diagnosed with arthritis, could not lie down, and walking was very painful. However, in my search for healing (and Lynn's as well), we found alternative education for what the causes might be. Using these alternative therapies, our backs became strong and the dis-eases that we had been labeled with disappeared. There are now new stories

---

27   Barry Gordon, *Family Constellation Therapist*, http://www.barrygordonlmft.com

in our family. Our family has strong healthy backs. I have not heard anyone repeat the old story and everyone now has a strong back. That old conversation and belief is gone. There is a new belief to be handed down. We have broken a negative pattern and replaced it with a positive one.

Jessica was healing the wounds of her past as well as those handed down through her family heritage. She wanted to end these hereditary patterns for current and future generations so she enrolled herself and her family in our Sunday Night Group Distance Healing sessions. In order for a healing to be received, each person's spirit has the free will to participate or not. I have experienced refusals despite my client requesting a healing, however ninety-nine percent of the time, spirit is happily willing to receive.

Jessica's mother, Monica, lives in Switzerland. She was eighty-eight years old, suffering with pneumonia and depressed over living alone. Jessica never told her mom that she was receiving the weekly healings but Jessica was elated with the results:

My mom is now more joyous than she has been in a long time. Her depression is gone and she enjoys her walks to the village.

My sister Vanessa, at the time she joined the distance healings, was recovering from breast cancer and surgery and had undergone several chemo treatments. At one point when we thought the treatments were over, the doctor said that her blood levels were not good. They thought that there might be a problem with her liver. The doctor was considering additional chemo treatments, which was not received warmly by the family.

I asked Kathy to perform an individual personal distance healing on Vanessa, which she did. No one can say what happened but the next time her blood levels were checked, they were normal and no further chemo was needed.

As part of Vanessa's healing, there was a conversation that needed to take place and since I do not speak German, Jessica agreed to be the neutral, non-judgmental, interpreter.

As Louise Hay writes in her book *Heal Your Body*, and this is my belief as well, cancer cells materialize from: Deep hurts; Longstanding resentment; Deep secret or grief, eating away at the self; Carrying hatreds; What's the use? thoughts.

There were questions I needed Jessica to ask Vanessa. Then, depending on the part of the body that the cancer was affecting, specific thoughts would need adjustments.

If an emotional or traumatic event happens and it is not dealt with in the moment, the emotion gets stuffed deep down in the physical body, and that is where the cancer manifests itself. I asked Jessica to speak with Vanessa regarding what she was suppressing.

Vanessa welcomed the healing. The vibration level was extremely high as I cleansed and purified her blood, vibrated all cancer cells up above her body and whisked them away. My intention was to replenish every particle of Vanessa's being with light and love, reconnect her to her river of wellness, and release old stories and beliefs that no longer served her.

She was available and open throughout the healing and allowed much work to be done. Her ability to receive was wonderful.

The message from my guides was emphatic, and was not just for Vanessa but for all of us:

There is only a steady stream of well-being. We are either in alignment with it, cruising along, enjoying life, feeling good, loving everyone, including ourselves...or...We are not in it. We are turned around, fighting the currents, struggling really hard trying to get upstream when, in fact, we are going in the wrong direction.

It does not have to be so hard. Relax. Enjoy. Breathe! You will never get it all done. All is well. No concerns. This is the feeling of well-being. Life is a journey, not a destination. Slow down and enjoy the moment-by-moment experience. Look for reasons to feel good.

Forgive yourself and others. Strive to see the gifts from every wound, hurt or disappointment. For instance, if "it" had not happened, who would you have missed out on meeting? If "it" had not happened, what direction might your life have gone? You are exactly where you're supposed to be. Right here, Right now.

Carlo Carretto is a wonderful example of turning a misfortune into a gift. Born in 1910 in northern Italy, he became a school teacher, a religious activist, and eventually a spiritual writer. Once a climber and runner, he suffered an injury in the desert. He wrote, "That mistaken injection that paralyzed my leg was not a stroke of bad luck. It was a grace. It was bad luck, yes. It was misfortune. But God turned it into a grace. I had a useless leg. I could not climb or run. My crippled leg helped me to stand firm and my misfortune thrust me onto new paths. So I got a jeep and became a meteorologist[28]."

---

28   Carlo Carretto, *Why, O Lord?*, (Darton, Longman and Todd with Orbis Books USA, 1986)

Rather than becoming angry and resentful, Carlo became a spiritual writer and his writings have helped many. "The challenge of the gospel, according to Carretto, was to make an oasis of love in whatever desert we might find ourselves.[29]"

Just like Carlo, YOU are the only one with the power to change your thoughts, your view of circumstances. Begin to notice what they are. Awareness is the first step.

Any time you find yourself worrying, stop, take a breath, and tell yourself "All is well. My body has the power to heal itself." Focus your attention on a better-feeling thought, a little higher than your present thought. Then another thought a little higher than that thought, and so on until you move to a place of well-being. This is how you raise your vibration level.

If it is your desire, you can experience peace and wellness at all times, regardless of your circumstances. It is a practice - like going to the gym to strengthen a muscle, or learning to play the piano. One day, wellness will become your new baseline.

When we send the 9 PM (EST) Sunday distance healing, it is 3 AM in Switzerland. Vanessa still receives the healings and looks forward to those evenings because she sleeps soundly and wakes up completely rested and calm. I recommended that every night, before she goes to sleep, she declare out loud to the Universe, "I AM perfectly healthy." Imagine if we all went to sleep with that thought on our minds.

Gratitude lists are a wonderful way to remind yourself, and focus on, what it is that you are grateful for. I highly recommend that you begin yours today. There is so much to be thankful for. Begin to appreciate your surroundings and the people in your life. For those of you having a hard time beginning your list, start with the conveniences of life such as indoor plumbing, or the ability to read, eyes, ears, teeth, - that sort of thing. For others it may be the people in your life that keep you going, or make you laugh, or the home you live in, or the contribution you get to make to others. Keep adding to your list. It's truly endless.

Make fun plans for the future and focus on living into them. Take the focus off your own illness and suffering and put your focus on making a difference in someone else's life. Be in service to others. Do for another that which you would want another to do for you. Be the one to forgive or apologize first. How important is it to be right? Maybe it's better to be happy? Remember, "Resentment is a poison you swallow hoping the other person suffers."

---

29 Carlo Carretto, *Letters from the Desert* (Maryknoll, N.Y.: Oros, 1972); Robert Ellsberg, Carlo Carretto: Selected Writings (Maryknoll, N.Y.: Orbis, 1994)

Having someone to share with is important, but what you share is even more important. Remember, you get more of what you focus on. Give up trauma sharing and talking about how bad things are. Start telling the story of how great your life is. Tell the story of how amazing your body is and about the parts that work. If you take the whole body and divide it into percentages, we tend to tell about the small percentage that is not working optimally. Talk about the larger percentage that is working. Be amazed at the ability your body has to function on its own without any input at all from you.

Make it your intention to release the stories and memories that do not serve your highest sense of well-being. Take the lesson learned, thank your teacher, and let it go. As the old stories disappear, there will be new freedom in your mental, emotional, and physical fields. Create new, more empowering stories of your life and tell them to anyone who will listen. Find reasons to live. Find reasons to be healthy. Share about how great your life is. What you share will attract to you more of that. It is the Law of Attraction.

As Abraham-Hicks says, "There is no dark switch." There is only light and love. Darkness is only the absence of light. Through our conversations and thoughts we are either allowing and receiving the light and love, or not. It is always our choice. Make it a new game and invite your family and friends to play your new *dare to dream game* with you. Have fun. Put more play in your life. Create a new dream and live into it.

———

Celiac disease is a digestive disorder which damages the small intestine and interferes with the absorption of nutrients from food. A person with celiac cannot tolerate gluten, a protein in wheat, rye, and barley but may also be in everyday products such as medicines, vitamins, and lip balms. The most common symptoms of celiac disease are abdominal bloating and pain, chronic diarrhea, vomiting, constipation, pale foul smelling or fatty stool, and weight loss.

According to the mayo clinic, no treatment can cure celiac disease, however, you can effectively manage celiac disease by changing to, and maintaining, a gluten-free diet.

However, this is not always the case.

Michelle Gibson, who lives in Florida, was visiting friends and family in New York. She had been suffering from the terrible effects of celiac disease for many years. During her visit, she came to see me for a hands-on healing. Michelle believed that her deceased father, Angelo, had unknowingly suffered with celiac disease through-out his life. Just as we started the healing, Michelle began to sob uncontrollably. I asked her what she felt was occurring and she replied, "I feel the presence of my father in the room, and it is very comforting." With that, I proceeded with the heal-ing. When my hands were on her abdominal area, I had a vision of a volcano spewing hot bubbling lava. Incredible heat was coming from the area, so I stayed there for a very long time sending calming and cleansing energy until the heat dissipated. (Many times when I am guided to stay in an area like this for an extended period of time, I go into a sleep-like trance, only to realize after it is completed, that a long period of time has elapsed.) As soon as the healing was complete, Michelle said:

This was an amazing experience. It felt as if your hands had gone through my stomach and into my intestines. It actually felt as if you were scrubbing the inside of my intes-tines. I was very skeptical at first, but I feel significantly better both physically and mentally. Having my father's presence with me was also extremely comforting.

The benefits of this healing lasted Michelle for many months. One day, she had a setback and called to request a healing and inquired whether I would be coming to Florida. As I was not traveling to Florida anytime soon, I explained that I could send her a distance healing which would be just as effective as if I were there with her. She agreed to give it a try. After the healing she wrote:

I felt your healing touch over 1,200 miles away. It felt exactly the same as when you performed the physical healing on me in New York. I could not believe that I felt your hands inside my stomach cleaning my small intestines. The results were phenomenal! Since you did the healings on me, my health has been better than ever. Thank you.

WAYNE

I learned the art of distance healing from Kathy and Lynn while I was attend-ing the healing program. The thought of doing such a healing seemed almost incomprehensible to me, but I soaked up their knowledge like a sponge and started practicing.

I began to speak openly about the ability to perform healings from a distance, and as a result, Sheri Perbeck, one of my classmates, asked me to perform a dis-tance healing on her to stop smoking. I promised Sheri I would send her an addic-tion healing sometime over the next few weeks.

When a person has a chemical addiction, there is a craving in that person's body for a particular substance, for instance nicotine in cigarettes. The addiction itself is a chemical reaction which creates a pattern of neurons firing in the brain[30]. Different addictions correspond to different chakras. Smoking pertains to the fifth chakra (communication/career) and the fourth chakra (heart/lungs – or love/taking in life fully- also the lungs store grief).

The intention of the addiction healing is to break these patterns. Since two things cannot occupy the same space at the same time, I start at the head and fill every cell in the body with golden energy to the point where it overflows from each cell thus forcing the craving out of the cell and ultimately out of the body. This creates new healthier neuron patterns.

One evening, about a week after we spoke, I sent the first of two distance healings. Sheri lives in Connecticut, and I live 80 miles away in New York. A few days later I emailed Sheri and asked her how she was progressing in her battle against smoking. Her response was:

Hey Wayne, what's up? Yes, I know when you are giving me a healing. It's incredible. In fact, one night I said to my husband while we were sitting on our sofa, "Wayne's working on me. Love it. Love it." It felt like I was spinning inside my head, dizzy, floating. I'll have you know that I have more energy now than I have had in a long time. I've been going to the gym. I haven't stopped smoking yet, but I have cut way back

---

30   *What the Bleep Do We Know?*, Betsy Chasse and Mark Vicente, Directors, *2004*.

and am still working on quitting it completely. I know that I will. I've been doing some self-work and have been bringing up some old stuff from my childhood. The amazing thing is that I have been going to the gym, and I no longer huff and puff when I work out. Before your healing, I could not walk up a flight of stairs without shortness of breath.

I was delighted with Sheri's response. I never told her when I was going to send that first healing, but it was that same evening she referred to in her email. When I performed the healing, I saw her lungs were charcoal black. I requested that my guides scrub Sheri's lungs until they were perfectly pink and natural. When Sheri reported she was no longer winded, I again thanked my guides for the magnificent job they did in the distance healing. Not long after the initial healing, Sheri completely stopped smoking and went on to say:

10 years ago I couldn't run three miles without being pushed by my younger brother. Now, at 40 years old, pushing myself, I can do four miles. It used to be that my lungs needed to catch up to my body. Now my body needs to catch up to my lungs. They feel that healthy. I keep putting my speed up on the treadmill, pushing myself beyond what I think is my limit. Even when I'm on the Stairmaster, I'm thrilled and excited about how much more stamina I have. I surprise myself. It's amazing. I feel like a million dollars. I don't even think about smoking anymore. As a matter of fact, when I see someone smoking or smell it, it actually repels me. And all the healings Wayne sent me were from a distance!

With an experience like this under my belt, my confidence was sky high, and I knew that my ability to heal from any location at any distance was limitless.

———

One of the most amazing distance healings that I have ever performed was on Cathy Nolte. Cathy told me she had a blocked kidney with blood in her urine and had suffered with this painful condition for eight years. In January, 2008 a sonogram revealed that the blockage was causing the kidney to enlarge, creating a dangerous situation. Her doctor recommended surgery to remove the blockage, but with surgery, there was a twenty percent chance she could lose the kidney. Cathy was scared to have the surgery and scared not to.

When Cathy related this story to me, I told her that I had developed skills as a healer and would like to send her a distance healing with my intention set on clearing her blockage. She lives about twenty miles from me.

Immediately after we ended our call, I focused on her kidney and sent the healing. Right away I knew that it was good and felt very optimistic that the blockage was gone. The next morning, I sent an additional healing and after that, Cathy disappeared from my thoughts.

Weeks later, my nephew called to say that I should get in touch with his mom, Cathy, right away as she was desperately trying to reach me.

Sometime after I had performed the healings, Cathy had a renal scan and the results showed that there was no blockage. The doctor could not believe it, and said that she had absolutely no medical explanation for what had happened. When I reached Cathy on the phone and asked what her reaction was, she exclaimed, "I cried, I laughed, and I jumped up and down." She knew that the distance healings I performed were responsible for the elimination of the clog in her kidney.

In November 2008, Cathy had another test performed which revealed that for the first time in eight years, there was no blood in her urine.

The doctor was in awe and had Cathy go for a battery of tests because she could not believe the blockage and blood in her urine, that she had been monitoring for eight years, just disappeared into thin air. Embarrassed to tell her of the healing, Cathy told the doctor she had people praying for her. When Cathy told me this, I asked, "Why didn't you tell the doctor you had a healer perform a healing on you?"

Cathy went back to her doctor, told her of the healing, and signed a waiver allowing me to discuss her case with the doctor. When I called the doctor and asked what she thought happened, she immediately said, "There is no way a blockage of this nature that I have been monitoring for eight years just disappeared into thin air. There is no scientific explanation for what happened."

When I asked the doctor if I could use her name and quote her in the book, she declined, but said that if I wanted to put my business cards in her office, she had no problem with that.

KATHY

For a long time I had a vision of performing distance healings simultaneously on massive numbers of people. I envisioned a stadium filled to capacity and me able to reach each person and tend to their every need, through my guides and theirs, with a distance healing. In order to make my dream become a reality, I created a website (www.globalhealings.com) where people can easily sign up and receive weekly healings at a minimal cost for themselves, their families and even their pets. This was my way of starting to change the world.

My plan was to have other healers working in conjunction with me during these sessions. This way, I knew that one or more of the healers would reach every participant, just in case, for some reason, my energy didn't. My goal was to amass a group of the most talented healers I knew who would commit to a weekly healing regimen.

Early on in the process, I shared my dream with Wayne and asked that he join me in this endeavor. He has the uncanny ability to tap into people's core energies and just loves their souls. I could not imagine anyone more dedicated or loving to have on this journey with me.

He immediately agreed and we designated Sundays at 9:00PM (EST) to co-deliver the Group Distance Healings. Regardless of where we are, together or not, that is the time when we deliver the group healing, and just like the pebble tossed into a pond, the ripple effect has been amazing and far reaching.

The Schroeder family serves as a great example of a large group that received major benefits from our healings. Gloria, and her husband John, had been receiving hands-on healings for a long time and wanted to reach out and help their children and grandchildren living in different areas. In January 2008, as they were going to Florida for an extended visit, they decided to enroll their family into the Group Distance Healings for a few months.

Their son John Jr. and their daughter Alison live in Massachusetts; their daughter Christine and her son Tommy live in New York; and their daughter Lori and her son Daniel live in Connecticut. Gloria explained:

I have suffered with rheumatoid arthritis on and off since I was five years old. It had been in remission for many years but became active again three years ago. I experienced extreme pain in most of my joints, and it became so bad that it was difficult to walk or use my hands. The arthritis was throughout my body, including my head, causing me to have extreme headaches. At one point I was hospitalized with a critical lung condition. The lung problem developed because my immune system had deteriorated so badly. At this point, my body was so debilitated that I was forced to be in a wheelchair.

I knew that my sister Doris had received healings from her son Wayne on her hip and was now walking perfectly with no pain, no limp, and no cane. I contacted Wayne and asked for help. I met with him and he applied his healing energy in a hands-on session. I immediately started to feel improvement. My husband, John, and I continued to follow up with Kathy and both of us have benefited enormously from these sessions. Because we travel a considerable amount of time, we signed up for the Sunday evening distance healings to continue to reap the benefits of these treatments.

I am now feeling much better and am able to live a normal life. I no longer suffer with extreme pain. My joints are not swollen and disfigured, and I no longer need a wheelchair. I believe in the power of energy healing, and Wayne and Kathy have this gift.

WAYNE

I remember that first healing with my aunt Gloria very well. My instincts told me her energy was greatly depleted. I had a strong connection and could feel energy moving rapidly through her body and filling all the deficiencies. I saw a beautiful spectrum of colors during the session. It was my request and intention that her energy be balanced and her body heal from the arthritis. What a great reward I received when my request was answered and my loving aunt benefited tremendously from these healings. I am very grateful for the success that has improved her quality of life and shown Gloria and the rest of her family that there is a non-medical way that can create miraculous results. I am also grateful for the courage of my mother, Doris, who introduced and encouraged her sister, Gloria, which caused the ripple effect for so many people.

It was during one of the first group distance healings that Gloria felt the energy and her body went into a spinal wave. Out of Gloria's previous participation in NSA, her body knows this technique and automatically uses it to disperse tension from her body.

John Jr. had long been suffering with a neck condition called spasmodic tor-ticollis (cervical dystonia), a painful condition where the neck muscles contract involuntarily, causing the head to twist or turn to one side and even lock up. Cervical dystonia can also cause your head to uncontrollably tilt forward or back-ward. John explained:

When it attacks, it pins my chin to my chest. Any stress, whether emotional or physical, makes it worse.

At this point, John had almost no head mobility, and his life was seriously diminished. Desperate for some relief, he started to receive Botox injections directly into his neck muscles, and his neck improved dramatically. In addition to the Botox injections, he had been practicing T'ai Chi for three years. For John, this is a practice of focusing on the tan t'ien[31], located two inches below the naval, bringing breath and focus in through the nose, down and around the tan t'ien, and back up the spine to exhale out through the injured or effected area of the neck. This creates a balancing of his energy, both physically and emotionally, and keeps his life force energy moving. He received one lesson per week and practiced daily.

After participating in our weekly Group Distance Healings, John's neck improved significantly and he was able to reduce his Botox injections from two vials of Botox every three months down to one and one half vials of Botox injec-tions every four months. John stated:

From time to time, I still have little tremors but basically, I have full mobility of my neck and I have my life back!

Gloria's twelve-year old grandson, Daniel, had been suffering from a plethora of undiagnosed symptoms which were affecting his schooling, athletics and his overall life. They had tried many procedures and medications but nothing had worked and they were resigned to their son being handicapped. The healings breathed new life into Daniel and his family. As one healing grows upon another, after a few of these Sunday sessions, there was dramatic, noticeable change in his life and behavior. His mother, Lori, recognized this and was elated. She wanted to share this with others:

---

31   This is considered the physical center of gravity of the human body and is the seat of one's internal energy.

Last year my son, Daniel, became quite ill. We were not sure of the diagnosis so he was being treated for both Lyme disease as well as Spondyloarothrophy. For several months Daniel struggled with terrible headaches, joint aches and extreme exhaustion. My mother, having suffered with rheumatoid arthritis on and off for most of her life, was extremely concerned for Daniel. She immediately contacted Wayne and Kathy for help. My mother and father have both received numerous hands-on and distance healings and felt that this was something that could help Daniel.

I was very skeptical but anxious to try anything at this point. We received these healings every Sunday for several months. On Sunday evenings Daniel and I would go into a quiet, dark room and open ourselves to the healing. Daniel started showing improvement almost immediately.

Daniel has been symptom free since February 2008! I know that if Daniel ever shows any of these symptoms again, I will run, not walk, back to Wayne and Kathy. I cannot thank them enough for the help they provided to Daniel.

The change in Daniel was so dramatic that one of Lori's friends, Christin, noticed the difference and asked Lori what she was doing for him. When Lori told her that she and Daniel were receiving distance energy healings, Christin wanted to know more. She thought that her daughter was suffering with Lyme disease. The symptoms were getting worse, and after hearing Lori and seeing the results in Daniel, she wanted to try these healings on her daughter. In June of 2008, Christin sent the following e-mail to Wayne:

I am writing to you after speaking with my friend, Lori Crowley, in regard to our daughter, Victoria, being sick for a long time. We have been to Lyme specialists, an endocrinologist, taken way too many tests, and still no one can figure out what she has.

Since Daniel has gone through similar symptoms and been on antibiotics like Victoria, and now is functioning better than ever, Lori mentioned to me about the healings you and Kathy provide for the family. She said that Daniel receives a healing every Sunday and they have really made an impact in his life. Since we truly believe in healing, we would love to get in touch with Kathy so that she might be able to help Victoria as well.

Christin comes from Norway and is a loving wife and devoted mother of three young girls. As a result of her Norwegian upbringing she has a different awareness of natural remedies versus standard medical treatments. She shared the following history:

My thirteen-year-old daughter, Victoria, was extremely lethargic. Her short-term memory was disappearing. She could not talk and appeared to have all of her energy blocked. She would sleep until noon each day, was very sensitive to any kind of bright lights, and in addition to having a locked jaw, suffered with terrible pains in her head.

One day after I drove Victoria to school, she deteriorated so quickly that she had to be picked up an hour later. As her condition continued to worsen, she was unable to attend school and actually missed a total of six weeks.

The first time it hit was June of 2007 and Victoria missed school on and off over a five-week period. She got somewhat better and the doctors felt that something they tried helped, but did not know what. It was March 2008 when this affliction hit for the second time. Her skin took on a very strange color of blue and white and there were dark circles under her eyes. Obviously I was very concerned and took Victoria to many doctors in an attempt to solve this puzzle. At one point we went to a major New York City specialist. After extensive testing, the results of which were all negative, the specialist felt sure that Victoria had Lyme disease and treated her accordingly. She underwent a brain scan and a MRI and the only thing that showed up was something very minor.

In June of 2008, Victoria went for homeopathic treatments that measured the vitamins and minerals in her body. The results showed that her liver and kidneys were shutting down. They then started to work on rebuilding her immune system.

Christin was afraid Victoria was going to die. Her short-term memory was almost completely gone. She could barely speak and appeared to be gasping for air with every breath. Christin felt that the antibiotic dosage prescribed by the specialist was so high that "it could kill a cow." The doctor had stated that he wanted to keep Victoria on these antibiotics for up to a year, if necessary.

Christin was desperate for another solution. While at a hair appointment she expressed her concerns to friends in the salon. One woman who believed in alternative medicine related a story about her husband who had to have surgery and went to a healer to reconcile his problems. After hearing this story, Christin wanted to look into alternative medicine. She went to a psychic and wanted to know if her daughter was going to live or die. The psychic told her that Victoria's brain was fogged and that there appeared to be mold throughout her head. She also told Christin that Victoria will have a full life and become an accomplished doctor or research specialist.

Christin scheduled Victoria for a hands-on healing with Kathy. After a lengthy consultation and chakra reading, Kathy determined that every one of Victoria's chakras was blocked. Christin stayed in the room throughout the healing and observed:

As Kathy worked on Victoria's head, I was amazed to see a huge aura of gray misty-looking energy around and behind my daughter's head. I also saw a golden glowing light around Victoria's entire body. It was very close to her physical body. I had never seen anything like this before and was amazed. I was very thankful because I knew that my daughter was finally getting the help she needed.

After the healing, Kathy explained that Victoria would now begin to open up. Victoria had been in a deep sleep while on the healing table and the peaceful serenity that accompanied this sleep was exactly what she needed.

I continued to be amazed! While on our trip home, she began to talk. It was random things. Victoria said, "I love that music." She followed this with numerous other little positive comments that I had not heard for a long time.

We went back for several more physical healings, and each time Victoria improved. Shortly after this she was able to return to school.

Christin was now a big believer in the power of energy healings and decided to address some of her own needs. She scheduled an appointment with Kathy to resolve the problems she had regarding her father.

During the first healing I saw colors of purple, green and yellow. There was a peaceful serenity that overwhelmed my body and mind. I recalled childhood problems, and when the healing was completed all the worries of life were replaced with a feeling of relief.

After this, Christin registered her entire family in the weekly Sunday evening distance healings. Several members of her family had no idea that they were receiving the healings, however, Christin was monitoring any changes that took place within their lives. Her observations revealed:

Over the summer it was like a snowball effect. We were on a mission and something wonderful was happening within my family.

My oldest daughter, Maren, had a close friend pass away. She began negative questioning. "Is there a God? Why did he take my friend? Why did he not take me instead?"

Maren went into a dark space. She started to do spiritual things even though she believed in nothing.

Very odd things were happening in my home. I felt a ghost in my dining room, each time I would walk past the chair I would step around his legs. There was also a feeling of darkness, or gloom, in one corner of my living room. It was very uncomfortable and none of us would go in there. Because of these odd things, I decided to have the house cleansed for spirits by a woman who specialized in this sort of thing. It was a sage cleansing, the purpose of which was to remove negative energy from the home. Maren walked in while this was taking place and freaked out. "My mother is a witch!"

Kathy said that the distance healings would help Maren open up a new line of communication. Maren was traveling in Florence, Italy when unbeknownst to her she received the first Sunday healing. On Tuesday she called home, and I could not stop her from talking. She talked about the people she was meeting, the flight she took and about her experiences. She called every day. Since this time, the relationship between my daughter and I has grown better than I could ever imagine. There was no doubt in my mind that this reborn relationship was a direct result of these distance healings.

My third daughter, Emilie, was suffering from a haunting sleep disorder which kept her and everyone else in the family up each night. She would go to sleep and hear people and noises downstairs. She heard them coming up the stairs and was afraid that someone would kill her parents. This had started when she was one or two years old. She would wake up screaming, and it took at least twenty minutes before she could recognize anyone in the family. As time went on the severity of the dreams was not as bad but they continued every night.

Kathy recommended that we do a past life healing on Emilie. In one life Emilie envisioned herself as a male guard on post who fell asleep. The guard was awakened by an insanely irate commander who picked up a rock and crushed the guard's skull. In the second past life healing, she was a young girl who lived with her parents on a prairie. The parents were brutally killed, but the little girl managed to hide and eventually escape.

The results of these past life healings were a Godsend to Emilie and the entire family. The dreams went away right after the healings began. Emilie had a complete week of peaceful sleep with no dreams. As her spirit wrestled with the concept of whether she wanted to hang on to these fears from long ago, Emilie had two consecutive nights of dreams. Immediately thereafter she released them forever and has not had a recurrence since.

Christin was now on a spiritual path. She saw the remarkable change in her family and with the distance healings, provided healing for all of them without arousing a wrath of skepticism. Now it was her time. As she grew stronger and stronger, and one healing grew upon the other she commented, "I am getting back to who I am." She was preparing to deal with anger that had built up over decades with her estranged father and the resulting distant relationship that had evolved with her mother.

Her dad was dying of cancer.

"I hoped that he would soon pass, and yet I had this deep anger pent up inside me about all the bad things that he had done to the family. He was so mean. How do I deal with this?"

Kathy recommended that Christin attend a Family Constellation Therapy session, which is a powerful healing technique conducted in a group setting. Participants arrange their chairs in a large circle around the room leaving one empty chair beside the Family Constellation Practitioner. One participant volunteers to address a family issue or upset that is currently happening in their life, or an issue that has been handed down through generations. This person moves to the open seat and then chooses participants from the circle to become representatives of their family members, relatives, ancestors, countries, illnesses, addictions, and so on. Once the representatives have been placed within the circle, an enactment unfolds regarding the energy that had been amassed in the family dynamics over generations and very often there is an extensive release of unhealthy patterns. The volunteering person, and often their families, experience resolution and forgiveness. Just like the energy healings, this therapy has the potential to heal and clear seven generations back and seven generations forward.

This is exactly what took place for Christin. In her constellation, she chose representatives for her father, her father's parents and a stillborn sister that would have been named Catherine. This constellation centered on her father, and as a result, many of her questions were answered. As her processing would continue to unfold, bits and pieces of awareness would become clearer over time. Her practitioner suggested Christin not to speak to anyone about her experience for a month so that she may process the information without any outside influence or interpretation.

The following week Christin's father passed away, and she returned to Norway for the funeral. Christin knew that she had made peace with her father however she did not participate in his desire to have his ashes spread at sea.

When she returned home she saw a huge eagle by her house, something she had never seen before. A week later she saw it again and felt that it was some kind of sign.

Suddenly, she was faced with a sequence of strange events. Her vacuum cleaner burnt out, lamps didn't work, and light bulbs began to pop. She sensed that something was not normal about these events. Christin spoke with her sister in Norway and found she was having the same kind of unexplained events in her life. They requested help from a psychic who immediately felt the presence of their father. She said that their father was not letting go and would not cross over until he felt forgiven by his daughters. The psychic told Christin to visualize herself as an eagle and to see her world through the eyes of that eagle. The psychic asked the father to cross over and as soon as Christin's sister was able to forgive, his presence left her alone.

However, Christin was still bothered and she sent pictures of the rooms in her house to the psychic. Once again the psychic stressed the father's desire for forgiveness. Christin asked, "Why were you so mean?" She received an answer, "I'm sorry." Christin sat down and wrote all of the good things that she remembered her father doing. She then was able to achieve total forgiveness and he crossed.

The psychic noted that there were four other spirits in Christin's house. One was named Adam, who was always in her dining room in a certain chair. He had a male friend who also inhabited the house. The psychic helped them both cross. There were also spirits of two little girls in Christin's bedroom. They appeared like street urchins and were somehow associated with her father. With the help of the psychic, they were able to cross.

Christin is now a very happy person. She, in particular, and the rest of her family have had huge clearings. She is at peace and attributes all of her newfound freedom to the releases generated through Kathy's guidance into constellation therapy and by the transformational energy healings they received in-person and long-distance.

——— — ———

The beauty of distance healings is that they are not restricted by time or space. Whether sitting back and relaxing, out and about running errands, or skiing in the Alps, the benefits will still be received. Those who are active or preoccupied at the time of the healing may not actually feel the healing coming in, but most certainly, the healing will be reflected in their lives.

As one healing grows upon another, the more healings received, the better life will get.

These benefits may show up in relationships with family members and an increasing ability to get along with others. Many experience greater mental clarity and an improved ability to complete projects that were once overwhelming. People often comment on how much younger you look, the spring in your step, the smile on your face, and as you experience the joy in your heart, life will get better and better.

CHAPTER 22

I AM THAT AM

WAYNE

I have received many healings from Kathy, each one different, but in March 2008, I was blessed with a healing that far exceeded anything that I might have expected.

Kathy started at my feet and a feeling of peace and relaxation spread slowly up my legs to my torso and finally to my head. I saw colors of green with varying shades of red and orange.

It felt as if a new birth was about to take place, and it was *Me*!

I felt very emotional and had tears of joy running down my cheeks while an indescribable sense of elation engulfed every cell in my body. I was spouting bursts of laughter and relished the feeling of ultimate elation! Every cell in my body felt so alive and so good, from the hair follicles on the top of my head to the tips of my toe nails, every cell of my being felt better than I had ever felt in my life. I thought that if this feeling is what we have to look forward to after we die then perhaps death is not so scary. It was an indescribable feeling of magnificence. My next thought was that if this is available once, it must be available at any time and with that thought, I was suddenly in a hall of pure white and my entire team was with me.

For the first time ever, there was a gathering of the troops. On my left side were my four guardian angels, Simon, Cary, Joseph and Uncle Charlie. On my right, my power animal, Eddie the eagle, my dad, my Indian Shaman Milachichonk, and lastly, the spirit of Kathy joined us.

A beautiful glowing figure entered from the right and stopped directly in front of us. He was elevated as if he was at a podium or up on a stage and his countenance was that of a golden aura with an almost blinding light radiating forth. He was tall and lean with long flowing white robes, glowing with the same magnificence as the human core, and I could not take my eyes off of him. As blinding as this vision was, I craved to behold him. We all knew that this was the creator of the universe, the creator of all life. There was a wonderfully warm feeling that accompanied his presence, and I did not want to remove my eyes from such beauty. I asked him his name.

He responded, "I AM THAT AM."

This did not make any sense to me, and I thought that I had heard the name incorrectly. "Did you say, I am what is?"

The telepathic response was faster than immediate, "I AM THAT AM."

There was no mistaking the response. Without saying a word, his message was etched in my spirit. I knew that he could appear in any image he wanted, but he presented himself in an image that allowed me to see him in my perception of magnificence. Faster than I could even formulate the questions with my mind, the answers were back to me. I knew that he was channeling Kathy and me in the completion of this book and that his desire for mankind is to attain a higher quality of life. He wants all to know that these gifts – the ability to heal ourselves and each other, the ability to connect to the creator, and the support of our guardian spirits - are available to everyone. When the receiver is ready, the gifts will appear. The time has come to change the course and to pay attention to what he has given us. Stop looking outside of Self to fulfill the emptiness. It cannot be filled with "things". We must look inside. Connect with our Self. This will give us the connection that we are all searching for.

As suddenly as the vision began it ended, and I realized I was on the healing table and aware of my physical body. Kathy had her hands on my shoulders which helped me to feel grounded. I noticed a pulsation in my left forearm and as she finished the healing at my head, there was a heightening of my senses. My hearing was the most noticeable. Before the healing my ears had seemed a little stuffed, now I could hear a pin drop.

I feel blessed to have had an experience like this bestowed upon me. This was the greatest of gifts, and I will remember it for all time. I was eager to tell Kathy and hear her perspective on what this revelation meant.

She said, "The name, I AM THAT AM, means that he is everything. He is all that is. He has a line that goes out to every core. The core in each of us is a part of the whole, of all that is. When we declare our self as I AM _____ (fill in the blank) we make a declaration to the Universe (Source/God/Good) and the Universe lines up all cooperating components. Become aware of what you are declaring."

I know that if everyone would look within his/herself, and use the gifts that have been bestowed upon each of us in positive and empowering ways, that real change on the planet will start to become a reality.

COMMENTS BY KATHY: *What Wayne experienced, the connection to Source, to all that is, is something that I too have experienced only in a different way. I did not see the same vision that Wayne saw. My connection was, and is, more of the Angelic realm. I have been in the presence of magnificence. I have asked questions. For me, it is more of a telepathic experience. Like Wayne, the answer was given before the thought was even completed. This is something that once experienced, one never forgets. It is a knowing as opposed to a wondering.*

There is no doubt in Wayne's mind, or mine, that this really happened. "I AM THAT AM" – Source/God/Good - or in Wayne's case, the Creator, is inclusive of everything.

As I said, my experiences have been more of the Angelic realm. I have been wrapped in the giant angel wings of Archangel Michael. I have played charades with Archangel Rafael, and have had many of these telepathic conversations that Wayne experienced. Our Source/ guardian angels are available to each and every one of us at our request, and yet very few ever ask them for help or even ask them their names. And even if you don't believe in angels ... angels believe in you!

If you would like to know your angel's name(s), take a moment right now. Close your eyes. Put your feet on the floor. Ask your angel(s) to reveal their name(s) to you. Then listen to the name(s) that come into your mind. It may not be a name you were expecting. Once you have their names, ask for their help. You have free will. They cannot help unless you ask. Ask for guidance. These are the ambassadors of I AM THAT AM.

Several days later, I remembered the story written in the Bible of the Burning Bush speaking to Moses. (Exodus 3:14). He realized that the bush was afire and yet the bush was not burning. As he got closer, a voice spoke to him from the bush. He questioned the voice, and asked for its name. The voice said, "I AM THAT I AM." This has also been interpreted as, "I AM WHO I AM" and "I AM WHAT I AM". Depending on which version of the Bible that you read, there are alternate interpretations of the ancient Hebrew into English.

However, there is not a doubt in my mind as to what I saw and the name that I heard.

"I AM THAT AM"

CHAPTER 23

What is a Healing

In reading this book, you have traveled with us on a journey into our evolution as healers. All of the people you have read about have had their lives affected in very positive ways and many of them considered their experience a miracle. This ability to heal is not restricted to a select few but is embedded in every human being.

In March 1978, 28 year-old Russian crane operator, Yuliya Vorobyeva, received a 380 volt shock in a mine near Donetsk, Ukraine and was pronounced dead.[32] Her body was placed on a slab in the morgue and two days later during the autopsy, she regained consciousness. She was unable to sleep for six months but eventually, fell asleep and slept for "a long time". When she awoke, she found that she had many powers. She said, "I went shopping one morning. I got to the bus stop and a woman was stand-

---

32   Ukraine newspaper *Izvestia* article dated June 14, 1987.

ing there. Suddenly, I was struck by horror. I thought I could see right through this woman like a television screen."

Yuliya was interviewed by a reporter and was able to tell him what he had eaten simply by looking at his stomach. Because of this amazing skill, she was hired by the Donetsk hospital to diagnose rare illnesses. Dr. A. Swedlerova later said that Yuliya, "never made a single mistake."

Where did this newfound ability come from? Could it be that she had this ability all along and the shock that she received just triggered its awakening?

As healers, we also have been able to use the abilities we have been given and the skills we have developed for the betterment of our fellow man.

Healings have been practiced in various forms and cultures for thousands of years and throughout generations many people who spoke about or practiced such things were ostracized or killed, including Jesus Christ. The Bible, considered one of the most important books ever written, contains parables and stories of miracles which many people readily accept as truth.

We believe that the miracles of two thousand years ago can still be performed by people today. The great yogi masters practice healings and in native tribes throughout the world, in some of the most isolated places, shamans perform what are considered miracles as well.

However, many people still doubt that these practices work and do not seem comfortable unless they are utilizing the medical model when dealing with their afflictions.

But there are also many people who come to us with severe psychological or physical problems that have been in treatment by the medical model for years with mixed results. At some point, these people become desperate and are willing to try alternative methods to improve their conditions. They usually come to us when they have reached a critical point in their lives. It is very gratifying and rewarding for us to be able to help people in such desperate straits. The elation that people exhibit after a healing is indescribable. Imagine if they had come to us before they had reached the desperation stage? Before they had had the surgery or the complications? Prevention is always preferred.

As we have stated earlier in the book, every story you have read is true. Every person mentioned in this book is a real person who had real life experiences.

Although we cannot predict what will happen during or after a healing, every healing is beneficial to both the healer and the person receiving the healing. We have highlighted some of the more dramatic results, however, there are many times when people receive modest results. A person may experience relaxation for the first time and a deeper level of peace than they have ever felt in their lives. Often, minor aches and pains simply go away and there are times when severe chronic pains also disappear. For many, the worries about everyday life dissipate. Concerns about bills, family problems, and even death, can completely dissolve. People also report that life becomes easy. Serendipity becomes the norm and new opportunities open up.

There are also times when a person can be confronted by the outcome of the healing. Many people have a tendency to build up anger and resentment with themselves, or others, at events that did not go their way. Often, they do not realize they are mad or what they are mad about. Sometimes a suppressed memory will surface, and the person will experience the fear, hurt, anger or betrayal that they felt when the original event took place.

Emotions are energy in motion and if repressed, will cause pain and illness. If the person is ready and willing to release the energy, a major healing will take place.

Although these experiences may not seem joyful, they are the gateways to growth and development. Once an old feeling surfaces it can be explored and viewed from a different perspective, resolved by forgiveness of self or another, or dealt with by making a course correction in one's life.

However, people have choice and if one chooses to ignore the new awareness and continue with the old patterns the probable outcome for their health and life could be worse than before. They say "ignorance is bliss", but "knowledge is power". Sometimes the familiarity of the affliction is preferable to the resolution. To have something be different, you must do something different.

Just like a pebble in a pond, every healing creates a ripple effect. When one person shifts, it creates a ripple that affects their friends, loved ones, and even their enemies.

Remember, forgiveness opens a magical door that leads to love, which is fruit for the soul. To those who can attain this state the ability to heal is limitless. For those who cannot do this for themselves, there are a growing number of healers who can help them until they recognize the gifts that they have.

A healing can be as simple as opening up a person's energy channels and balancing the energy throughout their body, or it can be as complex as healing the most intricate afflictions known to man, and not necessarily from this lifetime. As healers, we have the ability to channel energy through our bodies and into the person we are healing. We are guided by Universal Source Energy to meet the needs of the person receiving the healing. Although we cannot foretell what the outcome will be, our intention is always for the highest and best good of the person.

There is an increasing awareness in the world about the capabilities of healers and that means all of us. You have the ability to heal yourself and others. Like any skill or gift, practice enhances the ability. Try it for yourself - the next time you, or someone else, experience pain or injury, set your intention, and if they give their permission, gently place your hands on the injured site. Ask for a healing for their highest and best good.

We live in an environment rife with negativity. Most people awake each morning and either turn on the TV to watch the news or read the newspaper. They are greeted with disaster: who has been murdered; who has been raped; who has been robbed; and who has been affected by some other financial catastrophe. As the day proceeds and we communicate with others: Do you know who lost their job? Do you know the family who lives in the house on the corner that is in foreclosure? Did you hear who has illness, surgery, cancer? In the evening, you listen to the news and there are politicians who were caught cheating on their income taxes, and that is followed by a plane crash with no survivors. On top of this you have to worry about having a job, and can you pay your bills? Does any of this sound familiar?

To be faced with this barrage every day is almost incomprehensible. The result of this environment is dis-ease. Under these conditions we have no time to recognize our potential and greatness.

Start to change this pattern today!

Exercise #1: Begin by blocking out all of the negativity that you are bombarded with from your daily life. Laughter is healing. Watch comedies, play games, talk about the good things in your life. Begin a Gratitude List and add to it daily. Forgive yourself and others.

Exercise #2: Look in the mirror and say, "I love you. I forgive you. I appreciate you. Blessed am I to live in such a magnificent temple."

Exercise #3: When you retire for the evening, to calm your mind, focus on your breathing. Breathing in through your nose and out through your mouth is a calming breath. There is a powerful healing exercise that can have a monumental impact on your health and well-being when practiced regularly.[33] As you close your eyes, picture an infant just above your forehead. The infant is perfect in every way. Surround this infant with a glowing white light. This is the light of eternal existence. Picture the perfect cells and organs within the infant. Focus in on the perfection of this beautiful image as you are relaxing and beginning to fall asleep. Know that all of this perfection is yours for the asking. This is your birthright. As you sleep through the night, your body, mind and spirit will start to adopt the perfection of this divine infant. When you awaken, and before you start your day, refocus for a short while on this image and be willing to accept your legacy.

When you are able to forgive yourself and others, to be grateful for everything that you have, and to love yourself and others, there is nothing that cannot be healed. These three exercises will create new patterns and an extremely high and joyful vibration in your cells. It will feel as if you have been ignited with a new spark for life. When you live at this vibration, you live a vibrant, healthy, joyful, and creative life.

Follow these procedures every day, and you will begin to notice change in short order. You will begin to greet the day with a new energy. Pain and ailments will begin to disappear. For those able to go deep within themselves and recognize their own divinity, the change in body, mind and spirit will be nothing short of a miracle.

———

In early 2008, off the coast of New Zealand, two pigmy sperm whales became confused and headed toward the beach. Swimmers watched the whales' progress carefully, concerned that they would beach themselves and die. The whales came closer and closer to the shallows and tragedy seemed inevitable. However, a hero appeared. A beautiful dolphin swam into view, signaling and clicking madly as she headed for the two whales. As the swimmers watched in amazement, the dolphin put herself directly between the whales and the beach, blocking their access.

---

33 Baird T. Spalding, *The Life and Teachings of The Masters of the Far East*, six volume series, (DeVorss & Company, 1986)

The whales stopped. She then escorted them from the shallows to the safety of the deeper waters and watched diligently until they swam away.[34]

What possibly could have prompted this heroic dolphin to rescue these two whales? The dolphin had nothing to gain. Was it love or instinct that prompted this dolphin to act for the betterment of the oceans and the species that reside therein?

There is a huge lesson to be learned here. For those willing to listen and follow their instincts, the open seas and untold freedom to reach new heights lie ahead. Never think that you are too small or insignificant to make a difference, or that no one will ever listen to you. Those who are willing to follow their instincts, and courageously speak their truth, will be the leaders.

Oprah is the first person of star status who had the courage to lead the masses in the first of its kind, 10-week worldwide podcast with Eckhart Tolle, causing an awakening on the planet.[35] She truly is a world leader. As are you!

If you see the beacon of knowledge held within this book, follow your instincts and allow your spirit to burn brightly in attaining your limitless capabilities.

---

34   There were numerous accounts one of which is: http://www.msnbc.msn.com/id/23588063
35   Eckhart Tolle, *A New Earth,* (New York: Plume, 2006)
http://www.oprah.com/oprahsbookclub/Watch-A-New-Earth-Web-Classes-on-Oprahcom

CHAPTER 24

How Can I Get There From Here

KATHY

There are many areas that comprise a full life: health, family, friends, relationship, hobbies, contribution, growth and development, spirituality/religion, leisure, wealth and career.

If all of these areas are working in harmony, you are most likely living a life you love and loving the life you live. Keep doing what you are doing. You are living the life that is available for all of us. You are the example of what we are entitled to. This is our divine birthright.

However, if there is an area of your life that is not working as well as you would like, (the one you complain about constantly) then you must do something different. Insanity is doing the same thing over and over and expecting different results.

In reading this book you have done something different. Dare to dream and then pursue your dreams with passion. Be the magnificent creator you are designed to be.

For those of you who have been or know someone who has been diagnosed incurable or terminal and are not ready to accept that diagnosis, you, or they, must go inside (in-curable) to find the cure. Healing takes place from the inside out. The answers will come from inside of you. Take the time, listen to your Higher Self and be willing to take the action steps that are necessary. Embrace *change*!

It has been my experience that the action step could be forgiveness of another, but more often, forgiveness of one's self. If you resist forgiveness of another, then you get to be right - righteous, justified in holding your position, but more often than not, if you are pointing a finger at someone else there are three fingers pointing back at you. Release the guilt. Forgive yourself for whatever part you played. That is where the real gift is. You are the common denominator in every experience of your life. And – you give the experience meaning.

Taking responsibility for your life and health is where all the power is. For example, a person who is not being responsible for their own well-being crosses the street at a crosswalk, doesn't look both ways before proceeding, and gets hit by a car. They get to be dead right. If they had taken responsibility for their life, they would have looked both ways before crossing and would still be alive. It's as simple as that. Be present in every moment. Do not follow the crowd.

Take responsibility for your health and well-being. To accelerate the process, think of a situation in your life where you are resisting forgiveness of yourself or another, and say these words aloud: "I love you, I'm sorry, please forgive me, thank you.[36]" This is an ancient Hawaiian healing technique called Ho'oponopono.

Abraham[37] says, "There is not a body so ill that it cannot achieve perfect health!"

This is also my personal belief, as I have seen miracles and continue to expect them. I also believe that we have only touched the tip of the iceberg with regards to what is available for human beings through non-invasive healing modalities be it changing our thought processes, connecting with our bodies through breathing, placing our hands on the area that hurts and asking/listening for guidance or receiving the gentleness of energetic healings.

If you are asking "How can I do this? How can I get to health from this place of illness? How can I get there from here?"

The answer is *Baby Steps*.

---

36 Ho'oponopono - The ancient Hawaiian healing technique http://www.holisticharmony.com/archives/capsules/hopono.asp

37 Abraham-Hicks, http://www.Abraham-Hicks.com

Begin today. Start a Healing Journal and document your journey. Follow these steps:

- First, you are exactly where you are supposed to be. Your life and health are simply a reflection of what you currently know. Write down everything that is going on with your body, mind and spirit. This is a reference point in time which will document and reinforce the progress you make.

- Be kind to yourself. Begin to notice your thoughts. Write them down. Start to be your own best friend. Start to treat yourself better. Be willing to recognize your magnificence. Forgive yourself for the past.

- Use our Resource Guide. Read some of the books, watch some of the movies and take some of the courses. Choose the ones that feel right for you. Do not compare yourself or your journey to anyone else.

- Give yourself permission to explore new ideas and to think new thoughts. Keep what you want, release the rest. You are on a journey – take the time to enjoy the scenery along the way.

- Practice being present: "Be still" in your body, and get in touch with your internal guidance system. Learn to listen to your Higher Self, your voice of wisdom. This is not the voice that ridicules and beats you up, that is your "survival identity/ego (Wayne Dyer calls it <u>e</u>dging <u>G</u>od <u>o</u>ut)". Listen to the other voice – the one that says, "Reach for the stars!" and "You can do it!" You may need to practice this a few times before you can hear this kinder voice because we are taught to push that voice away in order to please others. The following technique will help you to hear the voice of your Higher Self:

  > Sit with your feet on the floor. Place your hands in your lap, palms facing up, fingers touching or not. If you are lying down, uncross your ankles and allow your hands to rest at your sides. Close your eyes. Become present to your surroundings and aware of your body. Notice your breath. How do you breathe? Where does the breath go in your body? If possible, breathe in through your nose and out through your mouth. Notice if this changes your thoughts or feels different? Focusing on your breathing will help to quiet your mind.

If there is an area of your body that is distressed in some way with pain, injury, stiffness, or an area that you are concerned about or just doesn't feel right, place your hands (one on top of the other) on that part of your body. If the feeling amplifies and becomes overwhelming, take your hands off your body and then just breathe in your nose and out your mouth. Revisit this area at another time.

If it was not overwhelming and your hands are still on your body, exhale and allow yourself to make the sound that is trapped in this area. Groan, scream, moan, squeak, sigh or whatever the sound may be. It will most likely be an ugly sound. If it's painful, do not hold your breath and suffer in silence. That is how the pain got locked in there. Keep bringing breath to this area and as you exhale, make a sound. Any sound. Even a tiny sound will help to release the suffering. You are where you are and it's perfect. Just notice your experience, do not judge it. Notice your breath, your thoughts and what is happening in your body.

With your hands still touching your body, ask the area, "What can I do to help you feel better?" or "What 'action' do I need to take?" If you do not receive an answer, bring more breath to the area. Then ask the questions again. This may take practice. Do not quit on yourself.

The "answer" will come from your Higher Self, most likely as a thought that pops into your head. It may be a simple change – like drinking more water - or it may be a course correction in your life – like forgive someone who doesn't deserve it or change your career or end your unhealthy relationship. Are you willing to do what is needed? If you are, make the commitment. If you are telling the truth, the pain will lessen in intensity or it may release completely. You cannot lie to your body.

If you do not follow through on your commitment, the pain may return as a reminder of your unfulfilled agreement. Your body is your guidance system. I highly recommend that you get to know yours.

This technique may stir up thoughts, feelings or emotions that have been suppressed under the pain, which is good and part of the healing process. Pains and illnesses are the culmination of our blind spots. From the time we are very young, and throughout our lives, traumas happen: an argument, accident, injury, divorce, or death. Whether physical, emotional, mental, or spiritual, we experience an 'e-motion' (energy in motion) of fear, rage, anger, hurt, frustration, sadness, loss, or even ultimate elation. In the moment it happens, we only deal with as much as we can handle. Perhaps there are other people around us, or we have to be the strong one during a situation. Maybe we receive horrible news and then immediately have to go into a meeting and pretend everything is fine. The remainder of the emotional trauma is stored away to be dealt with later. Because life stops for no one, later turns into someday, and over time, becomes forgotten. This is how we survive.

However, just because the emotions are forgotten, does not mean they are gone. They are filed into the cellular structure of our body, each type accumulating in a specific area. As the years go by the places in our bodies where we stored the forgotten emotions start to overflow and become painful. Pain is the body's way of getting our attention to let us know something needs to be addressed.

Many of us are taught that pain is bad and we should move away from "It". We learn to disconnect from our bodies as if they are separate from us. For example, saying, "My back is killing me," implies it is separate from me. If we don't deal with the emotions, we will need medications to suppress the pain. Eventually, the medications we use to help cover up the symptoms don't work as well as they once did. Because life events are still impacting us, and not being dealt with, it takes stronger medications to deaden the pain. If you are feeling numb to life, or are constantly on the verge of tears, it's because you are filled to the saturation point and are pinched off from your Higher Self.

The course correction, which was once a simple thought to stand up for one's self, becomes more challenging. Now we may have to change our job, ask for the raise we deserve, speak with our boss, spouse, parent, kids, stand up for ourselves in our relationships, or face some other confrontation that we're just not able or willing to do. It could be making a phone call or facing an uncomfortable situation. "It" is perceived as pain, and we move away from "It".

A great example would be: You bring a guest to a friend's dinner party and in front of your friends, your guest demands, "Get me a glass of wine." This is clearly an order, not a request. In the moment it's said, you have choices, and depending on the course of action you take, it will determine the energetic outcome for both people.

The first would be: You feel the uncomfortableness of being diminished in front of your friends, yet saying nothing you fetch the wine. Seething for the remainder of the night, you let the upset fester inside mixing with all the other times in your life that you felt diminished or humiliated by someone and said nothing. You are dis-empowered, while the person who demanded and received the wine feels rewarded, empowered and justified in repeating this behavior again. Tolerating this behavior creates a superior/inferior relationship, and will over time, destroy the relationship.

The second choice would be: In the moment you are given the order, you say "No".

"No" is a complete sentence however, there is a resistance – a confrontation and abruptness – putting both parties on the defensive and creating humiliation for the other person. This sets up a power play and the grounds for an argument.

There is a third choice: You can ask the person to join you away from the group and let them know the impact their demand had on you. Ask them to make requests rather than demands. This is communication – adult to adult – and there is no suppressed anger or resentment, and thus, no stuck energy. There is only freedom. You then have the option to create a new relationship called adult/adult, where they can make a request and you fulfill the request or not. This is as simple as rephrasing the demand into a question, "Will you please get me a glass of wine?" This is a request and implies you have an option and generates an atmosphere of respect. There is no upset, both parties are empowered, no one is diminished, and no energy is stuffed.

If you can't take the person aside in the moment, then make a commitment to yourself to have the conversation with them as soon as possible to clear the air between you so it won't happen again, and release the stuffed emotions.

Another area to bring awareness to is television. You may notice that many commercials recommend the usage of a drug to avoid feeling something. If you close your eyes so you don't see the happy people, and listen to these commercials instead, you will hear the side effects. "Take this product, your headache will go away," but the side effects can kill you. Just start listening. Magazines are similar. The eye catching color page advertisement will promote the positive benefits of the product but when you turn to the back of the page, the side effects can be devastating. Usually, the side effects page is in black and white and with much smaller print. Just start to notice these things.

Your body is designed to make you feel uncomfortable if your life is going in the wrong direction. Ignore the feelings, then mask the symptoms, and the symptoms turn to illness. Wait even longer and the illness can become chronic and sometimes even lead to surgery - the removal of the part that is energetically overloaded.

The point is - if we continue to avoid feeling, we disconnect from our bodies and ultimately may even disconnect from life itself.

If we are willing to connect and experience the full range of emotion that is stored, we may learn that a painful back means "I feel unsupported in my life." "I feel unloved." We can release the energy and be done with it. This requires a new awareness. The new awareness requires a new behavior. The new behavior could be as simple as declaring, "I stand up for myself!" That declaration supports the new behaviors of that person such that if they are ordered to do something, they can say NO. They are now supporting themselves from within and loving themselves because of it.

The key to health and well-being is to discover what our bodies are trying to tell us - that some little course correction is needed in our lives. Don't say "yes" if you really mean "no." For some, it may be a huge course correction such as I married the wrong person or even the wrong gender.

Take responsibility for your well-being. Be proactive. This is not a dress rehearsal. This is your life. If someone calls you selfish because you are pursuing your dreams and speaking your truth then perhaps it is only because you are not willing to do what they want. So who is really being selfish? You are the only person you go through your entire lifetime with. Make choices for yourself that honor your health and well-being.

I have seen miraculous reversals of symptoms and illnesses when we learn to communicate with our bodies. You may not like what you hear, but at least you'll have choice. Give yourself a chance to heal.

When you close your eyes at night, please set your intention to release all resentments that you might knowingly or unknowingly be harboring. Replace your resentments with forgiveness. This will be a gift you give to yourself and your health.

When Wayne and I perform a healing, our focus and intention is to open our clients' energy centers and connect them to their Source energy supply. We vibrate every particle of their being with the intention of perfect health. Our goal is to remove all blocks so that they have complete connection and a clear highway to heal themselves.

When we are connected to Source energy, anything is possible. Spontaneous healing is possible. Immediate healing is available. We are connected to "All That

Is", to "I Am That Am". We are one with the Universe. Every particle of our Being is aligned with Source energy. We are all One. Your mind – the machine - gets quiet and there is only the loving voice of the Self, which wants all good things for you. Love, peace and relaxation become present. Pain disappears and there is only love.

The key is maintaining the connection. This is your responsibility.

Say to yourself, "I am a magnificent human being". "I love myself".

LOVE IS THE HIGHEST VIBRATION AND THE MOST POWERFUL
HEALING TOOL.
TO LOVE YOURSELF YOU MUST RECOGNIZE YOUR OWN
MAGNIFICENCE.

To maintain the connection, we must learn to be true to ourselves, to quiet our minds so that we can hear the inner voice of our Higher Self and act accordingly. This voice never says "should or shouldn't". That is the mind speaking, the ego. The voice of the Self is kind and loving. It's a knowing. You just know.

You may ask, "How can I maintain the connection, and how can I quiet my mind?"

Use meditation or focused breathing. Be still and listen. Become aware of your thoughts. Awareness of what you think is extremely important.

Your mind never stops; it is a machine and designed to work for you. If you were your mind, you would not be able to observe your thoughts because you would BE your thoughts. You may be thinking, "What is she talking about?" THAT! That voice in your head that says, "What is she talking about?" For many reading this, it may be the first time you are aware of the voice in your head. That voice is your machinery, the voice of survival from your youth.

That voice is a culmination of the conversations you have heard or had since birth, the books and articles you have read, the things you have witnessed or experienced over your lifetimes, the music you have listened to, the television shows and movies you have watched, as well as the traditions and beliefs that have been handed down through the generations. The machinery takes in everything, like a giant computer. It is designed to give you more of what you think about. However, when it runs on automatic, without your awareness that it is running... people and events show up in your life that are a match.

Our society provides a daily bombardment of negative stuff to think about. That stuff then becomes our reality because we seek others to get their agreement that our point of view is correct, and that reinforces that we are right. That is the ultimate job of the machinery-your brain. To be right and survive! Then it brings you more of what you are right about. If you like your life the way it is just let those tapes run. If you don't like your life the way it is then you must interrupt those tapes and "awareness" is the access.

You get what you think about, most of the time. To have a different life or different health, YOU must reprogram your mind. YOU must think different thoughts. YOU must tell a different story.

Our minds are designed to bring us our every wish. "Your wish is my command", they say in *The Secret*[38]. It is true. It is the Law of Attraction.

It is in our conversations that our worlds are created. When you are alone or with others, what do you think and talk about? If we think and talk about illness... we see and often get more illness. If we think and talk about wellness, we get more wellness. Speak of poverty get more poverty. Speak of wealth receive more wealth. Speak of the absence of wealth receive more absence of wealth.

If you can begin to tell the story of how good you feel, and focus on how good you feel, and tell others of how good you feel, you will continue to maintain that connection and it will continue to grow out of your sharing and feeling. Life will improve.

Begin to notice your thoughts. Notice what you think about during the day. How much of your energy goes towards positive thoughts? How many of your conversations are about positive aspects of life? How much of your energy is given to negative thinking or conversations about how bad things are? Just begin to notice. What do you and your family, friends and co-workers talk about?

If you are not feeling good and want to feel better, think a better feeling thought. For example: Anger is a better feeling thought than depression. Begin to experience how each thought feels in your body. Sample a few thoughts. Does it feel bad or good? This is your emotional guidance system. You get what you think about. The Universe does not distinguish or judge. It gives you more of what you focus your attention on. Just like the *law of gravity*, it is always there, and just like the law of gravity, you can use it to your advantage, once you are aware of it.

Once you notice the conversations that you have with your family, friends, and co-workers you will begin to understand why your life looks like it does. If

---

38   *The Secret*, http://thesecret.tv/; Sean Byrne, Damian McLindon, Drew Heriot, Marc Goldenfein, Directors, 2006; Rhonda Byrne, Author, 2006

you like the way your life looks, keep doing what you are doing. If there is an area of your life that does not look the way you want it to, upgrade your conversations and thoughts in that area. Awareness is the key!

The most powerful words you can say are: **I AM** and **I HAVE**.

When you add these words to your desires, they become declarations!

The most powerful mantra for healing your body, mind and spirit is:

- **I AM MAGNIFICENT.**

- **I AM ONE WITH {THE CREATOR, GOD, ALL, UNIVERSAL ENERGY, SOURCE, OR WHATEVER 'IT' IS FOR YOU}**

- **I AM PERFECT HEALTH. I AM AMAZING HEALTH {IN THE IMAGE AND LIKENESS OF THE CREATOR}**

- **I AM PERFECT LOVE. I AM AMAZING LOVE {IN THE IMAGE AND LIKENESS OF THE CREATOR}**

- **AND ONLY PERFECTION CAN EXIST IN EVERY CELL, MOLECULE, FIBER AND 'GOD PARTICLE' THAT MAKES UP MY ENTIRE BEING**

To have the greatest success you must experience the *feeling* of your desire fulfilled. To prepare yourself for success, allow yourself to create a deep inner feeling of love, peace, serenity and appreciation for YOU, the Being you are. Focus on each word knowing with absolute certainty that your request will be granted.

We recommend you repeat this daily and often, with meaning, and allow these words to transform your cells. This is the greatest affirmation you can make each night before going to sleep and each morning upon awakening. Practice this behavior until it becomes a habit and watch your life transform.

We wish you an eternity filled with abundant
Love, Laughter, Health, Wealth, Joy and Passion for Life!
~ Kathy & Wayne ~

Our Gift to You

Gratitude

Thank you for reading our book.

To show our appreciation,

we offer you one (1)

FREE

GROUP

DISTANCE HEALING

To receive your FREE gift:

1) Visit our website: www.globalhealings.com

2) Select *GIFT*

3) Fill out the form. (Gift Code: love)

RESOURCE GUIDE

ENERGY HEALINGS:
[15]Available In-Person, Long-Distance, and by joining our Sunday Night, or Monday Morning, Group Distance Healings

Kathleen W Raymond
Wayne G Gabari
AADP Board Certified Holistic Health Practitioners, Transformational Energy Healing Educators and Practitioners
** See website for Workshops and Trainings **
www.GlobalHealings.com
globalhealings@gmail.com

Office location:	Mailing Address:
Katonah Healing Arts	Global Healings, LLC
15 Parkway	PO Box 74
Katonah, NY 10536	Katonah, NY 10536

RECOMMENDED SUPPLEMENT:
ASEA & RENU28 – *Native* to the body!
From the inside out or the outside in, this is the greatest scientific health and athletic breakthrough of our time!
http://moleculesforhealing.teamasea.com
aboutASEA@gmail.com

MAGNETIC ENERGY THERAPY:
[2] **Nikken**, Magnetic Energy Therapy and Wellness Products
Contact: **WayneGabari@gmail.com**

PSYCHICS/MEDIUMS:

Bob Buchanan

bbucha3458@aol.com

www.bobbpsychicmedium.com

Dennis Levesque

doc_denny@hotmail.com

Sheri Perbeck

fairyperbeck@yahoo.com

www.themysticalfairy.com

NETWORK SPINAL ANALYSIS AND SOMATO RESPIRATORY INTEGRATION:

[4] Network Spinal Analysis / NSA Chiropractic

[5] Somato Respiratory Integration (SRI)

Dr. Donald M. Epstein –

Wise World Seminars

444 N. Main Street

Longmont, CO 80501

Tel: (303) 678-8086

Fax: (303) 678-8089

www.wiseworldseminars.com

Dr. David B. Mehler –

(212) 229-0503

27 West 20th Street, Suite 306,

New York, NY 10011

www.vikaz.com

info@vikaz.com

FAMILY CONSTELLATION THERAPY:

[27] **Barry Gordon,** *Family Constellation Therapist,* Anger Resolution

(w) (203) 269-1300

aoa1@msn.com

www.barrygordonlmft.com

YOUNG LIVING ESSENTIAL OILS:
Terry Ferraro
www.terryferraro.com
terryferraro@gmail.com

OTHER WEBSITES:
Louise Hay
www.louisehay.com

[8] Royal R. Rife, *The Website of Royal Rife*, 1888-1971
www.rife.org/

[16] Landmark Worldwide: Innovative programs for living an extraordinary life
www.landmarkworldwide.com

[22] Patient's views of the side effects of prescribed medications
www.askapatient.com

[23] Rainbow Chakra Centers: Body-Mind-Spirit Connections (Chart #5)
www.InnerLightResources.com

[36] Ho'oponopono - The ancient Hawaiian healing technique
www.holisticharmony.com/archives/capsules/hopono.asp

[37] Abraham-Hicks, The Law of Attraction – Jerry & Ester Hicks
www.Abraham-Hicks.com

BOOKS:
[3] John E. Sarno, M.D., *Healing Back Pain – The Mind-Body Connection* (New York: Warner Books, Inc., 1991)

[6] Louise L. Hay, *Heal Your Body (condensed version)*, (California: Hay House, Inc., 1987)

[7] Tom Cowan, *Shamanism, As a Spiritual Practice for Daily Life* (California: The Crossing Press, 1996)

[9] Jamie Sams & David Carson, and illustrated by Angela Werneke, *Medicine Cards,* (New York: St. Martin's Press, 1988)

[11] Brian L. Weiss, M.D., *Many Lives, Many Masters,* (New York: A Fireside Book, Simon & Schuster, 1988)

[12] Lee Carroll, *The Parables of Kryon,* (California: Hay House, Inc., 1996)

[13] Eckhart Tolle, *The Power of Now – A Guide To Spiritual Enlightenment,* (California: New World Library, 1999)

[14] Doreen Virtue, *Angel Numbers 101,* (New York: Hay House, Inc., 2008)

[18] Donald M. Epstein, D.C., *The 12 Stages of Healing,* (California: Co-published by Amber-Allen Publishing and New World Library, 1994)

[19] Louise L. Hay, *You Can Heal Your Life (extended version),* (California: Hay House Inc., 1999)

[20] Ester and Jerry Hicks, *The Law of Attraction*, Hay House, Inc. USA 2006)

[21] Florence Scovel Shinn, *The Wisdom of Florence Scovel Shinn, Four Complete Books,* (New York: A Fireside Book, Simon & Schuster, 1989),
> *The Game of Life and How to Play It*
> *Your Word is Your Wand*
> *The Secret Door to Success*
> *The Power of the Spoken Word*

[24] Sylvia Brown with Lindsey Harrison, *Life on the Other Side,* (New York: New American Library, 2001), Exit points are specific moments in our lives when we have the option to choose to live or choose to die.

[25] Anita Moorjani, *Dying To Be Me*, (Hay House, Inc., 2012)

[33] Baird T. Spalding, *The Life and Teachings of The Masters of the Far East*, six volume series, (DeVorss & Company, 1986),

[35] Eckhart Tolle, *A New Earth*, (New York: Plume, 2006)
www.oprah.com/oprahsbookclub/Watch-A-New-Earth-Web-Classes-on-Oprah.com

Conversations with God, Neale Donald Walsch, (also the movie)

Saved by the Light, by Dannion Brinkley, Paul Perry, Raymond Moody

Blessings From The Other Side, by Sylvia Brown

The Journey Home, by Lee Carroll (channeled by Kryon)

Money & The Law of Attraction, by Abraham-Hicks (Jerry and Ester Hicks)

The Shack, by William P. Young

Your Erroneous Zones, by Dr. Wayne Dyer

Wishes Fulfilled, by Dr. Wayne Dyer

I Can See Clearly Now, by Dr. Wayne Dyer

Anything written by:
> Abraham-Hicks/Jerry & Ester Hicks
> Anthony Robbins
> Caroline Myss
> Debbie Ford
> Joe Vitale
> Kryon – Lee Carroll
> Louise Hay
> Marianne Williamson
> Wayne Dyer

MOVIES:

[30] *What The Bleep Do We Know?*, Betsy Chasse and Mark Vicente, Directors, 2004.

[38] *The Secret,* http://thesecret/tv, Sean Byrne, Damian McLindon, Drew Heriot, Marc Goldenfein, Directors, 2006; Rhonda Byrne, Author, 2006

Pay it Forward

Conversations with God

Resurrection (1980)

The Living Matrix

The Shift

Thrive

DEFINITIONS:

[10] Chakras are the energy centers/batteries of the body. They are unseen energetic vortexes that connect us to the earth and also to our higher selves (Source energy). There are seven major Chakras; each governs a different area of the body and the coordinated area of your life. Much like gravity: we know it exists, we cannot see it, yet it governs our life. All Chakras contribute to our well-being when they are open and charged. Energy flow through the body can be restricted if one or more of these centers are partially constricted or blocked.

For more information on the chakras, read: *Eastern Body, Western Mind – Psychology and the Chakra System as a Path to the Self* by Anodea Judith

MISC:

[26] Isaac Newton, *Quantum Physics Theory: Particle vs Wave,* (ScienceDaily, Feb. 27, 1998), www.sciencedaily.com/releases/1998/02/980227055013. htm

[28] Carlo Carretto, *Why, O Lord?*, (Darton, Longman and Todd with Orbis Books USA, 1986)

[29] Carlo Carretto, *Letters from the Desert* (Maryknoll, N.Y.; Oros, 1972); Robert Ellsberg, Carlo Carretto: Selected Writings (Maryknoll, N.Y.: Orbis, 1994)

~ NOTES ~

29354732R10187

Made in the USA
Middletown, DE
17 February 2016